THE FOOTNOTE

A Curious History

THE FOOTNOTE

A Curious History

ANTHONY
GRAFTON

HARVARD UNIVERSITY PRESS

Cambridge, Massachusetts

First Harvard University Press paperback edition, 1999

This work will be published as *Les Origines tragiques
de l'érudition: Une histoire de la note en bas de page*
as part of the series La Librairie du XXe Siècle,
edited by Maurice Olender.

Library of Congress Cataloging-in-Publication Data
Grafton, Anthony.
The footnote : a curious history /
Anthony Grafton. — [Rev. ed.]
p.   cm.
Original English ms. version was translated into German
and published under title: Die tragischen Ursprünge
der deutschen Fussnot (Berlin, 1995) ;
this is a revision of the original English version.
Includes bibliographical references (p.   ) and index.
ISBN 0-674-90215-7 (cloth)
ISBN 0-674-30760-7 (pbk.)
1. Bibliographic citations.   I. Title.
PN171.F56G73   1997
907'.2—dc21   97-17732

Designed by Gwen Nefsky Frankfeldt

CONTENTS

PREFACE

Many books offer footnotes to history: they tell marginal stories, reconstruct minor battles, or describe curious individuals. So far as I know, however, no one has ever dedicated a book to the history of the footnotes that actually appear in the margins of modern historical works. Yet footnotes matter to historians. They are the humanist's rough equivalent of the scientist's report on data: they offer the empirical support for stories told and arguments presented. Without them, historical theses can be admired or resented, but they cannot be verified or disproved. As a basic professional and intellectual practice, they deserve the same sort of scrutiny that laboratory notebooks and scientific articles have long received from historians of science.

Statements about the nature and origins of the footnote appear in histories of historiography and manuals for writers of historical dissertations. They are particularly likely to occur in polemics about the good old days when historians were men and footnotes were footnotes. These often suggest that at a particular date—usually the nineteenth century—and place—often the pre–World War I German universities—footnotes enjoyed a golden age of solidity and accuracy. Such statements, however, rarely rest on extensive research, and are often intended to support or attack the practices of a given school rather than to reconstruct their sources and development. The scattered studies that do exist, moreover, naturally reflect the limitations of their authors' specialized training and perspectives. Scholars have placed the birth of the footnote in the twelfth century, the seventeenth, the eighteenth, and the nineteenth— never without good reason, but usually without attending to the other chapters in this story. One point of my essay is, quite simply, to connect these scattered threads of research. Another, and more important one, is to show that, when woven together, these strands make up a story as full of unexpected human and intellectual interest as many more famous episodes in intellectual history. The footnote is not so uniform and reliable as some historians believe. Nor is it the pretentious, authoritarian device that other historians reject. It is the creation of a varied and talented group, one that included philosophers as well as historians. Its development took a long time and followed a bumpy path. And its story casts new light on many dark recesses in the unwritten history of historical scholarship.

ACKNOWLEDGMENTS

* I became interested in this subject as an undergraduate, when I read parts of Pierre Bayle's *Dictionary* and Arnaldo Momigliano's *Studies in Historiography*. A plan, conceived with friends, to create a pseudo-scholarly journal and devote a whole issue to the topic sadly failed. But I slowly continued to collect information. At last, a conference on Proof and Persuasion in History, held in 1993 at the Davis Center for Historical Studies, Princeton University, provided the impetus to assemble my materials and advance an interpretation of them. I owe warm thanks to Sue Marchand, with whom I organized the conference, and to Mark Phillips and Randolph Starn, who offered sharp and useful criticisms of my original paper. A revised version of this appears, with other papers from the conference, as "The Footnote from de Thou to Ranke," in *History and Theory*, Theme Issue 33 (1994; copyright Wesleyan University). Richard Vann kindly permitted me to reuse my original formulations in this book.

An invitation to spend the academic year 1993–94 at the Wissenschaftskolleg zu Berlin both enabled and stimulated me to attack the footnote a second time. The Wissenschaftskolleg provided free time for work in the city of Ranke and Meinecke. Gesine Bottomley and her staff in the Wissenschaftskolleg library found the most ordinary and the most obscure materials with equal ease and rapidity. They also guided me through the magnificent labyrinth of Berlin's collections of manuscripts and rare books. I feel a special debt to the staff of the Handschriftenabteilung of the Staatsbibliothek zu Berlin, Preussischer Kulturbesitz, Haus II, who helped me to explore the dark boxes, every one an Ali Baba's cave, that house the magnificent chaos of Ranke's Nachlass. The library staffs of the Freie Universität and the Humboldt Universität, especially those of the Meinecke Institut and the Seminar für Klassische Philologie at the Freie Universität, also gave me open access to their treasures. Earlier research was done chiefly in the Firestone Library of Princeton University and at the Bibliothèque Nationale de France; supplementary research at the British Library, the Fondation Hardt, the Warburg Institute, the Österreichische Nationalbibliothek, and, above all, the Bodleian Library, Oxford.

Many friends offered criticism and information. My thanks to J. W. Binns, Robert Darnton, Henk Jan de Jonge, Erhard Denninger, Carlotta Dionisotti, John Fleming, Simon Hornblower, Reinhart Markner, Reinhart Meyer-Kalkus, Grant Parker, James Powell, Wilhelm Schmidt-Biggemann, J. B. Trapp, Giuseppe Veltri, David Wootton, and Paul Zanker, all of whom made valuable suggestions or asked helpfully unanswerable questions. François Hartog, Glenn Most, and Nancy Siraisi criticized earlier versions of the text. Tim Breen, Christopher Ligota, and Wilfried Nippel invited me to present my arguments to well-informed and contentious seminar audiences. Had Arnaldo Momigliano not taught me so much about the subjects treated here, I would never have ventured to qualify one or two of his theses. Christel Zahlmann, whose death came as a heavy blow to so many friends in and outside Germany, saw the potential of a book about the footnote well before I did; Petra Eggers and Maurice Olender helped me realize it. And a number of the reviewers of the German edition—especially Patrick Bahners, Martin Giel, Herfried Münkler, and Helmut Zedelmaier—helped me to reshape the work for its appearance in this enlarged form.

Finally, my thanks to those who have commented on the English versions of this book. H. Jochen Bussmann, who produced the graceful translation published by Berlin Verlag in 1995 under the title *Die tragischen Ursprünge der deutschen Fussnote,* made many pointed observations on the original English text. So did Sue Marchand and Peter Miller. Jill Kraye and Randolph Starn, both of whom read the final English manuscript for Harvard University Press, subjected it to criticism as constructive as it was unsparing.

As successive directors of the Davis Center, Lawrence Stone and Natalie Davis made the History Department at Princeton a center for critical reflection on historical method. As historians, both have thought hard and written well about the nature of archival documents and the problems of historical documentation. As friends and advisers, both have given me and many others unstinting encouragement and constructive criticism. And both have written, and will write, many superb footnotes. This book is offered as a small tribute to two masters of the craft it discusses.

THE FOOTNOTE

A Curious History

CHAPTER ONE

Footnotes:
The Origin of a Species

✳ In the eighteenth century, the historical footnote was a high form of literary art. No Enlightenment historian achieved a work of more epic scale or more classic style than Edward Gibbon's *History of the Decline and Fall of the Roman Empire.* And nothing in that work did more than its footnotes to amuse his friends or enrage his enemies.[1] Their religious and sexual irreverence became justly famous. "In his Meditations," says Gibbon the historian of the emperor Marcus Aurelius, husband of the notoriously "gallant" Faustina, "he thanks the gods, who had bestowed on him a wife, so faithful, so gentle, and of such a wonderful simplicity of manners."[2] "The world," urbanely reflects Gibbon the annotator, "has laughed at the credulity of Marcus; but Madam Dacier assures us (and we may credit a lady) that the husband will always be deceived, if the wife

---

1. See in general G. W. Bowersock, "The Art of the Footnote," *American Scholar,* 53 (1983–84), 54–62. For the wider context, see the remarkable older study by M. Bernays, "Zur Lehre von den Citaten und Noten," *Schriften zur Kritik und Litteraturgeschichte,* IV (Berlin, 1899), 255–347 at 302–322.

2. E. Gibbon, *The History of the Decline and Fall of the Roman Empire,* chap. 4; ed. D. B. Womersley (London, 1994), I, 108–109.

condescends to dissemble."[3] "The duty of an historian," remarks Gibbon in his ostensibly earnest inquiry into the miracles of the primitive church, "does not call upon him to interpose his private judgment in this nice and important controversy."[4] "It may seem somewhat remarkable," comments Gibbon in a footnote which drops all pretense of decorum, "that Bernard of Clairvaux, who records so many miracles of his friend St. Malachi, never takes any notice of his own, which, in their turn, however, are carefully related by his companions and disciples."[5] "The learned Origen" and a few others, so Gibbon explains in his analysis of the ability of the early Christians to remain chaste, "judged it the most prudent to disarm the tempter."[6] Only the footnote makes clear that the theologian had avoided temptation by the drastic means of castrating himself—and reveals how Gibbon viewed this operation: "As it was his general practice to allegorize scripture; it seems unfortunate that, in this instance only, he should have adopted the literal sense."[7] Such cheerfully sarcastic comments stuck like burrs in orthodox memories and reappeared to haunt their author in the innumerable pamphlets written by his critics.[8]

Gibbon's artistry served scholarly as well as polemical

3. Chap. 4, n. 4; ibid., 109.

4. Ibid., chap. 15; I, 473.

5. Chap. 15, n. 81, ibid., 474.

6. Ibid., 480.

7. Chap. 15, n. 96, ibid. For a recent critical discussion of the story of Origen's self-castration, see P. Brown, *The Body and Society* (New York, 1988), 168 and n. 44.

8. This point is well made by Bernays. For more recent studies along the same lines, see F. Palmeri, "The Satiric Footnotes of Swift and Gibbon," *The Eighteenth Century*, 31 (1990), 245–262, and P. W. Cosgrove, "Undermining the Footnote: Edward Gibbon, Alexander Pope, and the Anti-Authenticating Footnote," *Annotation and Its Texts*, ed. S. Barney (Oxford, 1991), 130–151.

ends—just as his footnotes not only subverted, but supported, the magnificent arch of his history.[9] He could invest a bibliographical citation with the grave symmetry of a Ciceronian peroration: "In the account of the Gnostics of the second and third centuries, Mosheim is ingenious and candid; Le Clerc dull, but exact; Beausobre almost always an apologist; and it is much to be feared, that the primitive fathers are very frequently calumniators."[10] He could supply a comic parallel with a gravity usually reserved for the commendation or condemnation of a major historical figure: "For the enumeration of the Syrian and Arabian deities, it may be observed, that Milton has comprised, in one hundred and thirty very beautiful lines, the two large and learned syntagmas, which Selden had composed on that abstruse subject."[11] And he could salute the earlier scholars, good Christians all, whose works he drew upon for a thousand curious details, with a unique combination of amused dismissal of their beliefs and genuine respect for their learning.[12] Gibbon was certainly right to think that a comprehensive account of his sources, written in the same style, would have

9. For two helpful case studies see J. D. Garrison, "Gibbon and the 'Treacherous Language of Panegyrics,'" *Eighteenth-Century Studies,* 11 (1977–78), 40–62; Garrison, "Lively and Laborious: Characterization in Gibbon's Metahistory," *Modern Philology,* 76 (1978–79), 163–178.

10. Chap. 15, n. 32; I, 458.

11. Chap. 15, n. 9, ibid., 449.

12. See e.g. n. 98 to chap. 70, in which Gibbon expertly reviews and assesses the work of the indefatigable historian and editor of texts Ludovico Antonio Muratori, "my guide and master in the history of Italy." "In all his works," Gibbon comments, "Muratori approves himself a diligent and laborious writer, who aspires above the prejudices of a Catholic priest" (Muratori himself would have claimed that writing accurate history lay within a good priest's duties); ed. Womersley, III, 1061. On Muratori himself see S. Bertelli, *Erudizione e storia in Ludovico Antonio Muratori* (Naples, 1960).

been "susceptible of entertainment as well as information."[13] Though his footnotes were not yet Romantic, they had all the romance high style can provide. Their "instructive abundance" attracted the praise of the brilliant nineteenth-century classical scholar Jacob Bernays as well as that of his brother, the Germanist Michael Bernays, whose pioneering essay on the history of the footnote still affords more information and insight than most of its competitors.[14]

Nowadays, historians' arguments must still stride forward or totter backward on their footnotes. But the lead of official prose has replaced the gold of Gibbon's classic oratory. In the modern world—as manuals for writers of dissertations explain—historians perform two complementary tasks.[15] They must examine all the sources relevant to the solution of a problem and construct a new narrative or argument from them. The

13. "Advertisement," I, 5 (this text first appears, under the same title, on the verso of the half title to the endnotes in the first edition of the first volume of the *Decline and Fall* [London, 1776]).

14. The phrase "lehrreiche Fülle" is Jacob Bernays', as quoted with approval by Michael Bernays (305, n. 34). The relationship between the two deserves a study. Jacob mourned his brother as dead when he converted to Christianity: but Michael nonetheless emulated Jacob's analysis of the manuscript tradition of Lucretius in his own genealogical treatment of the editions of Goethe. For Jacob, see A. Momigliano, "Jacob Bernays," *Quinto contributo alla storia degli studi classici e del mondo antico* (Rome, 1975), 127–158; for his work on Lucretius, see S. Timpanaro, *La genesi del metodo del Lachmann,* 2nd ed. (Padua, 1985). For Michael Bernays, see W. Rehm, *Späte Studien* (Bern and Munich, 1964), 359–458, and H. Weigel, *Nur was du nie gesehn wird ewig dauern* (Freiburg, 1989). So far as I know, the third brother, Freud's father-in-law Berman, did not venture an opinion on Gibbon's footnotes.

15. See e.g. E. Faber and I. Geiss, *Arbeitsbuch zum Geschichtsstudium,* 2nd ed. (Heidelberg and Wiesbaden, 1992). For a detailed and judicious American guide to these issues, see F. A. Burkle-Young and S. R. Maley, *The Art of the Footnote* (Lanham, Md., and London, 1996).

footnote proves that both tasks have been carried out. It identifies both the primary evidence that guarantees the story's novelty in substance and the secondary works that do not undermine its novelty in form and thesis. By doing so, moreover, it identifies the work of history in question as the creation of a professional. Like the high whine of the dentist's drill, the low rumble of the footnote on the historian's page reassures: the tedium it inflicts, like the pain inflicted by the drill, is not random but directed, part of the cost that the benefits of modern science and technology exact.

As this analogy suggests, the footnote is bound up, in modern life, with the ideology and the technical practices of a profession. One becomes a historian, as one becomes a dentist, by undergoing specialized training: one remains a historian, as one stays a dentist, if one's work receives the approval of one's teachers, one's peers, and, above all, one's readers (or one's patients). Learning to make footnotes forms part of this modern version of apprenticeship. Most historians begin on a small scale, during the frenetic weeks they dedicate to writing papers that must be read aloud to their professor's seminar. At this point, their footnotes are only seen, not read. They form a blurred, closely printed mass of text vaguely glimpsed on the bottoms of pages which move up and down in the shaking hands of the nervous, mumbling speaker. Later, in the long months spent composing a dissertation, students move from craft to industrial styles of footnote production, peppering each chapter with a hundred or more references to show that they have put in hours of hard work in archive and library. Once elevated to the doctorate and employed, finally, active historians compose footnotes every time they write a monograph or an article for a learned journal.

Over time, however, the writing of footnotes usually loses its flavor: the thrilling claim of membership in a mysterious new profession, the bold assertion of one's right to take part in a learned dialogue, degenerates into a mere routine. Historians for whom composing annotations has become second nature—like dentists who have become inured to inflicting pain and shedding blood—may hardly notice any more that they still extrude names of authors, titles of books, and numbers of folders in archives or leaves in unpublished manuscripts. In the end, the production of footnotes sometimes resembles less the skilled work of a professional carrying out a precise function to a higher end than the offhand production and disposal of waste products.

Historians, however, cannot afford to ignore waste products and their disposal. The exploration of toilets and sewers has proved endlessly rewarding to historians of population, city planning, and smells. The stages of their development distinguish the textures of modern from premodern social life far more vividly than the loftier periodizations found in political and intellectual histories.[16] One who wishes to learn how a sixteenth-century French classroom differed most pungently from a modern one should not only examine Petrus Ramus' popular textbooks, but also ponder his biographer's statement that he bathed once a year, at the summer solstice.[17] Similarly, the study of those parts of history which lie beneath ground level may reveal hidden cracks and forgotten conduits in both

16. See A. Corbin, *Le miasme et la jonquille* (Paris, 1982); L. Chevalier, *Classes laborieuses et classes dangereuses à Paris pendant la première moitié du 19e siècle* (Paris, 1984).

17. P. Sharratt, "Nicolaus Nancelius, *Petri Rami Vita,* Edited with an English Translation," *Humanistica Lovaniensia,* 24 (1975), 238–239.

the modern practice and the millennial traditions of historical scholarship.

Even a brief exercise in comparison reveals a staggering range of divergent practices under history's apparently stable surface. At first glance, of course, all footnotes look very much alike. All over the modern historical world, articles begin with an industrialized civilization's equivalent to the ancient invocation of the Muse: a long note in which the author thanks teachers, friends, and colleagues. Prefatory notes evoke a Republic of Letters—or at least an academic support group—in which the writer claims membership. In fact, they often describe something much more tenuous, the group of those who the author wishes had read his work, offered him references, or at least given him the time of day. Hence they retain something of the literary—not to say fictional—quality of traditional poets' prayers. But sober daylight soon dispels the cool, fragrant shades of scholarly autobiography. Long lists of earlier books and articles and strings of coded references to unpublished documents supposedly prove the solidity of the author's research by rendering an account of the sources used. In fact, however, only the relatively few readers who have trawled their nets through the same archival waters can identify the catch in any given set of notes with ease and expertise.[18] For most readers, footnotes play a different role. In a modern, impersonal society, in which individuals must rely for vital services on others whom they do not know, credentials perform what used to be the function of guild membership or personal recommendations: they give legitimacy. Like the shabby podium, carafe of water,

18. Cf. V. Ladenthin, "Geheime Zeichen und Botschaften," *Süddeutsche Zeitung,* 8/9 October 1994.

and rambling, inaccurate introduction which assert that a particular person deserves to be listened to when giving a public lecture, footnotes confer authority on a writer.[19]

Unlike other types of credentials, however, footnotes sometimes afford entertainment—normally in the form of daggers stuck in the backs of the author's colleagues. Some of these are inserted politely. Historians may simply cite a work by author, title, place and date of publication. But often they quietly set the subtle but deadly "cf." ("compare") before it. This indicates, at least to the expert reader, both that an alternate view appears in the cited work and that it is wrong. But not everyone who reads the book will know the code. Sometimes, accordingly, the stab must be more brutal, more direct. One can, for example, dismiss a work or thesis, briefly and definitively, with a single set-phrase or well-chosen adjective. The English do so with a characteristically sly adverbial construction: "oddly overestimated." Germans use the direct "ganz abwegig" ("totally off the track"); the French, a colder, but less blatant, "discutable." All these indispensable forms of abuse appear in the same prominent position and carry out the same scholarly version of assassination. Anyone who has read a normal piece of professional history recently produced in Europe or America can supply details of these and analogous procedures. The professional codes and techniques behind them seem as universal in use as they are limited in appeal.[20]

19. Cf. B. Lincoln, *Authority* (Chicago and London, 1994).

20. For an elegant study (and satire) of these practices in German jurisprudence see P. Riess, *Vorstudien zu einer Theorie der Fussnote* (Berlin and New York, 1983–84), e.g. 3: "Die Fussnote ist (oder gibt vor, es zu sein) Träger wissenschaftlicher Information" ("The footnote is, or pretends to be, the bearer of scholarly information"). Footnote 5 (one of three to this phrase), on the word

Closer scrutiny of detail, however, reveals that appearances of uniformity are deceptive. To the inexpert, footnotes look like deep root systems, solid and fixed; to the connoisseur, however, they reveal themselves as anthills, swarming with constructive and combative activity. In Italy, for example, the footnote often operates as much by omission as by statement. The failure to refer to a particular scholar or work amounts to a polemical statement, a *damnatio memoriae,* which the circle of interested parties will immediately recognize and decode. But that circle has only a limited circumference. The author thus makes one point to the small community of specialists who know the native idiom, another to the much larger one of historians and other readers who might pick up the odd copy of a particular journal. Only those who have memorized the dots and dashes of citation code—a code which changes, naturally, by the hour—will read the lacunae as charged and argumentative. To outsiders the same notes will seem calm and informative. Many Italian historical texts with footnotes, in other words, tell not only the theoretically required two stories but three. They address not only the theoretically universal public of historians, the "community of the competent" in every nation, but a far smaller group, the coven of the well-informed. The combined precision and obscurity of the Italian citation code compel admiration—especially in light of the practical difficulties that confront any Italian scholar who wants to read a given work before not citing it. Italian historians work, in most cities, in inadequate collections of modern secondary literature, where the razors of unscrupulous readers have stripped many journals

---

"Information," reads: "Oder auch nicht." ("Or else it isn't"). See also pp. 20–21 and U. Holbein, *Samthase und Odradek* (Frankfurt, 1990), 18–23.

of their most influential articles, standard modern works and rare older materials often prove inaccessible, and foreign monographs are rarities. The enormous lists of works actually cited in Italian footnotes offer evidence for a continuing respect for erudition that itself deserves respect—as well as a background that vividly sets off intentional omissions.

In postwar Germany, by contrast, omission has been less a matter of particular than of general statement. West German historians loved to condemn others for their failure to cite "the older German Literature." They themselves, however, regularly failed to cite more recent work—especially on German history—in languages other than German, and often failed to notice or assimilate the newer, interdisciplinary forms of history that flourished in France and the United States. In doing so they did not reveal ignorance (perish the thought). Rather, they exhibited a conviction: that they inhabited a Middle Kingdom of the historical mind, one organically connected with the *Begriff*-stricken, German-dominated historical discipline of the nineteenth century. Hence they had no need to admit the barbarians outside—except in those few privileged cases where the barbarians had learned enough of the procedures and mysteries of German scholarship to become civilized themselves. The historical community so revealed coincided neatly, for all its divisions, with national borders.

At the same time, however, West German historians not only perpetuated a prejudice but carried on a research practice, one which dovetailed neatly with their sense of their own position in the world of learning. They (or their research assistants) usually worked in a specialized library designed to provide the basic literature of modern historiography: that of their university's historical institute or seminar. The holdings of this limited collection they cited in detail and extensively. Works not represented in the seminar, by contrast, might be drawn on for information, if one's student assistant could find them in the university library or obtain them by interlibrary loan. But they played no large role in forming historical debates and usually occupied little space in footnotes. Naturally, foreign books were likelier than German ones to lie deep in the stacks of the university library rather than to stand in plain view on the open shelves of the seminar. In Germany, moreover, unlike the United States and England, the books in large university libraries are usually stored in order of acquisition, not in systematic subject groupings. The stacks, which remain inaccessible to readers, serve only as storehouses. The practical difficulties of access thus reinforced the intellectual border guards already set in place by traditions of instruction and scholarship. East German historians, for their part, had flesh-and-blood border guards to contend with. They made their statements of intellectual centrality and allegiance more directly—above all, perhaps, by placing the works of Marx and Engels, out of alphabetical order, at the start of their lists of citations. The history of the footnote that the joint forces of eastern and western scholarship will create in a united Germany remains, of course, to be written.

As these cases suggest, the footnote varies as widely in nature and content as any other complex scientific or technical practice. Like "precise quantitative measurement," "controlled experiment," and other guarantees that a given statement about the natural world is rigorous and valid, footnotes appear in enough forms to challenge any taxonomist's ingenuity. Each has an organic relation to the particular historical community in which it was spawned—one at least as important as its relation to the supposedly international community of historians, that chimera imagined by the English Catholic historian Lord Acton, who did so much to introduce the methods of German scientific history into England. Acton hoped to edit a *Cambridge Modern History* in which the nationalities of contributors could not be inferred from the method and substance of their articles—a history which will be written when the seas turn to lemonade.[21]

Footnotes, moreover, vary in origin as well as style. Some consist of long lists of archival citations documenting a graduate student's hard-won individual knowledge of an obscure point; others, like those that decorated the erudite-looking articles and books on the history of German unions and politics by the East German leader Walter Ulbricht, result from collaborative work and offer information dug up after the text was written, in order to sustain a preexisting thesis. The two sorts of note look similar, but obviously have very different relations both to the texts they supposedly came into being to support and to the historical professions that supposedly regulated their production.[22]

Citations in scientific works—as a number of studies have

21. For Acton's program see *The Varieties of History,* ed. F. Stern, 2nd ed. (London, 1970), 249, and the commentary of H. Butterfield, *Man on His Past* (Boston, 1960), and J. L. Altholtz, "Lord Acton and the Plan of the *Cambridge Modern History,*" *Historical Journal,* 39 (1996), 723–736.

22. See e.g. W. Ulbricht, "Die Novemberrevolution und der nationale Kampf gegen den deutschen Imperialismus," *Beiträge zur Geschichte der deutschen Arbeiterbewegung,* 1 (1959), 8–25 at 17–18. The "Vorwort," p. 7, also emphasizes that the journal would publish "unveröffentlichte, für die Forschung wie für die Propagandaarbeit wertvolle Dokumente und Materialien" ("unpublished documents of value for research and for purposes of propaganda")—as it did, in articles grouped under the heading "Dokumente und Materialien."

shown—do far more than identify the originators of ideas and the sources of data. They reflect the intellectual styles of different national scientific communities, the pedagogical methods of different graduate programs, and the literary preferences of different journal editors. They regularly refer not only to the precise sources of scientists' data, but also to larger theories and theoretical schools with which the authors wish or hope to be associated.[23] Citations in historical writings show at least as many signs of their origin in fallible and prejudiced human effort.

One who actually follows historians' footnotes back to their sources, accordingly, taking the time to trace the deep, twisted roots of the blasted tree of scholarly polemic, may well discover much more of human interest than one would expect buried in the acid subsoil. Jacob Thomasius offered a neat taxonomy of the wrong forms of citation as early as 1673. Some authors "say nothing, at the most significant point, about one whom they then cite only on a point of no or little importance." Wickeder ones "take the most careful precautions never to mention [their source] at all." And the wickedest "mention him only when they disagree with or criticize him."[24] In addition to these "neg-

---

23. See in general B. Cronin, *The Citation Process* (London, 1984), with an extensive bibliography. On the social sciences see J. Bensman, "The Aesthetics and Politics of Footnoting," *Politics, Culture, and Society,* 1 (1988), 443–470 (reference kindly supplied by C. Gattone). The cartoonist Carole Cable makes a similar point more simply. She shows two academics facing each other, one of them holding a text and saying: "You've fine-tuned the footnote to a major networking device" (*Chronicle of Higher Education,* 11 April 1997, B13).

24. J. Thomasius, *praeses, Dissertatio philosophica de plagio literario,* resp. Joh. Michael Reinelius (Leipzig, 1692), §251, 106: "Nam qui loco maxime illustri tacent eum, quem in re demum nullius aut parvi pretii nominant, hi videlicet plagiariorum *technam* exercent, id agentium, ut accusati de silentio habeant,

ative" forms of mis-citation, Thomasius also described a "positive" procedure: that of the scholar-pickpocket. When caught in the act, the adept criminal begs his victim to take his wallet back quietly: as soon as the victim reaches for it, the thief cries out, "Help, he's robbing me!" Similarly, more than one scholar has plagiarized material from another while simultaneously accusing the victim, in the relevant footnote, of having done the same. Few readers will have the tenacity to check the story for its accuracy, and most will assume that the elegant pickpocket, not the disheveled victim, has told the truth.[25] The path of a fact or factoid from archive to notebook to footnote to book review is, in short, often anything but straight. In this case as in others, the critical reader may well find that "the journey, not the arrival, matters."

The footnote demands attention for other reasons as well: not only as a general part of the practice of science and scholarship, but also as an object of keen nostalgia and a subject of sharp debate. Twentieth-century historians have added one modern room after another to the traditional mansions of their discipline. In doing so, of course, they have sometimes blocked the windows, not to mention the prospects for promotion, of more traditional colleagues. The process has caused much pain, and the resulting clamor has more than once taken the form of

---

unde se utcunque tueantur. Nequiores illi, qui religiosissime cavent, ne uspiam nominent, cui plurima debent. Nequissimi, qui non nominant, nisi ubi absentiunt aut reprehendunt."

25. Ibid., §252, 107: "Caeterum ab hoc actu tacendi *negativo* distinguendus alter *positivus,* cum, quod alibi furati sunt, alibi ut suum defendunt quidam, negantque illi se debere, qui ipsis tanquam verus auctor obiicitur, aut hunc maiore malitia pro suo plagiario accusant."

sharp cries that the traditional footnote has fallen into disregard.

Some of the new forms of history rest on evidence that footnotes cannot accommodate—like the massive analyses of statistical data undertaken by historical demographers, which can be verified only when they agree to let colleagues use their computer files. Others rest on evidence that footnotes have not normally included—like the field notes of anthropologists, which record ephemeral events, from rituals to interviews, and document customs that change even as they are described. These cannot in principle be verified: as Heraclitus saw, no anthropologist can live and work in the same village twice. No two anthropologists will describe the same transaction in identical terms, or analyze and code the same description of a transaction in identical categories. Most serious of all, even one set of normal field notes usually bulks far too large to be published in any normal way.[26] Still other up-to-date historians muster and cite archival evidence in the traditional manner, but use it to answer new questions deriving from political economy, literary theory, and all disciplines between.[27]

A hundred years ago, most historians would have made a simple distinction: the text persuades, the notes prove.[28] As

26. See *Fieldnotes: The Making of Anthropology,* ed. R. Sanjak (Ithaca, N.Y., 1990), and R. M. Emerson, R. I. Fretz, and L. L. Shaw, *Writing Ethnographic Fieldnotes* (Chicago and London, 1995).

27. For a pioneering discussion of these points see L. Stone, *The Past and the Present Revisited* (London, 1987), 33–37.

28. See e.g. Ch.-V. Langlois and Ch. Seignobos, *Introduction to the Study of History,* tr. G. G. Berry (London and New York, 1898; repr. 1912), 305–306; for the original text see Langlois and Seignobos, *Introduction aux études historiques* (Paris, 1898), 264–266. And for a recent, highly critical discussion see P. Car-

early as the seventeenth century, after all, some antiquaries entitled the documentary appendices of their works simply "Preuves"—"Proofs."[29] Nowadays, by contrast, many historians would claim that their texts offer their most important proofs: proofs that take the form of statistical or hermeneutic analyses of evidence, only the sources of which are specified by notes. In each of these cases, for all their differences, many critics have responded much as a slow-footed fullback responds in a hard-fought soccer match to the evasive tactics of a fast-moving striker. Just kick the legs out from under your opponents—show that they have misread, or misinterpreted, the documents—and you need not bother to refute their arguments. Such criticisms vary radically in intellectual quality, scholarly rigor, and rhetorical tone. But most of them rest in part on a common and problematic assumption: that authors can, as manuals for dissertation writers say they should, exhaustively cite the evidence for every assertion in their texts.[30] In fact, of course, no one can ever exhaust the range of sources relevant to an important problem—much less quote all of them in a note. In practice, moreover, every annotator rearranges materials to prove a point, interprets them in an individual way, and omits those that do not meet a necessarily personal standard of relevance. The very next person to review the same archival ma-

---

rard, "Disciplining Clio: The Rhetoric of Positivism," *Clio,* 24 (1995), 189–204.

29. E.g. A. Duchesne, *Preuves de l'histoire de la maison des Chasteigners* (Paris, 1633). This accompanied Duchesne's work on the history of the family, as its title indicates.

30. For a provocative—and nostalgic—discussion of what footnotes can and cannot do, see G. Himmelfarb, "Where Have All the Footnotes Gone?" in *On Looking into the Abyss* (New York, 1994), 122–130.

terials will probably line them up and sort them out quite differently.[31]

A number of controversies about footnotes reveal some of the ways that polemicists have used—and misused—them: most often, perhaps, in order to make a charge of incompetence take the place of a counterargument. One in particular, provoked by an innovative outsider, sent waves of turbulence through the entire North Atlantic historical community.[32] Henry Turner, a senior historian of German business and the Nazis who teaches at Yale University, discovered early in the 1980s that a younger scholar at Princeton, David Abraham, had made mistakes in identifying and quoting archival documents in his *Collapse of the Weimar Republic: Political Economy and Crisis* (Princeton, 1981). Abraham's errors, so Turner and others argued, were not only gross but purposeful: Abraham had deliberately misdated, misattributed, and mistranslated archival texts in order to make the relations between the Nazis and the businessmen seem far closer than they had been. These critics denounced Abraham, absurdly, as a forger, instead of acknowledging that he had gone to German archives with highly developed theoretical interests, a novel point of view, and little active knowledge of the German language or the best techniques for taking notes.[33] As

31. Cf. P. Veyne, *Comment on écrit l'histoire* (Paris, 1977), 273–276.

32. For what follows, and for the published and unpublished texts to which the controversy gave rise, see P. Novick, *That Noble Dream* (Cambridge, 1988), 612–621; I should warn the reader that David Abraham was for several years my colleague at Princeton (cf. Novick, 612, n. 51).

33. This was not the first such attack Turner had mounted. See H. A. Turner, "Grossunternehmertum und Nationalsozialismus, 1930–1933. Kritisches und Ergänzendes zu zwei neuen Forschungsbeiträgen," *Historische Zeitschrift*, 221 (1975), 18–68, with the reply by D. Stegmann, "Antiquierte Personalisierung

often happens, in short, the critics refused to see the genuine
errors they discovered in perspective—or to admit their own
fallibility. When Turner's own book, *German Big Business and
the Rise of Hitler* (New York, 1985), also a polemical one, appeared, it too naturally attracted closer than usual scrutiny from
historians who did not share his sympathies. More than one
pointed out that Turner, too, had rearranged documents to
make them fit his thesis and failed to cite evidence that went
against him.[34] Abraham's proved mistakes were far more numerous than Turner's (as his book was far more intellectually
ambitious). But both cases exemplify the fallibility of all scholars—and the fact that a historical work and its notes can never,
in the nature of things, reproduce or cite the full range of
evidence they rest on.[35]

Still, the tactics of Abraham's critics continue to find application. Two distinguished anthropologists recently offered the
public a parallel cautionary tale. Both tried to explain a single
event: the death of Captain Cook. Each flailed the other's footnotes mercilessly in the hope of destroying the interpretations
given in the other's text. Each showed far more awareness of
the gaps in his opponent's record of his research in the sources
and the inferences he drew from them than of those in his own.

---

oder sozialökonomische Faschismus-Analyse?" *Archiv für Sozialgeschichte,* 17
(1977), 275–296.

34. See K. Wernecke, "In den Quellen steht zuweilen das Gegenteil," *Frank-
furter Rundschau,* 17 May 1986, ZB 4, and F. L. Carsten, review of H. A. Turner,
German Historical Institute, London, Bulletin, 22 (Summer 1986), 20–23; both
previously cited by Novick, 619, n. 60; "The David Abraham Case: Ten Comments from Historians," *Radical History Review,* 32 (1985), 75–96 at 76–77.

35. For another episode in some respects similar to the Abraham case, see
R. M. Bell and J. Brown, "Renaissance Sexuality and the Florentine Archives:
An Exchange," *Renaissance Quarterly,* 40 (1987), 485–511.

And neither showed any clear awareness of the necessary lacunae in normal citation procedure—at least as used by the other. Up-to-date academics often speak demeaningly of "positivism," by which they refer to a form of historical research that heaped up citations in the hope of arriving at the truth about the past, as an ancient superstition long abandoned by the enlightened. The hopeful energy with which these votaries of the once-proud craft of ethnography looked for salvation in the disciplines of historical pedantry shows that such pronouncements are exaggerated.[36]

Sharp controversies about footnotes are nothing new. Master, as well as apprentice, historians have provoked them. In 1927 Ernst Kantorowicz published his biography of the Holy Roman Emperor Frederick II of Hohenstaufen. A follower of Stefan George, Kantorowicz saw himself as tracing the history of a lost "other Germany." This enterprise would have no meaning if it failed to reach a nonacademic public. He brought out his passionately rhetorical work, unencumbered by footnotes but adorned, on its title page, with an elegant swastika, in the series Blaetter fuer die Kunst of the Berlin publisher Georg Bondi. The book became an instant best-seller, multiple copies of which appeared in the windows of fashionable bookshops on the Kurfürstendamm. But it also aroused the fury of academic medievalists, who denounced Kantorowicz for what they saw

36. See G. Obeyesekere, *The Apotheosis of Captain Cook: European Mythmaking in the Pacific* (Princeton and Honolulu, 1992), and M. Sahlins, *How "Natives" Think: About Captain Cook, For Example* (Chicago and London, 1995). Solely in terms of historical criticism, Sahlins has the better of the exchange, as I. Hacking rightly pointed out in his review of Sahlins's book, *London Review of Books,* 7 September 1995, 6–7, 9. But Sahlins too at times transforms what are clearly normal shortcuts in Obeyesekere's arguments into nonexistent errors.

as an intellectually dangerous tendency to mistake the myths
and metaphors of his sources for historical facts. Kantorowicz's
decision to publish the text, in the first instance, without apparatus did nothing to soften the tempers of his critics. They
found the omission all the more frustrating because they knew
that this dandified conservative ex-soldier was a master of the
crafts of textual editing and interpretation. He had stood out
in a famous generation of Heidelberg students for the depth of
his technical preparation and the passion of his commitment
to the study of primary sources. No one could doubt that he
knew the entire literature of his subject in minute detail.[37] But
his expertise made the format and style of his book even more
annoying to his critics.

Two years after Kantorowicz's book appeared, Albert Brackmann attacked it in public at a meeting of the Prussian Academy of Sciences. A report on his lecture appeared in an important Berlin newspaper, the *Vossische Zeitung,* and the whole text
was printed in the major German historical journal, the *Historische Zeitschrift.*[38] Kantorowicz had claimed that Frederick saw
himself, during his coronation in Jerusalem, as a holy king, the
direct successor to David, like Jesus himself.[39] Brackmann fo-

37. On Kantorowicz's early training, E. Grünewald, *Ernst Kantorowicz und
Stefan George* (Wiesbaden, 1982), offers much new information; for his time at
Heidelberg, see 34–56. Kantorowicz claimed that he had omitted footnotes for
two reasons: "Um einerseits den Umfang des Buches nicht zu vergrössern, an-
dererseits die Lesbarkeit nicht herabzumindern, unterblieb jede Art von Quel-
len- und Literaturnachweisen" ("All forms of references to sources and secondary
literature were omitted, in order to avoid making the book both longer and less
readable"). *Kaiser Friedrich der Zweite* (Berlin, 1927), 651.

38. Grünewald, 86–87; A. Brackmann, "Kaiser Friedrich II in 'mythischer
Schau,'" *Historische Zeitschrift,* 140 (1929), 534–549.

39. Kantorowicz, *Kaiser Friedrich der Zweite,* 184–186.

cused his critique on this thesis. When Kantorowicz replied, citing the German witness Marquardt of Ried, who had celebrated Frederick as God's servant, "famulus Dei," Brackmann was unmoved. Kantorowicz, he pointed out, had omitted from his book the crucial line in which Marquardt clearly distinguished between Jesus and Frederick: "Hic Deus, ille Dei pius ac prudens imitator" ("The one is God, the other the pious and prudent imitator of God"). In quoting this line in his rebuttal, Brackmann argued, Kantorowicz silently modified his book, in which he had translated different verses but omitted the salient one.[40] Yet Kantorowicz evidently stuck to his guns; in 1931, when he finally issued his supplementary volume of annotations, he still emphasized the celebratory tone of Marquardt's poem, not its distinction between the Emperor and the Savior. He added no reference to Brackmann's refutation, though he did cite his own article.[41] The point here is not that Kantorowicz or Brackmann was right, but rather that even now the reader cannot follow in full detail the movement of Kantorowicz's thought on this one, central source.

In the period just before and after he produced his volume of annotations, Kantorowicz made his commitment to historical erudition clear. His analysis of the sources for the life and reign of Frederick II remains standard, even though the biography it was meant to support, with its fervent rhetoric, plays little role in scholarly discussion.[42] He himself spent much of

40. Kantorowicz, " 'Mythenschau.' Eine Erwiderung," *Historische Zeitschrift,* 141 (1930), 457–471 at 469–470; Brackmann, "Nachwort," ibid., 472–478 at 476–477.

41. E. Kantorowicz, *Kaiser Friedrich der Zweite. Ergänzungsband* (Berlin, 1931; repr. Düsseldorf and Munich, 1964), 74.

42. D. Kuhlgatz, "Verehrung und Isolation. Zur Rezeptionsgeschichte der

his time—especially after he lost his professorship in Frankfurt because he was a Jew—as a guest in one of the citadels of German learning, the Berlin quarters of the *Monumenta Germaniae Historica,* where historians young and old collaborated in the production of meticulous editions of the primary sources for Germany history.[43] Did he change his mind? Did he decide he had been wrong to omit the line Brackmann emphasized? Did he have an answer to Brackmann's criticism? The documentation is unusually plentiful, but the full range of intellectual operations by which a given document became part of Kantorowicz's apparatus, and this in turn part of a story, an argument, and a set of footnotes, remains mysterious.

Both experience and logic, then, suggest that the footnote cannot carry out all the tasks that the manuals claim it does: no accumulation of footnotes can prove that every statement in the text rests on an unassailable mountain of attested facts. Foototes exist, rather, to perform two other functions. First, they persuade: they convince the reader that the historian has done an acceptable amount of work, enough to lie within the tolerances of the field. Like the diplomas on the dentist's wall, footnotes prove that historians are "good enough" practitioners to be consulted and recommended—but not that they can carry out any specific operation. Second, they indicate the chief sources that the historian has actually used. Though footnotes usually do not explain the precise course that the historian's interpretation of these texts has taken, they often give the reader who is both critical and open-minded enough hints to

---

Biographie Friedrichs II. von Ernst Kantorowicz," *Zeitschrift für Geschichtswissenschaft,* 43 (1995), 736–746.

43. H. Fuhrmann, with M. Weschke, *"Sind eben alles Menschen gewesen." Gelehrtenleben im 19. und 20. Jahrhundert* (Munich, 1996), 39, 100, 193–194, n. 229.

make it possible to work this out—in part. No apparatus can give more information—or more assurance—than this.

Even if the intentions of text and annotation have become somewhat blurred, however, the radical nature of the shift from providing a continuous narrative to producing a text that one has annotated oneself seems clear. Once the historian writes with footnotes, historical narrative tells a distinctively modern, double story. Traditional political historians, in the ancient world and in the Renaissance, wrote from within a rhetorical tradition, as statesmen or generals addressing their peers. The histories they produced reflected far more interest in virtue and vice than in sources and dating. Their works claimed universal validity; they eloquently described examples of good and evil, prudent and imprudent speech and action, that would provide moral and political lessons valid in all times and places.[44] Modern historians, by contrast, make clear the limitations of their own theses even as they try to back them up. The footnotes form a secondary story, which moves with but differs sharply from the primary one. In documenting the thought and research that underpin the narrative above them, footnotes prove that it is a historically contingent product, dependent on the forms of research, opportunities, and states of particular questions that existed when the historian went to work. Like an engineer's diagram of a splendid building, the footnote reveals the occasionally crude braces, the unavoidable weak points, and the hidden stresses that an elevation of the facade would conceal.

The appearance of footnotes—and such related devices as

44. See G. H. Nadel, "Philosophy of History before Historicism," *History & Theory*, 3 (1964), 291–315; R. Koselleck, *Vergangene Zukunft* (Frankfurt, 1984), 38–66; E. Kessler, "Das rhetorische Modell der Historiographie," *Formen der Geschichtsschreibung*, ed. R. Koselleck et al. (Munich, 1982), 37–85.

documentary and critical appendices—separates historical modernity from tradition. Thucydides and Joinville, Eusebius and Matthew Paris did not identify their sources or reflect on their methods in texts parallel to their narratives. This fact elicits cries of regret from hypocrites but also gives employment to squads of classicists and medievalists, who devote themselves to bringing about a return of the suppressed sources.[45] In the last two centuries, by contrast, most histories—except those written to inform and entertain the larger public of nonspecialists, and a few designed to irritate the small community of specialists—have taken some version of the standard double form.[46] Footnotes are the outward and visible signs of this kind of history's inward grace—the grace infused into history when it was transformed from an eloquent narrative into a critical discipline. At this point, systematic scrutiny and citation of original evidence and formal arguments for the preferability of one source over another became necessary and attractive pursuits for historians. As the *locus classicus* for these pursuits, the erudite footnote naturally formed a vital part of any solid work of history. Presumably the footnote's rise to high social, if not typographical, position took place when it became legitimate, after history and philology, its parents, finally married. The question, then, is simply to identify the church in which the wedding took place and the clergyman who officiated.

Or so, at least, I thought—until I began to examine modern studies of footnotes and of historiography, in search of the precise point when history publicly doubled back on itself. The

45. See Bernays.
46. For a recent and successful effort to annoy, see S. Schama, *Dead Certainties: Unwarranted Speculations* (New York, 1991).

harder I looked, the less secure my answers became. Most students of footnotes, in recent times, have come to bury, not to praise, them. A slew of recent articles and a few books discuss footnotes at length. But most of their authors are interested less in studying, historically and empirically, what footnotes have done and what they have suffered, than in making fun of them. American law students, for example, write parodies, in which every word has a footnote number leading to detailed citations, to elucidate the common law origins of baseball rules. German jurists write satires calling for the creation of new disciplines like "Fussnotenwissenschaft" and "Fussnotologie."[47] Both generally treat the footnote as the quintessence of academic foolishness and misdirected effort. The sterile pedantry of scholars makes a perpetually attractive theme, and the criticism is usually justified—especially in the law, where a single footnote in a judicial opinion or a code may exercise an immense influence on the lives of individuals and the fortunes of companies. The best students in America's best law schools—who devote much of their time, for a year or two, to checking and compiling exhaustive footnotes for the legal journals which they edit—have an especially good excuse for regarding footnotes with dislike, though their own occasional parodies of footnotes are rarely distinguished for their wit or tastefulness.[48] Nonetheless, what Peter Riess argued in fun is also true in fact:

47. See respectively "Common-Law Origins of the Infield Fly Rule," *University of Pennsylvania Law Review,* 123 (1975), 1474–1481, and Riess.

48. See the articles cited by B. Hilbert, "Elegy for Excursus: The Descent of the Footnote," *College English,* 51 (1989), 400–404 at 401; this article is one of several exceptions to the general description offered in my text above. On the perhaps excessive impact of some judges' footnotes, see A. Mikva, "Goodbye to Footnotes," *University of Colorado Law Review,* 56 (1984–85), 647–653 at 649.

"The frequency with which footnotes appear, particularly in legal scholarship, stands in striking contrast to the minimal amount of scholarly attention that footnotes as such have received."[49]

Most students of historiography, for their part, have interested themselves in the explicit professions of their subjects, rather than their technical practices—especially those that were tacitly, rather than explicitly, transmitted and employed. The philosophy of history has had far more attention than its philology. Most studies of the latter, moreover, have addressed themselves only to the ways in which historians do research—as if the selection and presentation of one's data did not affect it in fundamental ways.

The much-abused French historians Ch.-V. Langlois and Charles Seignobos, authors of a late nineteenth-century manual of historical writing so old-fashioned that parts of it now look strangely modern, at least admitted that "it would be interesting to find out what are the earliest printed books furnished with notes in the modern fashion." But they confessed that "bibliophiles whom we have consulted are unable to say, their attention never having been drawn to the point." And their own suggestion—that the practice began in annotated collections of historical documents—goes astray.[50] Annotation of documents—X writing commentary on Y—began in the an-

49. Riess, 3: "Die Häufigkeit der Fussnote, namentlich im rechtswissenschaftlichen Schrifttum, steht in einem auffälligen Gegensatz zu der geringen wissenschaftlichen Behandlung, die die Fussnote als solche erfahren hat."

50. Langlois and Seignobos, *Introduction to the Study of History,* tr. Berry, 299 and n. 1 (*Introduction aux études historiques,* 259 and n. 1). They remark: "It was in collections of documents, and in critical dissertations, that the artifice of annotation was first employed; thence it penetrated, slowly, into historical works of other classes."

cient world and has flourished in every culture that possessed a formal, written canon.[51] The complex texts, usually of diverse origins, that make up a society's holy scriptures normally include commentary of various sorts: perhaps they always do so. Thus Michael Fishbane has shown, in a remarkable book, how scribes and authors alike worked veins of commentary directly into the text of the Hebrew Bible. Brief glosses on unusual words and phrases became organic parts of the texts they clarified. Later books quoted and commented on earlier ones. Sometimes deliberately, sometimes inadvertently, the Scripture became its own interpreter.[52] Even later commentaries—like the so-called *Glossa ordinaria,* or extended word-by-word gloss, that wound itself around the Latin text of the Vulgate Bible used in the medieval West, or the gloss of Accursius, the medieval commentator on the Roman *Corpus iuris*—eventually came to be seen as integral parts of the texts they explicated. These were regularly taught with their commentaries.

Secular scriptures also breed explanatory remarks. Some of these are occasional and isolated, others systematic and extended. The Roman grammarians who lectured on Virgil in the last centuries of the Empire and the medieval grammarians who taught Horace in the twelfth century had to introduce their students to an alien language as well as to difficult poetic texts. Their glosses offer the historian rich information about the ever-edgy relationships among teachers, texts, and pupils. Elementary glosses led students through the obstacle course of Latin grammar and syntax; more advanced ones used the prin-

---

51. See e.g. J. B. Henderson, *Scripture, Canon, and Commentary* (Princeton, 1991); J. Assmann, *Das kulturelle Gedächtnis* (Munich, 1992), 102, 174–177.
52. M. Fishbane, *Biblical Interpretation in Ancient Israel* (Oxford, 1985).

ciples of rhetoric to justify the presence in the text of unexpected words; still more advanced ones offered allegorical explications of strange myths and apparently immoral stories. Many included long digressions on questions ranging from the natural to the moral sciences. Detailed autobiographical passages, as Jean Céard has pointed out, make some commentaries on texts surprisingly similar to the autobiographical *Commentaries* of Julius Caesar. Even the introspective, wide-ranging *Essays* of Montaigne sometimes resemble a set of commentaries set loose from the texts they originally applied to.[53]

Occasionally the writer served as his own explicator. Dante and Petrarch wrote formal commentaries on segments of their own poetic production—a tradition which continued, through the erudite commentaries of Andreas Gryphius on his gruelingly learned six-hour tragedies, down to T. S. Eliot's notes on *The Waste Land.*[54] Many Renaissance authors, from Petrarch on, came to see themselves as writing for a posterity as distant as they themselves were from the classics. Hence they began to

---

53. See the richly suggestive studies of R. A. Kaster, *Guardians of Language* (Chicago and London, 1988); S. Reynolds, *Medieval Reading* (Cambridge, 1996); J. Céard, "Les transformations du genre du commentaire," *L'automne de la Renaissance, 1580–1630,* ed. J. Lafond and A. Stegmann (Paris, 1981), 101–115.

54. B. Sandkühler, *Die frühen Dantekommentare und ihr Verhältnis zur mittelalterlichen Kommentartradition* (Munich, 1967); K. Krautter, *Die Renaissance der Bukolik in der lateinischen Literatur des xiv. Jahrhunderts: von Dante bis Petrarca* (Munich, 1983); W. Rehm, "Jean Pauls vergnügtes Notenleben oder Notenmacher und Notenleser," *Späte Studien* (Bern and Munich, 1964), 7–96 at 7–10; cf. Goethe's comment on the *Römische Elegien,* quoted ibid., 10: "Denn bei den alten lieben Toten / Braucht man Erklärung, will man Noten; / Die Neuen glaubt man blank zu verstehn; / Doch ohne Dolmetsch wird's auch nicht gehn" ("The reader who on dear old ancients dotes, knows that he needs good glosses, and wants notes. The moderns seem far easier, far straighter. Yet they too need a talented translator").

record in writing the sorts of historical and biographical information they themselves most prized when studying the Romans—as Petrarch did, imitating Ovid, in his prose letter to posterity and elsewhere. Johannes Kepler—whose historical sense was as acute as his scientific talent—wrote a formal commentary in middle age on his own first book, the *Mysterium cosmographicum,* in order to explain to readers in a distant future the personal circumstances and particular experiences that had given that book its shape and content.[55]

The historical footnote is also connected with a second older form of annotation—one that provides precise references to the section of an authoritative text from which a given quotation in a later work comes. Such references rarely appeared in ancient literary prose, since the well-educated author cited texts from memory, not from books, often introducing a slight change to show that he had done so.[56] Even the authors of works avowedly written as compendia did not always identify their sources precisely: if the elder Pliny listed the authors from whom he derived the matter of his *Natural History* and Aulus Gellius cited the authors, and sometimes the books, that he quoted in his *Attic Nights,* Macrobius often failed even to mention the writers whom he quoted word for word in his enormous, influential *Saturnalia.*[57] But Roman jurists provided very precise references

55. For Petrarch and Kepler see the provocative and insightful analysis of H. Günther, *Zeit der Geschichte* (Frankfurt, 1993). Kepler's commentary on the *Mysterium* appears in vol. VIII of his *Gesammelte Werke,* ed. M. Caspar et al. (Munich, 1937—).

56. See J. Whittaker, "The Value of Indirect Tradition in the Establishment of Greek Philosophical Texts, or the Art of Misquotation," *Editing Greek and Latin Texts,* ed. J. Grant (New York, 1989), 63–95.

57. See A. L. Astarita, *La cultura nelle "Noctes Atticae"* (Catania, 1993), 23–26.

to the earlier legal treatises they drew upon. The fourth-century *Collatio legum Romanarum et Mosaicarum,* for example—a treatise which argued that the laws of Moses were compatible with those of Rome—cites the former vaguely, but provides chapter and verse for every reference to the latter. Fragmentarily preserved notes on a legal lecture from the late fifth century C.E. reveal that professors referred students to their sources not only by book and chapter divisions, but also by the page number, in what were evidently uniform copies.[58] Medieval scholars who worked within the new schools of the twelfth century and the universities that took shape after them developed high standards of precision and neat sets of abbreviated reference forms for other disciplines as well as law. Evidently, precise citation comes with professionalization.

The margins of manuscripts and early printed texts in theology, law, and medicine swarm with glosses which, like the historian's footnote, enable the reader to work backward from the finished argument to the texts it rests on. Peter Lombard, the theologian whose commentaries on the Psalms and the Letters of Paul "are probably the most highly developed of glossed books," systematically named his sources in marginal glosses, creating what Malcolm Parkes has called "the ancestor of the modern scholarly apparatus of footnotes."[59] Peter certainly de-

---

58. For the *Collatio* see the edition by M. Hyamson (London, 1913). The *Scholia Sinaitica* are to be found in *Fontes iuris romani anteiustiniani,* ed. S. Riccobono et al. (Florence, 1940–1943); see P. Stein, *Regulae iuris* (Edinburgh, 1966), 115–116.

59. See the seminal article of M. B. Parkes, "The Influence of the Concepts of *Ordinatio* and *Compilatio* on the Development of the Book," in *Mediaeval Literature and Learning,* ed. J. J. G. Alexander and M. Gibson (Oxford, 1976), 115–141 at 116–117; cf. also P. Lombard, *Sententiae in iv. libris distinctae,* Spicilegium Bonaventurianum, 4 (Rome, 1979), I, pt. 1, prolegomena, *138–139*.

serves credit for one typically modern feat: provoking the first controversy over a wrong reference in a note. One of his glosses mentioned St. Jerome as a source for the story, a popular one in the twelfth century, that the Salome mentioned in the Gospel of Mark was not a woman but the third husband of St. Anne. His student Herbert of Bosham, who attacked this thesis, argued fiercely that Peter's gloss was wrong. As a good pupil, though, he preferred to ascribe the mistake to an ignorant scribe rather than his learned teacher.[60] Experimentation with new and safer forms of reference began early: the thirteenth-century encyclopedist Vincent of Beauvais tried to avoid scribal errors by incorporating his source references into his texts, presumably on the theory that glosses were more vulnerable than the text proper to errors in copying.[61]

But no traditional form of annotation—from the grammarian's glosses to the theologian's allegories to the philologist's emendations—is identical to the historical footnote. Modern historians demand that every brand-new text about the past come with systematic notes, written by its author, on its sources. This is a rule of professional historical scholarship. It has no obvious connection with the long-established historical fact that all writings deemed important by a scholarly or religious community have received commentaries from later interpreters. Scriptural commentaries buttress a text which draws its main authorization from qualities that histories cannot

60. P. Lombard, *140. For the full text see *Patrologia Latina,* 190, 1418 B-C; for the context see B. Smalley, "A Commentary on the *Hebraica* by Herbert of Bosham," *Recherches de théologie ancienne et médiévale,* 18 (1959), 29–65 at 37–40.

61. Parkes, 133. See also J. P. Gumbert, " 'Typography' in the Manuscript Book," *Journal of the Printing History Society,* 22 (1993), 5–28 at 8, and, for the general context, M. A. Rouse and R. H. Rouse, *Authentic Witnesses* (Notre Dame, 1991), chaps. 4–7.

boast: the fact that its author was divine or, more often, divinely inspired, its antiquity, its literary form. Such notes act as intermediaries between a text considered to be of eternal value and a modern reader whose horizons are necessarily limited by immediate needs and interests. Some annotators see the scriptures as a bomb that may go off if roughly handled by ordinary people, others as a bulwark to theological and social order.[62] All of them agree, however, that the text, like an everlasting beacon, sends out a message of eternal value and relevance. Human readers need commentaries only because their parochial needs and interests may blind or distract them.

Historical footnotes resemble traditional glosses in form. But they seek to show that the work they support claims authority and solidity from the historical conditions of its creation: that its author excavated its foundations and discovered its components in the right places, and used the right crafts to mortise them together. To do so they locate the production of the work in question in time and space, emphasizing the limited horizons and opportunities of its author, rather than those of its reader. Footnotes buttress and undermine, at one and the same time.

Nor does the historian's apparatus derive from late medieval and Renaissance authors' commentaries on their own works. The historian who builds a literary house on a foundation of documents does not address the same task as the author of a

---

62. See e.g. E. B. Tribble, *Margins and Marginality* (Charlottesville and London, 1993), chap. 1. On the distinction between the different forms of commentary and the footnote see also J. Kaestner, "Anmerkungen in Büchern. Grundstrukturen und Hauptentwicklungslinien, dargestellt an ausgewählten literarischen und wissenschaftlichen Texten," *Bibliothek: Forschung und Praxis,* 8 (1984), 203–226.

religious, literary, or scientific work who tries to fix the text's message unequivocally for posterity. The one explains the methods and procedures used to produce the text, the other the methods and procedures that should be used to consume it. Finally, the historian who cites documents does not cite authorities, as the theologians and lawyers of the Middle Ages and the Renaissance did, but sources. Historical footnotes list not the great writers who sanction a given statement or whose words an author has creatively adapted, but the documents, many or most of them not literary texts at all, which provided its substantive ingredients. The modern professional historian is not in any simple way the direct descendant of the professional intellectual of the medieval schools or the Renaissance court.

In this necessarily speculative essay, I will try to find out when, where, and why historians adopted their distinctively modern form of narrative architecture—to learn who first erected this curious arcade with its ornate *piano nobile* and its open bottom floor that offers glimpses of so many alluring wares. My answers will necessary be schematic and tentative, but I hope to show that the footnote has a longer pedigree than we have been accustomed to believe—and that the beast's origins shed a light of their own on its nature, functions, and problems.

CHAPTER TWO

Ranke: A Footnote about Scientific History

✳ Every schoolboy knows—at least every German high school student once knew—what scientific history is and who invented it. Scientific history rests on primary rather than secondary sources: Leopold von Ranke, the Protestant jurist's son from the wonderfully named Thuringian town of Wiehe a. d. Unstrut who became one of the dominant figures of the nineteenth-century University of Berlin, was its first famous practitioner. Though Ranke became the academic historian par excellence, moreover, his achievements were of far wider than merely academic interest. His university was founded after Prussia's defeat by Napoleon. Designed by Wilhelm von Humboldt to foster original research, it formed an organic part of the effort to renew Prussian culture and society that also led to the building of official Berlin's splendid classical island of museums and the propounding of Hegel's splendidly unclassical philosophy of history.[1] By the middle of the nineteenth century,

1. On the founding and early history of the University of Berlin see the complementary accounts by U. Muhlack, "Die Universitäten im Zeichen von Neuhumanismus und Idealismus: Berlin," *Beiträge zu Problemen deutscher Universitätsgründungen der frühen Neuzeit,* ed. P. Baumgart and N. Hammerstein, Wolfenbütteler Forschungen 4 (Nendeln/Liechtenstein, 1978), 299–340, and C.

the university had established worldwide preeminence in natural science, systematic philosophy, and philological scholarship. It made the appropriate stage for a grand intellectual drama in the realm of history—the realm in which, many German thinkers of different schools agreed, the spirit of the age must manifest itself. Ranke's books thrilled thousands of readers, while his lectures and seminars won dozens of earnest young men to the belief that history, properly studied, would enable them and their country to master the chaos of the modern world. He made a crowd-pleasing hero for this attractive series of scenes.

No one, certainly, believed this more firmly than Ranke himself. Other historians complain about having to read dull sources in dusty archives far from home. But collections of primary sources and folders of archival acts acted on Ranke like clover on a pig. His letters evoke the pleasures of document-diving with a vividness seldom attained in this context. Here he is in 1827, happily ensconced in the archives at Vienna:

> After three I make my way to the archive. Hammer is still working here, on his Ottoman affairs, and a Herr von Buchholtz, who wants to write a history of Ferdinand I. It is really a complete office. One finds one's pens, pen-knife, scissors, and so on, all ready for one, and has one's own well-defined workplace. Usually it becomes dark rather soon, and I find it very pleasant, when the overseer calls out "A Liecht" ["A light," in the Viennese dialect]: at once the servant brings two for each person who is working there.[2]

McClelland, " 'To Live for Science': Ideals and Realities at the University of Berlin," *The University and the City,* ed. T. Bender (New York and Oxford, 1988), 181–197. On the remaking of German cultural institutions in this period, see the informative work of T. Ziolkowski, *German Romanticism and Its Institutions* (Princeton, 1990).

2. L. von Ranke, *Das Briefwerk,* ed. W. P. Fuchs (Hamburg, 1949), 131–

Here he is again in August 1829, this time in the libraries of Rome:

I find the fresh, cool, quiet evenings a great pleasure. The Corso is busy until midnight. The cafés stay open until 2:00 or 3:00 A.M., and the theater often does not close until 1:30. Then one dines. Not I, naturally. I hurry into bed, since I would like to be at the Palazzo Barberini by 7:00 the next morning. There I use a room belonging to the librarian, which receives the north wind; my manuscripts are piled up there. My scribe arrives soon after I do, and slips in with a "Ben levato" ["Good morning"] at the door. The librarian's servant, or the servant's wife, appears before me, and offers me their services with the usual "Occorre niente?" Also the librarian, named Razzi, is really good and has given me and other Germans excellent help.—A few steps from there is the Biblioteca Albani, where Winckelmann wrote his history of art . . . I use two other libraries, making good progress. How quickly one studies the day away![3]

132: "Nach drei Uhr begebe ich mich nach dem Archiv. Hier arbeitet noch Hammer (an den osmanischen Sachen) und ein Herr v. Buchholtz, der eine Geschichte Ferdinands I. schreiben will. Es ist eine völlige Kanzlei: man findet Federn, Federmesser, Papierschere usw. vorbereitet, hat seinen umzäunten Platz. Gewöhnlich wird es bald etwas dunkel, und ein angenehmer Augenblick ist mir, wenn der Vorsteher ruft: 'a Liecht,' worauf der Diener für jeden, der da arbeitet, deren zwei bringt." Ranke's working companions were the historians Franz Bernhard von Buchholtz and Joseph Freiherr von Hammer-Purgstall.

3. Ibid., 194: "Ein grosser Genuss sind die frischen, kühlen, stillen Abende und Nächte. Bis Mitternacht ist der Corso belebt. Die Cafés sind 2–3 Uhr nach Mitternacht eröffnet. Das Theater schliesst oft erst halb zwei. Dann nimmt man noch die Cena ein. Ich natürlich nicht. Ich eile ins Bett; ich möchte gerne des andern Morgens um sieben beim Palast Barberini anlangen. Dort benutze ich ein Zimmer des Bibliothekars, welches die Tramontana hat, wo meine Manuskripte aufgehäuft sind. Bald nach mir langt mein Schreiber an und huscht mit einem Ben levato! zur Tür herein. Der Diener des Bibliothekars oder die Frau des Dieners erscheint und bietet mir mit dem gewöhnlichen: occorre niente? ihre Dienste an. Auch der Bibliothekar namens Razzi ist wahrhaft gut

With these vivid words Ranke evoked what became, for many German scholars and many non-German admirers, one of the great discoveries of early nineteenth-century history: the pleasures of the archive.[4] For Ranke, despite the charm of his style and the profundity of his historical thought, won his status as the founder of a new historical school by the rhetorical appeal of his documentation.

Late in life, Ranke dictated a sketchy autobiography. He dramatized his life as the story of a vocation as irresistible and unique as Bertrand Russell's call to philosophy. His early education had been classical: he had mastered Greek and Latin at an old and famous secondary school, Schulpforta, where young philologists were stuffed like Strasbourg geese with ancient literature. Then he had learned the methods of modern classical philology at the University of Leipzig, where he studied with a pioneering student of Greek tragedy, Gottfried Hermann. Gradually, however, he had developed an interest in history— both that of modern Europe, including the life of Martin Luther, and that of ancient Rome, which he studied in the pioneering critical treatment of Barthold Georg Niebuhr. While teaching in the Gymnasium, or high school, at Frankfurt an der Oder, Ranke fell in love with Sir Walter Scott, whose novels brought the Middle Ages and the Renaissance back to life for

---

und hat mir und anderen Deutschen die besten Dienste geleistet.——Wenige Schritte von da ist die Bibliothek Albani, wo Winckelmann die Kunstgeschichte schrieb . . . Noch zwei andere Bibliotheken besuche ich mit gutem Fortgang. Wie bald ist ein Tag wegstudiert!"

4. A. Farge, *Le Goût de l'archive* (Paris, 1989)—a wonderful description of the nature of archival work in one of the great national collections. For vivid and insightful descriptions of archival work in other locales, see also S. Nievo, *Il prato in fondo al mare* (Rome, 1995), and R. Hilberg, *The Politics of Memory* (Chicago, 1996).

him as they had for many others. But the love affair was deeply troubled. Scott proved as unreliable as he was charming. Comparison with the historical tradition, as preserved by the chronicler Philippe de Commines and contemporary reports, revealed that the Charles of Burgundy and Louis XI portrayed in Scott's *Quentin Durward* had never really lived. Ranke found these errors—which he took as deliberate—unforgivable. But he also found them inspiring: "In making the comparison I convinced myself that the historical tradition is more beautiful, and certainly more interesting, than the romantic fiction." So he set out to write his *Geschichten der romanischen und germanischen Völker (Histories of the Latin and German Peoples)* from contemporary sources alone. Unfortunately, these too disagreed; hence Ranke had to build his narrative by dismantling those of his predecessors, each of whom—even the German ones—proved unreliable on some points. Only close, comparative study could produce a critical history.[5]

The work that appeared in 1824 brought Ranke everything he could have wanted. His still immature narrative style, with its classicizing and Gallicizing turns of phrase, aroused objections. He had meant to reach the middle of the sixteenth century, but allowed his publisher—who began setting the text sooner than Ranke had thought possible—to bring out a truncated version of his original project, one that ended in the 1510s. But the same novelist's ability to find vivid details that would later enliven his letters on libraries had already given fire and ceremony to his discussion of critical research. Ranke's

---

5. Ranke, *Sämmtliche Werke,* 53/54 (Leipzig, 1890), 61–62: "Bei der Vergleichung überzeugte ich mich, dass das historisch Ueberlieferte selbst schöner und jedenfalls interessanter sei, als die romantische Fiction."

preface to his long second volume, *Zur Kritik neuerer Geschichtsschreiber (On the Criticism of Modern Historians)*, portrayed the contact between the critical historian and his sources as complex and ceremonious, strenuous but rewarding:

> Consider the strange feelings that would arise in someone who entered a great collection of antiquities, in which genuine and spurious, beautiful and repulsive, spectacular and insignificant objects, from many nations and periods, lay next to one another in complete disorder. This is also how someone would have to feel who found himself all at once within sight of the varied monuments of modern history. They speak to us in a thousand different voices; they reveal the most widely different natures; they are dressed in all the colors.[6]

The library and archive transform themselves through Ranke's glamorous metaphors into a gallery of three-dimensional antiquities, the sources assembled in them into precious objects. The historian, for his part, turns into the man of taste, whose sense of what is genuine and false becomes a touchstone. By applying this deftly, the astute and critical historian performs magic: he reassembles the dusty thrift shop of the past into a modern museum, in which the visitor encounters coherent sets of material from distinct historical periods, organized room by room, dated, labeled, and attested. Ranke himself underwent

6. Ranke, *Geschichten der romanischen und germanischen Völker von 1494 bis 1514, Zur Kritik neuerer Geschichtschreiber* (Leipzig and Berlin, 1824), iv: "Wie einem zu Muth seyn würde, der in eine grosse Sammlung von Alterthümern träte, worin Aechtes und Unächtes, Schönes und Zurückstossendes, Glänzendes und Unscheinbares, aus mancherley Nationen und Zeitaltern, ohne Ordnung neben einander läge, so etwa müsste sich auch der fühlen, der sich mit Einem Mal im Anschaun der mannichfaltigen Denkmale der neuern Geschichte fände. Sie reden uns in tausend Stimmen an: sie zeigen die verschiedensten Naturen: sie sind in alle Farben gekleidet."

a similar metamorphosis, as a great writer and teacher emerged from the chrysalis of the provincial Gymnasium teacher. He found himself the possessor of a chair at Berlin, the recipient of special permission to use the archives, and the beneficiary of grants for travel to foreign archives and libraries.

Ranke's "method of research" had an intellectual edge fully worthy of his brilliant style. The history of the Italian wars of the early sixteenth century by Machiavelli's friend Francesco Guicciardini had long been thought the most accurate and the most profound account of those terrifying years, when huge French and Spanish armies, equipped with cannon and muskets in unprecedented quantities, fought their way up and down the Italian peninsula. Even the most powerful Italian states found themselves reduced by their lack of military force to pawns in a game of power politics which they had traditionally dominated by guile. As part of the foundation for his own political analysis of Italy's failure to resist the great powers from the north, Guicciardini quoted the speeches of many political actors in full. Moreover, he described any number of events in which he or friends of his had taken part. In sum, Guicciardini lived up to all the demands traditionally made of historians in the classical tradition: that they themselves have had political and military experience, that they report as eyewitnesses or on the basis of interviews with other eyewitnesses, and that they manifestly love the truth.[7] Evidently Guicciardini deserved the faith reposed in him by Ranke's most eloquent and recent predecessor, the Genevan philosopher Sismonde de Sismondi.[8] His

7. G. Nadel, "Philosophy of History before Historicism," *History and Theory*, 3 (1964), 291–315.
8. On whom see e.g. P. B. Stadler, *Geschichtschreibung und historisches Denken in Frankreich, 1789–1871* (Zurich, 1958), chap. 5.

eight-volume history of the Italian republics in their medieval
heyday of political freedom and artistic creativity reached its
melancholy climax in the High Renaissance, when the downfall
of Italy and the hegemony of Spain brought progress to an end.
Sismondi's close-packed footnotes referred to all major chroniclers of the sixteenth century, but he relied especially heavily
on Guicciardini.

Ranke appreciated the depth and intricacy of Guiccardini's
political analyses, which he saw as typically Florentine. The
passage he devoted to characterizing the historian is a little
masterpiece of cultural history in its own right:

> He wants to show what was to be expected in each case, what
> was to be done, what the real reason of an action was. Therefore
> he is a true virtuoso and master in his explanations of the extent
> to which each human action derived from an inborn passion,
> from ambition, from selfishness. These discourses are not the
> product of Guicciardini's wit alone. They depend, in two re-
> lated ways, on the condition of his Florentine fatherland. On
> the one hand, Florentine power was not independent, and the
> situation in public affairs often swung from one extreme to the
> other. Therefore men spontaneously directed their attention to
> affairs and their possibility of success . . . That is the one side.
> But their manner was the same in domestic matters. To un-
> derstand the origin of a work like Guicciardini's, one must first
> read in Varchi and Nerli how much thought, gossip, trading,
> suspicion, and judgment took place before the election of a
> gonfaloniere [an official of the Commune]. Relationships, al-
> liances, and counter-alliances were formed in this small circle,
> just as in European affairs, to win a few more black beans [in
> the selection process]. A vast range of things had to be taken
> into account: observations, rules, and counsels took shape.[9]

9. Ranke, *Zur Kritik*, 47–48: "Was in jedem Fall zu erwarten, zu thun, was

Ranke traced the connections between the arts of politics and history, showing that a single cultural style determined Florentine political behavior and historical exposition. No wonder that his student Jacob Burckhardt, who later applied a similar method to a much wider range of cultural forms, from statecraft to the dance, found his method inspiring.[10] Never before had historical method been analyzed with so much intensity or the results presented with such brilliance. Yet Ranke's central conclusions were negative. The same skills that won Renaissance writers like Guicciardini high office and inspired their brilliant political reportage produced bad history. Because Guicciardini cared only about his actors' motives, intentions, and skills, Ranke argued, he allowed his larger narrative to become confused and shapeless. Still worse, because the establishment of facts did not matter greatly to Guicciardini, he made no systematic effort to obtain first-hand information. In fact, he cop-

---

der eigentliche Grund einer Handlung gewesen, will er zeigen. Daher ist er in den Erläuterungen, in wiefern eine jede menschliche Handlung aus angeborner Leidenschaft, Ehrgeiz, Eigennutz, komme, ein wahrer Virtuos und Meister. Diese Discorsen sind nicht eine Hervorbringung von Guicciardini's Geist allein; sie ruhen, und zwar in doppelter Hinsicht, nur allzuwohl auf dem Zustand seiner Vaterstadt Florenz. Erstens nämlich, da die Macht von Florenz nicht selbständig war, und die Lage der öffentlichen Angelegenheiten zuweilen von dem einen Extrem zum andern schwankte, richtete sich die Aufmerksamkeit unwillkürlich auf die möglichen Erfolge der Dinge . . . Das ist das Eine. Aber auch in den innern Angelegenheiten pflegen sie derselben Art und Weise. Wenn man in Varchi und Nerli liest, wie viel vor einer Gonfalonierewahl gesonnen, geschwatzt, unterhandelt, vermuthet, geurtheilt ward, wie man in diesem kleinen Kreis, so gut als in den europäischen Angelegenheiten, Verwandtschaften, Bündnisse, Gegenbündnisse schloss, um einige schwarze Bohnen mehr zu bekommen, wie viel es da zu berücksichtigen gab, wie sich nun Beobachtungen, Regeln, Rathschläge entwickelten, so versteht man erst den Ursprung eines Werks, wie Guicciardini's Werk ist."

10. W. Kaegi, *Jacob Burckhardt: Eine Biographie,* II (Basel, 1950), 54–74.

ied materials from other historians not only in the earlier part of his histories, which covered the years of his childhood, but even for the events of his maturity.[11]

Guicciardini also made plenty of mistakes. His reports on treaties, for example, had won him particular respect as a researcher: "Francesco's nephew Agnolo, who edited his history, maintains that his uncle showed special industry in exploring the public monuments [sources], and had excellent access to them."[12] In fact, however, many errors disfigured these passages. Even the famous speeches lacked historical credibility. Some differed from the texts actually delivered, while others lacked any confirmation from external sources. Not one of Guicciardini's set-piece orations, Ranke argued, could be proved to have been delivered as the historian recorded it. Rather, they exemplified the typical methods of Renaissance historians, who tried to emulate the ancients and show their brilliance at formal rhetoric, just as Livy had. They did not report, but composed, speeches which might provide sharp political commentary on a situation but "had nothing in common with historical sources."[13] For all his political insight, Guicciardini was not a "documentary" historian. Therefore the crit-

11. Ranke, *Zur Kritik,* 8–20.

12. Ibid., 38: "Agnolo, der Neffe Franzesco's, der Herausgeber dieser Geschichte, behauptet, sein Oheim habe mit besonderem Fleiss die öffentlichen Denkmäler (pubbliche memorie) erforscht, und habe vielen Zugang zu ihnen gehabt." Ranke goes on to remark: "Wir sahen, wie Johann Bodin auf diese originale Kunde der Beschlüsse und Bündnisse einen besondern Werth legte"— "As we saw, Jean Bodin attached special value to these original reports about decisions and alliances." For the importance of Ranke's use of Bodin, see Chapter 3 below.

13. Ibid., 27: "mit historischen Monumenten so gut wie nichts gemein hatten."

ical modern scholar who wished, as Ranke did, to learn and show "wie es eigentlich gewesen," "how it really was," should not cite him.[14]

Footnotes, in other words, were not enough. Sismondi had plenty of those. Ranke even counted them, establishing that Sismondi's 27 references to François Beaucaire in chapter 104 and at least 27 more in chapter 105 put the French historian in second place, behind Guicciardini, among Sismondi's sources. But the peppering of short references to authors, titles, and page numbers that supposedly proved Sismondi's conscientious workmanship in fact revealed only that he had failed to ask the right question in the first place: "who, of these many writers, possesses information that is really original with him: who can offer us real instruction?"[15] A historical account that marched on Guicciardini's evidence was doomed to suffer fallen arches, if not worse:

> Let us clearly acknowledge, once and for all, that this book does not deserve the unconditional respect it has enjoyed up to now. It should be described not as a source, but only as a re-working of sources, and a faulty one at that. If we accomplish that, we will have reached our goal: the Sismondis will have to stop citing Guicciardini at the bottom of every page, and always the same Guicciardini. They will have to know that he does not provide any proof.[16]

14. Ranke exaggerated here: see e.g. E. Schulin, *Traditionskritik und Rekonstruktionsversuch* (Göttingen, 1979), 48–50; and more generally the classic work of F. Gilbert, *Machiavelli and Guicciardini* (Princeton, 1965).

15. Ranke, *Zur Kritik*, v: "wem von so Vielen eine originale Kenntniss beygewohnt, von wem wir wahrhaft belehrt werden können."

16. Ibid., 36: "Erkennen wir klar, dass das unbedingte Ansehen, welches diess Buch bis jetzt genossen, ihm mit Unrecht gewährt worden, dass es nicht eine Quelle, eine Urkunde, sondern allein eine Bearbeitung, und zwar eine

Only the right footnotes, not a random assembly of references, could enable a text to stand proud under critical scrutiny.

Ranke's apparatus, by contrast, attested to his systematic, original, critical research. Even while teaching in book-deprived Frankfurt an der Oder, he had managed to obtain the main printed histories of the Renaissance from the Royal Library in Berlin, the patience of whose staff he tried (when he received his call to Berlin, the joke went round that it had been necessary either to bring the whole library to Ranke or to bring him to the library; given his small size, the latter course had proved easier).[17] He had also learned from an older student friend, Gustav Stenzel, who himself became a distinguished medievalist, that the historian should begin work on a given reign or period by making systematic excerpts from the sources.[18] These amounted, in effect, to long, closely written summaries of the texts, in German. Ranke divided the pages of his folio notebook into two columns, one devoted to Guicciardini, the other to complementary or divergent accounts. Systematic comparison revealed the Florentine historian's dependencies and defects. As Ranke set out to explain his conclusions, the notebooks metamorphosed almost spontaneously into a radical critique. It became clear almost at once, both to Ranke and his publisher, that this material, far more than his narrative, would excite the public: it amounted to the dynamiting of what had

mangelhafte zu nennen ist, so ist unser Zweck erreicht; so müssen die Sismondi aufhören, unter jeder Seite den Gucciardini und immer den nämlichen zu citiren; sie müssen wissen, dass er nicht beweist."

17. For Ranke's use of the Royal Library see C. Varrentrapp, "Briefe an Ranke . . .," *Historische Zeitschrift,* 105 (1910), 105–131, and Ranke, *Neue Briefe,* ed. B. Hoeft and H. Herzfeld (Hamburg, 1949), 22, 24–25, 39, 41–42, 44–45, 54–55.

18. See the excellent account in Schulin, 49.

looked like historical bedrock. As Ranke wrote to his brother
in October 1824,

> You will probably still remember the handwritten notebook in
> folio (or rather the not-yet handwritten one) in which I entered
> all my notes about the historians whom I read. I could not
> avoid offering some justification for my treatment of these his-
> torians in my history. So I made the folio notebook into a quarto
> one, and the quarto one in turn is being transformed into a
> printed octavo. They predict that this will bring me more suc-
> cess than the other.[19]

19. Ranke, *Das Briefwerk,* ed. Fuchs, 65: "Du wirst Dich wohl noch auf das
geschriebene Foliobuch besinnen (vielmehr das noch nicht geschriebene) in das
ich alle Notizen über die Geschichtschreiber, die ich las, eintrug. Nun war es
unerlässlich, dass ich meine Behandlung dieser Geschichtschreiber in der Geschichte selbst einigermassen rechtfertigte. Da habe ich nun aus jenem Foliobuch eins in quarto gemacht, und daraus wird eins in octavo gedruckt; aus diesem
prophezeit man mir einen grössern Erfolg als aus dem andern." Students of
Burckhardt will recall that he, too, excerpted primary sources with remarkable
energy and assiduity (W. Kaegi, *Jacob Burckhardt: Eine Biographie,* III [Basel,
1956], 383–396); his cultural history of the Renaissance also came together as
he reworked a vast mass of excerpts. Cf. his famous letter to Paul Heyse of 14
August 1858, quoted ibid., 666: "Gestern habe ich zum Beispiel 700 kleine
Zeddel nur mit Citaten aus Vasari, die ich in ein Buch zusammengeschrieben
hatte, auseinandergeschnitten und sortiert zum neuen Aufkleben nach Sachen.
Aus andern Autoren habe ich noch etwa 1000 Quartseiten Excerpte über die
Kunst und 2000 über die Cultur. Wie viel von all diesem werde ich wohl
wirklich verarbeiten?" ("Yesterday, for example, I cut up 700 little slips, with
quotations from Vasari alone, which I had written down in a book, and rearranged them to be glued up again, organized by topics. From other authors I
have some 1000 more quarto pages of excerpts on art and 2000 on culture.
How much of all this will I really be able to process?") On Burckhardt's working
methods see P. Ganz, "Jacob Burckhardts *Kultur der Renaissance in Italien.* Hand-
werk und Methode," *Deutsche Vierteljahrsschrift für Literaturwissenschaft und Geistesgeschichte,* 62 (1988), 24–59, and E. H. Gombrich, *In Search of Cultural History*
(Oxford, 1969). Next to the unwritten history of annotation that haunts historical libraries wails the ghost of the even thicker history of note-taking. See
for now the rich survey by A. Moss, *Printed Commonplace-Books and the Structuring*

The prophets were right. Ranke's first readers had many doubts about his narrative. But almost all of them—from Stenzel to the old Göttingen scholar Arnold Heeren to the German exile Karl Benedikt Hase, a brilliant lexicographer and deft forger whose diary, in classical Greek, affords unique guidance through the brothels and cafés of Balzac's Paris—agreed that they had never seen such brilliant, cogent, and polished critical argument carried out by so young a scholar.[20] A favorable reviewer in the *Allgemeine Literatur-Zeitung* emphasized the iconoclastic brilliance of Ranke's analysis of his sources, which stripped hallowed texts of their aura of authority: "He illuminates the works of the historians who have previously been considered the chief sources for the history of the period in question . . . as well as the personalities of their authors with the torch of his uncompromising, strict criticism. Pitilessly he deprives both of the aura, in which they previously glowed: or at least he determines precisely the extent to which they really deserve and do not deserve belief, and in general how far they should be considered *true sources*."[21] Even the most savage of Ranke's

---

of Renaissance Thought (Oxford, 1996), which ranges far more widely than its title promises.

20. See the materials published by Varrentrapp in *Historische Zeitschrift*, 105 (1910), 109 (Heeren), 112 (v. Raumer), 114 (Schulze), 115 (Kamptz); A. von Hase, "Brückenschlag nach Paris. Zu einem unbekannten Vorstoss Rankes bei Karl Benedikt Hase (1825)," *Archiv für Kulturgeschichte*, 60 (1978), 213–221 at 215. On Hase himself see the witty and erudite article of P. Petitmengin, "Deux têtes de pont de la philologie allemande en France: le *Thesaurus linguae Graecae* et la 'Bibliothèque des auteurs grecs' (1830–1867)," *Philologie und Hermeneutik im 19. Jahrhundert*, II, ed. M. Bollack and H. Wismann (Göttingen, 1983), 76–98.

21. Anonymous review of Ranke, *Ergänzungsblätter zur Allgemeinen Literatur-Zeitung* (February 1828), nos. 23–24, cols. 183–189 at 183–184: "Mit der Fackel einer unbestechlichen, strengen Kritik beleuchtet er die Werke der bisher

critics admitted that his "contributions to the criticism of modern historians" were "the best part of Mister Ranke's work; at least they reveal that he has compared the different extracts in many ways."[22]

In the next few years, Ranke's interest in historiography would die down as his interest in documents blazed up. He concluded his *Zur Kritik neuerer Geschichtsschreiber* not with a final analysis of published histories but with a chapter entitled "What Is Still to Be Done." Here he argued that historians must now go beyond the printed texts. Everywhere in Europe, but above all in Germany, the original sources lay unexplored and inaccessible: "For this period we have files of documents, letters, biographies, and chronicles of the highest importance, which remain in the state they would have been in if printing had never been invented."[23] Even the qualities of the best modern historians mattered less than those of the primary sources, the documents that revealed the real intentions of politicians and generals. To lay these open must become the vocation of a chosen individual, one who would travel with the boldness of

als Hauptquellen für die Geschichten der bezeichneten Periode . . . geachteten Historiker wie die Persönlichkeit ihrer Urheber, und beraubt beide schonungslos des Nimbus, worin sie bisher geglänzet, oder bestimmt wenigstens genau, in wie fern und in wie fern nicht sie wirklich Glauben verdienen, überhaupt in wiefern sie als *wahre Quellen* zu achten seyen."

22. "H. L. Manin" [H. Leo], review of Ranke, *Ergänzungsblätter zur Jenaischen Allgemeinen Literatur-Zeitung*, 16 (1828), nos. 17–18, cols. 129–140 at 138: Ranke's "Beyträge zur Kritik neuerer Geschichtschreiber" were "das Beste an Hn. *Rankes* Arbeit, und zeigen wenigstens zugleich von mannichfacher Vergleichung der verschiedenen Excerpte unter sich."

23. Ranke, *Zur Kritik,* 177: "Es sind über diese Zeit Acten, Briefe, Lebensbeschreibungen, Chroniken von der grössten Wichtigkeit vorhanden, für die es aber ist, als wäre die Buchdruckerkunst noch gar nicht erfunden."

the eighteenth-century explorer of Arabia, Carsten Niebuhr, not into some African or Near Eastern desert but into German hearts of archival darkness:

> What we need is a man equipped with reasonable knowledge, lavish letters of recommendation and good health, who would traverse Germany in all directions in order to hunt down the remains of this world, which is half sunken and yet so close to us. We pursue unknown grasses into the deserts of Libya: how can the life of our forefathers, in our own country, not deserve the same zeal?[24]

The right man, of course, was Ranke himself. He was inspired by the first publications of the young G. H. Pertz, a better-off scholar who had already begun the German invasion of Italian libraries, and who would soon lead the greatest of all German historical publishing enterprises, the *Monumenta Germaniae Historica*.[25] Ranke was also exalted by the success of his first book. He sent a flurry of letters and complimentary copies off to scholars, to ministers, and to the intellectual and statesman Barthold Georg Niebuhr, who was both a former ambassador to Rome and a historian. In short, Ranke solicited anyone and

24. Ibid., 181: "Hier wäre ein Mann erforderlich, der mit leidlichen Kenntnissen, sattsamen Empfehlungen und guter Gesundheit ausgerüstet, Deutschland nach allen Seiten durchzöge, und die Reste einer halb untergegangenen und so nahe liegenden Welt aufsuchte. Wir jagen unbekannten Gräsern bis in die Wüsten Libyens nach; sollte das Leben unserer Altvordern nicht denselben Eifer in unserm eigenen Land werth sein?"

25. Ranke, *Das Briefwerk*, ed. Fuchs, 70. For Pertz see H. Bresslau, *Geschichte der Monumenta Germaniae Historica* (1921); D. Knowles, *Great Historical Enterprises: Problems in Monastic History* (Edinburgh, 1963), chap. 3; H. Fuhrmann, with M. Wesche, *"Sind eben alles Menschen gewesen." Gelehrtenleben im 19. und 20. Jahrhundert* (Munich, 1996).

everyone who, he thought, might help him to obtain a university teaching post, travel grants and the keys to archival kingdoms at home and abroad.[26]

The exploration and exploitation of the primary sources of history—in the first instance the reports of Venetian ambassadors to their government, but in the end many sorts of public and private papers—became the guiding principle of Ranke's working life. From the later 1820s Ranke cocooned himself in the original materials of history. He regularly traveled, with official help, to gain access to what were in the early years still closely guarded archives.[27] He judiciously exploited the post-revolutionary book market, in which many Italian families put their papers up for sale. He systematically used the human copying machines who came long before the microfilm camera and the Xerox machine, the professional scribes who produced fair copies of archival documents for a fee. Continuous purchase of such important new editions as those contained in the *Monumenta* produced the mountain of books and manuscripts now preserved at Syracuse University in New York. A photograph shows the old historian dwarfed, almost crushed, by the material embodiment of his erudition.[28]

26. See e.g. Ranke, *Neue Briefe,* ed. Hoeft and Herzfeld, 56–59.

27. For a fascinating study in the glacial opening up of one of Europe's richest archives, see H. Chadwick, *Catholicism and History* (Cambridge, 1978).

28. For Ranke's practices see U. Tucci, "Ranke and the Venetian Document Market," in *Leopold von Ranke and the Shaping of the Historical Discipline,* ed. G. G. Iggers and J. Powell (Syracuse, N.Y., 1990), 99–107; for an image of him in his library see the frontispiece, ibid. See also the remarkable catalogue by E. Muir, *The Leopold von Ranke Manuscript Collection of Syracuse University* (Syracuse, N.Y., 1983). And for the larger history of the notaries and others who produced precise copies before the age of photography, see the fascinating work of H. Levine, *The Culture of the Copy* (New York, 1996), chap. 6.

Ranke did not simply accumulate: what he read and had copied, he used. He represented his history of Germany in the Reformation, for example, his chief work of the 1830s and 1840s, as the result of a triumphal progress across the German archives. In words that became famous, Ranke prophesied that this heavy book was only the first small swallow, the harbinger of a historical revolution: "I can see the time approach when we will no longer have to base modern history on reports, even those of contemporary historians—except to the extent that they had first-hand knowledge—to say nothing of derivative reworkings of the sources. Rather, we will construct it from the accounts of eyewitnesses and the most genuine and direct sources."[29] His excitement lasted through years of hard work, of searching and copying, assessing and editing, comparing printed editions with manuscript texts. As he prepared the documentary appendix of the history of the Reformation, for example, Ranke drew up repeated drafts for an introduction in which he called for "readers who take part in the work," "participatory readers." He admitted that he could not print all the relevant sources, or all those he had used: "Nobody would want to publish whole archives." But he insisted that intelligent

29. Ranke, *Deutsche Geschichte im Zeitalter der Reformation,* ed. P. Joachimsen et al. (Munich, 1925–26), I, 6*: "Ich sehe die Zeit kommen, wo wir die neuere Geschichte nicht mehr auf die Berichte, selbst nicht der gleichzeitigen Historiker, ausser insoweit ihnen eine originale Kenntnis beiwohnte, geschweige denn auf die weiter abgeleiteten Bearbeitungen zu gründen haben, sondern aus den Relationen der Augenzeugen und den ächtesten unmittelbarsten Urkunden aufbauen werden." Despite considerable progress in the study of Ranke and his Nachlass, some of which has resulted in important corrections to the work of Joachimsen and his collaborators, his introduction to this edition remains one of the finest treatments of Ranke's scholarship and thought. It is reprinted in his *Gesammelte Aufsätze,* ed. N. Hammerstein (Aalen, 1970–83), I, 627–734; on Ranke's thought and scholarship see also 735–758.

readers should work through at least the documents he did print. He urged them to overcome what he described as the minor linguistic difficulties posed by the sources, to follow the "particularly lively" accounts of great events that the original documents offered. If possible, they should work through text and documents together—a recommendation that suggests that Ranke's method was not so naive as some nowadays suppose.[30] Ranke himself never ceased to feel the sharp joy of discovery when a new set of sources became available. Each new kind of document widened his point of view, he thought, and enabled him to be more objective. When some of the documents originally kept in the Spanish archives at Simancas turned up in the accessible Archives du royaume in Paris, for example, he had the exciting opportunity to compare the reports of the diplomats of the Holy Roman Empire from the French court with those of the French diplomats at the imperial court. Even someone naturally inclined to impartiality, he reflected, could not read these sharply contrasting documents in tandem without feeling even more disposed to admire the representatives of both sides and be fair to them.[31] At the same time, he nourished no illusions about his ability to reconstruct all important events in exact detail. Over the years, as Ranke produced new editions of his history of the Reformation, he continued to find new sources. These added graphic details to, for example, his precise and passionate account of the social and religious revolution that took place in Münster in the 1530s, the Anabaptist Kingdom of God. But he admitted in the fourth edition of his work that the exact sequence of events that led

---

30. Ranke, *Deutsche Geschichte im Zeitalter der Reformation,* VI, 3–4: "Wer will auch die ganzen Archive drucken lassen?"

31. Ibid., III, ix.

up to the fall of the city remained problematic.[32] In such cases, Ranke's footnotes taught lessons in the fallibility of even the most scientific historians.

Ranke also devoted much attention to his sources in his teaching—especially in the seminar which he organized in his own home. He explained, in the Latin speech of 1825 with which he opened this informal but essential institution, that he would have liked to concentrate entirely on selected problems emerging from the primary sources. For the best students, this would have been the ideal approach. They, he explained, "have decided to dedicate their lives to learning history in a really deep way: I think that a sort of impulse of the soul and a particular quality of mind brings them to these studies. They will certainly want to know the springs from which histories are derived: they will not be content to have read the standard, required authors, and will wish to know the suppliers of every narrative."[33] Even less dedicated historians, if of high ability, "are not content to accept, believe, and teach, to trust others, but wish to use their own judgment in these matters."[34] Ranke

32. Ibid., 441–442, n. 1 (from 441), ending: "Doch bescheide ich mich, dass hier, wie oft in ähnlichen Fällen, immer noch gewisse Zweifel möglich bleiben" ("Yet I accept, that here, as often happens in similar cases, it remains possible to entertain certain doubts").

33. Leopold von Ranke Nachlass, Staatsbibliothek zu Berlin Preussischer Kulturbesitz (Haus II), 38 II A, fol. 72 recto: "eorum, qui historiae rerum discendae penitusque imbibendae vitam suam dicare constituerunt. Istos animi quodam impetu ingeniique sui natura ad haec studia ferri credo. Hi sine dubio fontes, e quibus historiae hauriuntur, cognoscere volent. Non satis habentes scriptores perlegisse quos schola suppeditat, promos omnis relati volent cognoscere." On this text (and Ranke's seminar) see the exemplary monograph of G. Berg, Leopold von Ranke als historischer Lehrer (Göttingen, 1968), 51–56 at 52 and n. 2.

34. Ranke Nachlass, 38 II A, fol. 72 recto: "Non tamen satis habent accipere ea, credere, docere, fidem aliis habere, sed suo ipsorum judicio in his rebus uti cupiunt."

would have liked to teach, rigorously, for the first group only: "I would set out a series of *loci classici* and have them read them: then I would remove the difficulties that struck them as they read. We would treat medieval history in the same way."[35] He decided not to do so only because he had students of quite varied abilities and interests, for some of whom such critical study was too hard. No one could have left Ranke's seminar without grasping his strong preference for the really gifted students who insisted on uncovering the treasures of the original texts on their own, or at least refused simply to repeat what they read in secondary works, without knowing what the sources of their information were. The seminar naturally concentrated—though not exclusively—on source criticism, and this interest moved with his students to other centers of historical research, like Munich, where the gifted and charismatic Heinrich von Sybel founded a seminar on the model of Ranke's.[36]

Most of Ranke's lecture courses also began with detailed accounts of the primary documents and some reference to the particular difficulties they posed.[37] Even at the end of Ranke's life, when he had ceased to teach and worked only with great physical difficulty, he still devoted hours every day to his favorite study. Surrounded by the irretrievably confused contents

35. Ibid., fol. 72 verso: "Si primum tantum genus hic adesset, rem ita instituerem—diger⟨er⟩em seriem locorum classicorum—eos legendos proponerem. Difficultates, quae legentibus offendunt, e medio tollere curarem. Eadem ratione historiam medii aevi tractaremus."

36. L. von Ranke, *Aus Werke und Nachlass,* ed. W. P. Fuchs et al. (Munich and Vienna, 1964–1975), I, 83–84. Cf. more generally *Geschichtswissenschaft in Berlin im 19. und 20. Jahrhundert* (Berlin, 1992), and for Sybel's Munich seminar see V. Dotterweich, *Heinrich von Sybel* (Göttingen, 1978), 255–284.

37. See Berg; Ranke, *Aus Werke und Nachlass,* ed. Fuchs et al., IV.

of his private library, the largest one in Germany, he listened to his young secretaries reading aloud excerpts from the documents he could no longer read himself—and stopped them, almost as soon as they began, when his uncanny sixth sense told him that a given passage was relevant and what it meant. Ranke insisted that only he knew what treasures the unpublished sources could yield. Neither his rival historians, who worked from mere selections, nor the archivists themselves could match his combination of detective instinct and historical insight.[38]

Even more important than this rich germ plasm of erudition, of course, were the books spawned in it: the endless series of histories of medieval and early modern Europe (and much more), each attended by a stately row of liveried documents and supported by a mass of footnotes providing not only references but whole passages from the sources. Ranke produced a new theory of history and wrote with a cosmopolitanism that would not be rivaled for a century. Long before Fernand Braudel became famous for his enormous, glitteringly detailed recreation of the economy and society of the sixteenth-century Mediterranean world, Ranke drew from the reports of Venetian ambassadors a vivid and pointed account of the societies of the two powers that dominated that world, Habsburg Spain and Ottoman Turkey.[39] He ranged with bravura across time and

38. T. Wiedemann, "Sechzehn Jahre in der Werkstatt Leopold von Ranke's," *Deutsche Revue*, November 1891, 177–179.

39. See L. Ranke, *Fürsten und Völker von Süd-Europa im sechszehnten und siebzehnten Jahrhundert. Vornehmlich aus ungedruckten Gesandtschafts-Berichten*, 2nd ed. (Berlin, 1837–1839), I, translated by W. K. Kelly as *The Ottoman and the Spanish Empires in the Sixteenth and Seventeenth Centuries* (London, 1843). For an expert assessment of this prescient work see J. H. Elliott, *Europe Divided* (London, 1968; repr. 1985), 418.

space, tackling subjects as varied as the English revolution of the seventeenth century, the Serbian revolution of his own time, the history of the Reformation and that of the early modern papacy. With these achievements I am not directly concerned.[40] But he also created and dramatized a new practice, based on a new kind of research and made visible by a new form of documentation. Each serious work of history must now travel on an impregnably armored bottom, rather like a tank. Failure to live up to this ideal of discovery and presentation brought disaster to such adherents of traditional method (or the absence of method) as Froude—whose name, like Holland's, came to designate a recognizable disease.[41] Living up to it meant, in the first instance, producing a large and informative apparatus, a set of juicy footnotes that the next scholar could productively squeeze—as Ranke indicated, implicitly, when he had his secretary read aloud extracts not from the text, but from the footnotes, of Droysen's *History of Prussia* while he prepared his own treatment of the same subject.[42] The man, the moment, the method come together with a neatness that immediately awakes suspicion.

Ranke insisted that his kind of history imitated no existing

40. See the masterly appreciation of F. Gilbert, *History: Politics or Culture?* (Princeton, 1990). For a more critical point of view, one which emphasizes the breadth and originality of eighteenth-century historiography (and brings out aspects of that tradition, like its interest in cultural and social history, which are not treated here), see P. Burke, "Ranke the Reactionary," in *Leopold von Ranke,* ed. Iggers and Powell, 36–44.

41. For "Froude's disease" see Ch. V. Langlois and Ch. Seignobos, *Introduction to the Study of History,* tr. G. G. Berry (London and New York, 1898; repr. 1912), 124–128.

42. T. Wiedemann, "Sechzehn Jahre in der Werkstatt Leopold von Ranke's," *Deutsche Revue,* December 1891, 322.

model.[43] In terms of source criticism, as we will see, he exaggerated his own originality—as the most original historians often do. But in another sense he was right: earlier historians did not anticipate Ranke's ability to bring the flavor and texture of the documents into his own text. When Ranke used account books, ambassadorial dispatches and papal diaries to characterize the austere, willful, and determined Franciscan who became Pope Sixtus V, and rebuilt the city of Rome into a magnificent stage for Catholic festivals and triumphal processions, he made his book into a sort of archive. He enabled the reader to share something of the impact of his own direct encounter with the sources.[44] In Ranke's own day, accordingly, his rhetoric generally carried conviction. Experienced haunters of archives like the Königsberg historian Johannes Voigt felt that Ranke had somehow given them a voice, or a language, with which they could for the first time explain the importance of what they had long been doing.[45] Practitioners of quite dif-

43. Ranke, *Sämmtliche Werke,* 53/54, 62.

44. See Ranke, *Die römischen Päpste in den letzten vier Jahrhunderten,* book IV, in Ranke, *Sämmtliche Werke,* 38 (Leipzig, 1878) = *The Popes of Rome* (Glasgow and London, 1846–47), I, 278–377. Cf. more generally C. Ginzburg, "Veranschaulichung und Zitat. Die Wahrheit der Geschichte," *Der Historiker als Menschenfresser. Über den Beruf des Geschichtsschreibers* (Berlin, 1990), 85–102.

45. See Voigt's letter to Ranke, surprisingly humble for the compiler of the entire Prussian *Codex diplomaticus* and the author of the heavily documented and methodologically innovative *Geschichte Marienburgs* (Königsberg, 1824) and *Hildebrand* (Weimar, 1815), in Varrentrapp, 127–128, and his strategic citation of Ranke's lines on the coming age of manuscript-based history, quoted above, in his *Briefwechsel der berühmtesten Gelehrten des Zeitalters der Reformation mit Herzog Albrecht von Preussen* (Königsberg, 1841), [v]. Admittedly, Voigt was a far less original and critical historian than Ranke, and ended up a disappointed man, unable to obtain leaves to do research and outdated in his critical technique. See e.g. the long and well-documented article on Voigt in the *Allgemeine Deutsche Biographie;* H. Prutz, *Die Königliche Albertus-Universität zu Königsberg i. Pr. im*

ferent fields acknowledged that Ranke's kind of history was
something radically new. In 1863 the classicist Heinrich Nissen set out to show, in his famous study of Livy and his sources,
that ancient historians had normally worked not like modern
historians but like modern journalists. They had drawn their
information, he argued, from one principal source, only occasionally using other texts to correct or supplement it. Nissen
based this thesis partly on an ingenious use of various forms of
collateral evidence—like the fact that ancient books, being
scrolls, would have been almost impossible to collate with one
another systematically.[46] But he received his main impetus from
Ranke—who, he thought, had shown that medieval and Renaissance historians still worked in the same way, if in very
different literary circumstances.[47] "Nissen's law"—as it came

---

neunzehnten Jahrhundert (Königsberg, 1894), 186–188; G. von Selle, Geschichte
der Albertus-Universität zu Königsberg in Preussen (Königsberg, 1944), 278–280.
But Voigt's testimony is therefore all the more representative.

46. H. Nissen, *Kritische Untersuchungen über die Quellen der vierten und fünften
Dekade des Livius* (Berlin, 1863), 70–79. For a recent discussion of how ancient
historians used their predecessors—one which shows both how useful and how
limited Nissen's perspective was—see S. Hornblower, "Introduction," *Greek Historiography*, ed. S. Hornblower (Oxford, 1994), 1–71 at 54–71.

47. Nissen, *Kritische Untersuchungen*, 77: Livy "steht unter dem Einfluss des-
selben Grundgesetzes, welches die ganze Historiographie bis auf die Entwicklung der modernen Wissenschaft beherrscht. Ranke hat zuerst in glänzender
Weise an einer Reihe von Geschichtsschreibern des 15. und 16. Jahrhunderts
nachgewiesen, wie sie die Werke ihrer Vorgänger in der Art benutzten, dass sie
dieselben einfach ausschrieben" (Livy "reflects the influence of the same fundamental law, which determined all historical writing until the development
of modern scholarship. Ranke was the first who used a whole series of historians
from the fifteenth and sixteenth centuries to prove, in a brilliant manner, that
the way they used the works of their predecessors amounted simply to direct
copying"). Ranke, of course, would never have confused Thucydides with the
journalists of his own time—or treated the whole tradition of historiography as
uniform.

to be called—was as exaggerated as it was ingenious, and reflected its creator's tendency to make wild hypotheses into solid facts.[48] Ranke's own view of the historical tradition was far more complex. But Nissen's version of Ranke became a central principle of research in ancient history for many years after he advanced it. For almost a century after Ranke's time, his disciples would repeat like a mantra an exaggerated version of what Ranke himself had taught them to believe: "The proposition that before the beginning of the last century the study of history was not scientific may be sustained in spite of a few exceptions . . . Erudition has now been supplemented by scientific method, and we owe the change to Germany." So J. B. Bury ecumenically declared in his Cambridge inaugural address of 1902, at the height of Anglo-German imperial rivalry.[49]

Doubts arose, to be sure, even in the later years of Ranke's exceptionally long life—especially as his appeal as a teacher began to fail. It became evident that he had unjustifiably accepted certain classes of documents—like the official reports of Venetian ambassadors to their Senate—as transparent windows on past states and events rather than colorful reconstructions

48. "Das liegt in seinem schleswigholsteinernen kopf," wrote Hermann Usener plaintively, explaining how he had failed to persuade his old friend not to argue that the ancient kings of Latium somehow represented the biblical days of Creation. H. Diels, H. Usener, and E. Zeller, *Briefwechsel,* ed. D. Ehlers (Berlin, 1992), I, 425. The work in question was Nissen's *Das Templum* (Berlin, 1869), at 127. Nissen received some sharp criticism: see e.g. L. O. Bröcker, *Moderne Quellenforscher u. antike Geschichtschreiber* (Innsbruck, 1882). But the age of *Quellenforschung* which began with his work was also largely governed by his spirit of reckless simplification: see C. Wachsmuth, *Einleitung in das Studium der Alten Geschichte* (Leipzig, 1895), 55–56, and the erudite (if peculiarly organized and written) work of B. A. Desbords, *Introduction à Diogène Laërce* (Diss., Utrecht, 1990).

49. See *The Varieties of History,* ed. F. Stern, 2nd ed. (London, 1970), 211.

of them, whose authors wrote within rigid conventions, had not heard or seen everything that they reported, and often wished to convince their own audience of a personal theory rather than simply to tell what had happened. Like the splendid Venetian processions recorded by Carpaccio, the rich Venetian documents Ranke loved told a story about elite values and beliefs in their city of origin, as well as about the events and institutions they described. More generally, it became evident that in his reliance on central archives and great families' papers Ranke had accepted, without reflecting hard enough, a certain interpretation of history itself: one in which the story of nations and monarchies took precedence over that of peoples or cultures, which had initially won his interest for the past.[50]

Ranke's claims to originality in method, however, took far longer to attract critical scrutiny than his claims to objectivity in results. In the nineteen-forties and after, non-German scholars began to study the history of historical thought in a systematic way. Not bound by what had become traditional assumptions, far less inclined than their predecessors had been to accept a German account of "how it really was," Arnaldo Momigliano and Herbert Butterfield did not accept what had seemed as obvious to Acton as to Ranke: that the application of minutely precise critical scrutiny to the full range of historical sources was part of the intellectual revolution set off in German universities around 1800 by the louder revolution that began in the Paris streets and led to the forcible opening of some of Europe's once secret chanceries and archives. Ranke's account

50. See esp. E. Fueter, *Geschichte der neueren Historiographie* (Munich and Berlin, 1911), 480–482; H. Butterfield, *Man on His Past* (Cambridge, 1955; repr. Boston, 1960); G. Benzoni, "Ranke's Favorite Source," *Leopold von Ranke,* ed. Iggers and Powell, 45–57.

of the development of his discipline was what historians of science call "disciplinary history" rather than the history of the discipline. He told his own story, in other words, to enhance the technical and emotional appeal of the sort of history he practiced, rather than to offer a full-scale, documented account of the development of historiography. In doing so, moreover, Ranke considerably exaggerated the archival component of his work. When the English Reformation scholar A. G. Dickens analyzed the footnotes to Ranke's history of the Reformation, for example, he discovered that fewer than 10 percent of them cited archival sources. The rest referred, for the most part, to the wealth of primary sources that earlier German scholars had published between the sixteenth century and the early nineteenth—a result that does as much to confirm the quality of Ranke's knowledge of historical literature as to undermine his reputation as a spelunker in deep archival shafts.[51] The first task that faces us, then, is simple: we must develop this critique, abandon Ranke's own, retrospective schema and return—as he always urged—to the documents. These are fortunately plentiful, both in print and in manuscript, and recent scholarship has already called attention to many of them. Taken together, neglected sources and novel works of scholarship make it possible to tell a quite different story about both Ranke and the tradition with which he claimed to have made a radical break.

51. A. G. Dickens, *Ranke as Reformation Historian,* Stenton Lecture 13 (Reading, Eng., 1980), 12–17, summarized in Dickens and J. Tonkin, with K. Powell, *The Reformation in Historical Thought* (Cambridge, Mass., 1985), 174–175. Cf. also E. Armstrong, "Introduction," L. von Ranke, *History of the Latin and Teutonic Nations (1494 to 1514),* tr. G. R. Dennis (London, 1909), ix–xxiv at xiii–xvi.

CHAPTER THREE

How the Historian Found His Muse: Ranke's Path to the Footnote

✳ The road that Ranke followed as he learned to dramatize the central importance of documents to the historian's enterprise was in some ways more direct, in others much more crooked than he remembered as an old man. To follow Ranke back to the origins of his new German history, we must begin in the middle of the American Middle West. Around the turn of the century, many American universities began to make themselves over, following what they saw as the German model. Professors, many of whom had enjoyed the adventure of studying in scholarly Göttingen, romantic Heidelberg, or metropolitan Berlin, began to enroll graduate students and offer specialized seminars at home. They carved out new spaces for these advanced courses—often within the impressively crenelated university libraries of the time, in rooms equipped with reference books and primary sources. Students from Berkeley to Baltimore could learn dead languages, master bibliographies, and apply sophisticated research techniques, just as their teachers had. And they could do so without having to live in Germany, drink beer, and translate texts, extemporaneously, into as well as out of Gothic and Anglo-Saxon, as German professors required the members of seminars to do.

The discovery of the truth about the past—to be obtained by German forms of scholarship—took on the moral prestige of a crusade and the cultural allure of a fashion. It captured academic hearts in Middle America as well as on the coasts.[1] Before the First World War, the historians at the University of Illinois decided to create a historical seminar of the German kind. To adorn their meeting room they bought portraits of the greatest American and the greatest non-American historian they could think of: respectively Francis Parkman and Edward Gibbon. Though Ranke lost out in the competition to have his picture on the wall, he received a consolation prize. A letter of his, bought from a dealer in Frankfurt, was also framed and hung in the seminar whose patron saint he naturally was. Years later, when the university found a new function for the room, the letter disappeared. Perhaps some historical aficionado of wide interests and low morals stole it.

Fortunately, a copy of this lost manuscript has survived. Ranke directed the letter—one of the few early ones that have been published—to his publisher, Georg Reimer, a great literary entrepreneur, who brought out such fundamental works of German literature and scholarship as the *Fairy Tales* of the brothers Grimm. In it Ranke addressed, with understandable anxiety, the delicate question of whether his first book could survive the state censorhip unharmed.[2] But he also raised, with even more anxiety, the question of the footnote. Surprisingly—especially to the late-twentieth-century reader, who expects learned authors to demand space for footnotes and harddriving publishers to refuse it—Ranke insisted that he had felt

1. See e.g. B. Perry, *And Gladly Teach* (Boston and New York, 1935).
2. On Reimer see G. Lüdtke, *Der Verlag Walter de Gruyter & Co.* (Berlin, 1924; repr. Berlin, 1978), 51–62.

it necessary to use notes only because a young author had to cite his sources. At all events, he had kept the distasteful things as short as possible: "I carefully avoided going in for real annotation. But I felt citation was indispensable in the work of a beginner who has to make his way and earn confidence." Ranke still hoped to find a way to avoid disfiguring his text with footnote cues and his pages with swelling feet of claylike annotation. Perhaps, he suggested, one could number the lines on each page or in each section, as was already normal practice in editions of classical authors, and put the notes at the end, keyed to the text. At best he saw the presence of annotation in his work as a necessary evil.[3]

Historians, young or old, are not on oath in letters to their publishers. But when the young and unknown Ranke professed his lack of interest in the formal aspects of documentation and his distaste for the appearance of pedantry, he was not striking a pose—even though he knew that his publisher cared as much about style as about science. The collection of Ranke's papers in Berlin includes not only his working notebooks, but part of the manuscript of his first book. Like the references in his finished book, those in the draft are the extremely short citations Ranke claimed to prefer: authors, titles, page numbers. Some pages have no footnotes at all; others have several footnote numbers, but not all of the references are filled in. And many footnotes give the author's name and the title, but no page number. All of the notes, finally, were added after Ranke had written

3. G. Stanton Ford, "A Ranke Letter," *Journal of Modern History*, 32 (1960), 143: "Sorgfältig habe ich mich vor der eigentlichen Adnotation gehütet: das Citat schien mir in dem Werk eines Anfängers, der sich erst Bahn machen und Glauben verdienen soll, unerläszlich."

out the entire text.[4] The document yields at least two obvious inferences. In the first place, Ranke, the founding father of the modern historian's craft, practiced it with no more discipline than his professional grandchildren and great-grandchildren. He composed his text as a whole. Only then did he search his books and notes, extracts and summaries, for the evidence to support it: he used a salt-shaker to add references to an already completed stew. This seems to have been Ranke's consistent practice. Even when, as an old man, he worked with and through secretaries, his methods underwent no fundamental change. The young men had to chase up references, for which Ranke supplied only hints, and which now and then did not exist at all, "a point on which Ranke was always very hard to convince."[5]

In fact, the scantiness of the notes in Ranke's *Geschichten* led to the worst public embarrassment of his career. In 1828 he learned that he had offered powerful ammunition to his fiercest critic. Heinrich Leo, another young Berlin historian, responded to his rival's rapid ascent to the academic stratosphere with understandable jealousy—as well as a passionate desire to save the literary ideal of history that he cherished from Ranke's many stylistic and intellectual sins. He did his best to puncture what he saw as the hot air balloon of Ranke's purported scholarship. In a long and dismissive review, he criticized Ranke's style and his philosophy, predicting that his inchoate, sentimental book would find its warmest reception "among learned

4. Ranke Nachlass, Staatsbibliothek zu Berlin, Preussischer Kulturbesitz (Haus II), Fasz. 1, I.

5. T. Wiedemann, "Sechszehn Jahre in der Werkstatt Leopold von Ranke's," *Deutsche Revue,* December 1891, 333: "wovon Ranke immer nur sehr schwer überzeugt wurde."

ladies"—"bey gelehrten Weibern." Worse still, Leo identified
many passages where Ranke's text did not correspond precisely
to the source quoted in the footnotes.[6] Ranke was appalled and
infuriated by this "devilish review," which attacked him "on
the most sensitive point of his research."[7] In a long reply he
argued that support for every assertion Leo had contested could
be found in one of the texts he had cited—though not necessarily in the passage referred to by any given footnote. The
reader who wished to test Ranke's use of the originals must
compare all of them systematically, as Leo had evidently failed
to. "I cite," Ranke wrote in an indignant foonote, "for those
who want to find, but not for those who look in order *not* to
find. Incidentally, this book is not the sort that one can scru-
tinize over a cup of coffee, with just one of the editions I cited
in one's hand."[8] Leo's rejoinder to this rebuttal was even more

6. "H. L. Manin" [H. Leo], review of Ranke, in *Ergänzungsblätter zur Jenaischen Allgemeinen Literatur-Zeitung,* 16 (1828), nos. 17–18, cols. 129–140,
esp. 136: "Doch wozu noch mehr anführen?—Man schlage nach, auf jedem
Blatte fast wird ein verdrehtes, ein nichtssagendes oder nachlässig benutztes
Citat zu finden seyn. Heisst das nun nackte Wahrheit? Heisst das gründliche
Erforschung des Einzelnen?" ("But why cite more evidence? One need simply
look, and on every page one finds a distorted, a meaningless or a carelessly used
quotation. Should this be called the naked truth? Should this be called thorough
research into the details?"). On the philosophical dimension of the debate between Leo and Ranke see G. G. Iggers, *The German Conception of History* (Mid-
dletown, Conn., 1968), 66–69, and S. Baur, "Rankes Historik, Teil I: Der junge
Ranke" (Diss., Freie Universität Berlin, 1996), 125–138.

7. L. von Ranke, *Das Briefwerk,* ed. W. P. Fuchs (Hamburg, 1949), 156–
161, 165, 168, 240: "auf dem kitzlichsten Punkt der Forschung."

8. L. Ranke, "Replik," *Intelligenzblatt der Allgemeinen Literatur-Zeitung* (May
1828), no. 131, cols. 193–199, at 195–196 n.: "Ich citire für die, welche finden
wollen, aber nicht für solche, die da suchen, um *nicht* zu finden. Bey einer Tasse
Kaffee, mit einem einzigen der citirten Ausgaben in der Hand, lässt sich übri-
gens diess Buch nicht prüfen"; cf. *Das Briefwerk,* ed. Fuchs, 159.

dismissive than his original review, and his judgment of the
Geschichten even more absurdly negative. But he had no trouble
using Ranke's own words to show that his victim's practices as
a writer of footnotes were genuinely problematic. Leo advised
Ranke to give up footnotes entirely in the future. A simple list
of the sources used in each section would serve the reader better
than annotations randomly attached to portions of the text "in
which one finds things completely different from those in the
citations."[9] Michael Bernays described the footnotes in Ranke's
first book as exemplary: "No one who deserves to read Ranke
would want to do without notes of this kind. But everyone
realizes that the material they contain could not be moved into
the text."[10] No praise would have pleased its recipient more.
But not all his original readers would have agreed.

For all his modern erudition, Ranke evidently retained his
allegiance to the classical notion of what a history should look
like. Far from joyously accepting that a history should tell the
double story of the historical past and the historian's research,
Ranke shied away from disfiguring his powerful narrative and
set-piece battle scenes with the ugly contrivances of scholarly
mechanics. In this he was far from alone among Germany's
historical revolutionaries. Barthold Georg Niebuhr, the revisionist who won fame by insisting that the traditional narrative
of Rome's early history must be dissected by source-criticism

9. H. Leo, "Replik," *Intelligenzblatt der Jenaischen Allgem. Literatur-Zeitung*
(June 1828), no. 39, cols. 305–312 at 310: "in denen ganz andere Dinge zu
finden sind, als in den Citaten."

10. M. Bernays, "Zur Lehre von den Citaten und Noten," *Schriften zur Kritik
und Litteraturgeschichte,* IV (Berlin, 1899), 333: "Keiner, der Ranke zu lesen
verdient, möchte Noten dieser Art entbehren; jeder aber sieht ein, dass ihr Inhalt
sich in den Text nicht schicken würde."

and then reframed as a social analysis of the city's rise, loved the details of historical investigation and lectured about them to his students at Berlin.[11] He too, however, thought that the best historical narrative was a classical one, free of notes. He longed to write without a learned apparatus, if he could only solve all the technical problems and then push them out of the way: "Should the learned work, which reconstructs the material, ever be finished, I found it an appealing thought to write a straight narrative history of the Romans, without investigations, proofs, and erudition, as it would have been written 1800 years ago."[12] For Niebuhr as for Ranke, the hope proved impossible to fulfill: the historian who had eaten from the tree of source-criticism could not regain the innocence needed to write a simple narrative. But their aspirations remained rhetorical and literary, to an extent that would surprise many later professional historians. Some American scholars of an older generation, sure of their own right to claim professional descent from Ranke, regarded writing well as incompatible with the duties of a professional historian.[13] In doing so they hardly followed their master.

11. See now the remarkable study by G. Walther, *Niebuhrs Forschung* (Stuttgart, 1993), with ample references to the older literature.

12. B. G. Niebuhr, *Briefe. Neue Folge, 1816–1830,* ed. E. Vischer, IV: *Briefe aus Bonn (Juli bis Dezember 1830)* (Bern and Munich, 1984), 117: "Es war für mich ein reizender Gedanke, wenn dies gelehrte Werk, wodurch der Stoff wieder geschaffen wird, vollendet seyn würde, eine ganz erzählende Geschichte der Römer zu schreiben, ohne Untersuchung, Erweis und Gelehrsamkeit; wie man sie vor 1800 Jahren geschrieben haben würde." Cf. W. Nippel, " 'Geschichte' und 'Altertümer': Zur Periodisierung in der Althistorie," *Geschichtsdiskurs,* ed. W. Küttler et al., I (Frankfurt, 1993), 310–311.

13. For Ranke's qualities as a writer see the fine account by P. Gay, *Style in History* (London, 1975), chap. 2. Two further acts of resistance against the necessity of providing footnotes, both carried out by distinguished historians who had minutely precise knowledge of the documents they used, are described in

Ranke, after all, wished—as he said in an all-too-often quoted and all-too-rarely analyzed phrase—"only to say, how it really was"—"nur sagen, wie es eigentlich gewesen."[14] But what does that mean? As Hajo Holborn and others have shown, Ranke's famous dictum about his intentions as a historian was in fact a strategically placed citation of an even more famous passage from Thucydides (1.22).[15] One who cited the most profound of Greek political historians as his model for serious, accurate exposition could hardly be eager to obscure the literary relation between their texts by adding a commentary to the body of his own work.

More than one recent critic has pointed out that footnotes interrupt a narrative. References detract from the illusion of veracity and immediacy that Ranke and so many other nineteenth-century historians wished to create, since they continually interrupt the single story told by an omniscient narrator (Noel Coward made the same point more memorably when he

---

a characteristically elegant essay by J. H. Hexter, "Garrett Mattingly, Historian," *From the Renaissance to the Counter-Reformation,* ed. C. H. Carter (London, 1966), 13–28 at 15–17, and in the sharply contrasting treatments of G. H. Selement, "Perry Miller: A Note on His Sources in *The New England Mind: The Seventeenth Century,*" *William and Mary Quarterly,* 31 (1974), 453–464, and P. Miller, *Sources for "The New England Mind: The Seventeenth Century,"* ed. J. Hoopes (Williamsburg, Va., 1981); on the second case cf. D. Levin, *Exemplary Elders* (Athens and London, 1990), 30–32.

14. For the wording of this text see W. P. Fuchs, "Was heisst das: 'bloss zeigen, wie es eigentlich gewesen'?" *Geschichte in Wissenschaft und Unterricht,* 11 (1979), 655–667, showing that in 1874 Ranke changed the original phrase quoted in the text, to make it read "bloss zeigen, wie es eigentlich gewesen."

15. H. Holborn, *History and the Humanities* (Garden City, N.Y., 1972), 90–91; K. Repgen, "Ueber Rankes Diktum von 1824: 'Bloss sagen, wie es eigentlich gewesen,' " *Historisches Jahrbuch,* 102 (1982), 439–449; R. S. Stroud, " 'Wie es eigentlich gewesen' and Thucydides 2.48.3," *Hermes,* 115 (1987) 379–382 (who refutes much of Repgen's analysis). Cf. F. Gilbert, *History, Politics, or Culture?* (Princeton, 1990).

remarked that having to read a footnote resembles having to go downstairs to answer the door while in the midst of making love).[16] Ranke's desire to imitate a classical historical model and his modern tastes both militated against the heavy use of notes. No wonder, then, that Ranke struggled to preserve the coherence of his narrative—and even tried, by placing the full texts of documents after his own text, to give the reader the experience of two kinds of authenticity, the literary and the documentary. No wonder, either, that modern scholars are not sure whether to treat him as the first scientific historian or the last Romantic.[17] Many distinguished later historians also rebelled against the need to provide rich documentation. Fustel de Coulanges, a passionate believer in the importance of full and accurate use of sources, only gradually and grudgingly accepted what he saw as the new fad of providing extensive formal documentation.[18] Ernst Kantorowicz, as we have seen, caused

16. L. Gossman, *Between History and Literature* (Cambridge, Mass. and London, 1990), 249–250; F. Hartog, *Le xixe siècle et l'histoire* (Paris, 1988), esp. 112–115; G. Pomata, "Versions of Narrative: Overt and Covert Narrators in Nineteenth Century Historiography," *History Workshop,* 27 (1989), 1–17. Coward attributed a stronger version of the remark to John Barrymore: C. Lesley, *Remembered Laughter* (New York, 1976), xx.

17. He seems to play both roles in Pomata, 12 and 14.

18. See Fustel's declaration, published by Camille Jullian in 1891, in Hartog, 360: "J'appartiens à une génération qui n'est plus jeune, et dans laquelle les travailleurs s'imposaient deux règles: d'abord d'étudier un sujet d'après toutes les sources observées directement et de près, ensuite de ne présenter au lecteur que le résultat de leurs recherches; on lui épargnait l'appareil d'érudition, l'érudition étant pour l'auteur seul et non pour le lecteur; quelques indications au bas des pages suffisaient au lecteur, qu'on invitait à vérifier. Depuis une vingtaine d'années les procédés habituels ont changé: l'usage aujourd'hui est de présenter au lecteur l'appareil d'érudition plutôt que les résultats. On tient plus à l'échafaudage qu'à la construction. L'érudition a changé ses formes et ses procédés; elle n'est pas plus profonde, et l'exactitude n'est pas d'aujourd'hui; mais

a scandal with his brilliant, best-selling *Kaiser Friedrich II,* which at first possessed no apparatus at all.[19] They and others were Ranke's heirs to an extent that they and their critics did not suspect.

Ranke, then, had footnotes forced upon him. But what of the second, and more important, component of his learned apparatus—the extended commentary on his sources, in the form of an essay on historians or a selection of primary documents with commentary? Appendices in fact formed the more distinguished and distinctive part of Ranke's commentary on his own text. They called forth his best efforts as researcher and as writer. They made clear to intelligent readers that his views about the possibility of obtaining absolute accuracy in describing the past were nowhere near so simple as modern versions

---

l'érudition veut se montrer davantage. On veut avant tout paraître érudit." ("I belong to a generation no longer young, in which researchers followed two rules. First of all, they approached each subject through direct and close study of all the sources. Then they offered the reader only the results of their researches, sparing him the paraphernalia of learning. Learning was reserved for the author alone, and not for the reader. Some references in footnotes sufficed for the reader, who was thus invited to make his own verification. Some twenty years ago, normal methods underwent a transformation. Today, the standard practice is to present the reader with the paraphernalia of learning rather than the results. The scaffolding matters more than the structure. Learning has changed its forms and methods. It is no longer deep, and precision is not a virtue of the present day. But learning wishes to make more of a display of itself. Scholars wish above all to appear learned.")

19. See e.g. Y. Malkiel, "Ernst H. Kantorowicz," in *On Four Modern Humanists,* ed. A. R. Evans, Jr. (Princeton, 1970), 150–151, 181–192. Malkiel points out that Kantorowicz's views changed considerably in later life, when he normally wrote in English, without artistic ambitions and with a sharp sense of the dangers that historical theses not derived from documents posed. He attacked a proposal to eliminate footnotes from *Speculum,* the main American journal of medieval studies, and supplied the work that he wrote in Berkeley and Princeton with a splendidly elaborate technical apparatus.

of his thought, whether intended as praise or as caricature, have suggested. And they gave the experience of reading Ranke something of the same symphonic density, the same continual interplay between chronological narrative and systematic reflection, that Gibbon offered his readers.

For all its originality and its impact, however, Ranke's textual apparatus also came into being in a different, and a more complex, way than he himself claimed. In his late dictations Ranke portrayed his turn to criticism as a conversion experience, with all the unpredictability and shock value that normally invests such moments. Like someone falling through a weak spot in an apparently solid floor, he recalled, he suddenly saw that history must rest on thick pillars and joists which only criticism could fashion and put in place. That insight became the foundation of the second volume of his *Geschichten,* in which he dealt with the sources and their problems. No one, he thought, had anticipated his moment of revelation—even the classical scholars, whose revolutionary work on Greek and Roman history and literature presented some apparent parallels to his own enterprise. Ranke expected Niebuhr's support, but recognized no fundamental debt to Niebuhr's method: "Here I had regard neither for Niebuhr, who really wanted more to provide the tradition with a meaning, nor, in particular, for Gottfried Hermann, who criticized authors on points of detail—though I promised myself that great men of this sort would applaud me."[20]

20. Ranke, *Sämmtliche Werke,* 53/54 (Leipzig, 1890), 62: "Ich habe hier weder auf Niebuhr, der eigentlich mehr der Tradition einen Sinn verschaffen will, noch vollends auf Gottfried Hermann, der die Autoren im einzelnen kritisirt, Rücksicht genommen, obwohl ich mir bei grossen Männern dieser Art Beifall versprach."

This late testimony in fact conflicts with what Ranke himself would have considered the more authoritative evidence: that of earlier and original sources. In the first place, historians before Ranke were not all innocent and uncritical compilers. Recent research has shown that a number of the critical techniques that Ranke used—systematic comparison of all the sources for a given event, identification of those that were produced closest to it or rested on official documentation, elimination of later sources, the information in which is derivative—came into being in the Renaissance. Italian and northern humanists, following up hints in classical models, exposed authoritative texts as forgeries by applying these practices systematically. Lorenzo Valla, for example, demolished the *Donation of Constantine.* This text, long treasured in the papal curia, purported to tell the story of how the grateful emperor Constantine, cured by the pope of his leprosy, gave the papacy in return the entire western half of the Roman Empire and hared off to Constantinople. Valla, a deep student of Latin usage and a master of the ancient rhetorical tradition, used this knowledge to show that the *Donation* could not have been written by a Roman in the fourth century. A classical text—even a late-classical one—would be cast in the language used by other writers in its period, and composed, in accordance with the principle of decorum, to fit its author, its recipients, and its situation. The *Donation* haplessly violated all these principles, in ways Valla could pin down and expose with contemptuous ease: "You address me in the words of a barbarian; do you want me to think it is the language of Constantine or Lactantius?" He also showed that none of the sources that should have mentioned the *Donation* and its results actually did so. Along the way, Valla took the time to make clear that among the sources for Roman history, the learned antiquary Varro offered better information about early tradition than the nostalgic historian Livy, and Livy, in turn, better information than the compiler of anecdotes, Valerius Maximus—and to suggest that a similarly unsparing critique of modern traditions revealed the falseness of the supposedly sacred objects and images shown to pilgrims in dozens of Roman churches.[21] Valla exaggerated, of course: he laid his whole work

21. L. Valla, *De falso credita et ementita Constantini donatione,* ed. W. Setz, *Monumenta Germaniae Historica,* Quellen zur Geistesgeschichte des Mittelalters, 10 (Weimar, 1976), 117–118: "Quis unquam phrygium Latine dici audivit? Tu mihi dum barbare loqueris videri vis Constantini aut Lactantii esse sermonem?" For the Roman historical tradition, see 148–151; for the pious frauds of the Roman churches, 141–144. Setz reviews earlier literature and offers an interpretation of his own in *Lorenzo Vallas Schrift gegen die Konstantinische Schenkung* (Tübingen, 1975). See also M. P. Gilmore, "The Renaissance Conception of the Lessons of History," in *Facets of the Renaissance,* ed. W. H. Werkmeister, 2nd ed. (New York, Evanston, and London, 1963); P. Burke, *The Renaissance Sense of the Past* (New York, 1969); D. R. Kelley, *Foundations of Modern Historical Scholarship* (New York and London, 1970), chap. 2; J. M. Levine, "Reginald Pecock and Lorenzo Valla on the *Donation of Constantine," Studies in the Renaissance,* 20 (1973), 118–143; and R. Fubini, "Contestazioni quattrocentesche della Donazione di Costantino: Niccolò Cusano, Lorenzo Valla," in *Costantino il Grande dall'antichità all'umanesimo,* ed. G. Bonamente and F. Fusco (Macerata, 1992), I, 385–431 (English summary: "Humanism and Truth: Valla Writes against the Donation of Constantine," *Journal of the History of Ideas,* 57 [1996], 79–86). On the role of rhetoric in Valla's argument see H. H. Gray, "Renaissance Humanism: The Pursuit of Eloquence," *Journal of the History of Ideas,* 24 (1963), 497–514, reprinted in *Renaissance Essays from the Journal of the History of Ideas,* ed. P. O. Kristeller and P. P. Wiener (New York, 1968), 199–216; G. Most, "Rhetorik und Hermeneutik: Zur Konstitution der Neuzeitlichkeit," *Antike und Abendland,* 30 (1984), 62–79; V. de Caprio, "Retorica e ideologia nella *Declamatio* di Lorenzo Valla sulla Donazione di Costantino," *Paragone,* 29, no. 338 (1978), 36–56; S. I. Camporeale, "Lorenzo Valla e il 'De falso credita donatione': Retorica, libertà e ecclesiologia nell '400," *Memorie Domenicane* n.s. 19 (1988), 191–293 (English summary: "Lorenzo Valla's *Oratio* on the Pseudo-Donation of Constantine: Dissent and Innovation in Early Renaissance Humanism," *Journal of the History of Ideas,* 57 [1996], 9–26); C. Ginzburg, "Préface," in Lorenzo

out as a denunciatory oration, indicted the papacy as well as the *Donation,* and took no argumentative prisoners. Parts of his argument came, as Riccardo Fubini has shown, from Nicholas of Cusa, who had already pointed out the absence of the *Donation* from sources where one would expect it to appear. But no later text showed more dramatically than Valla's how the sharp blade of criticism could cut its way through the contradictions and errors of tradition.

In the sixteenth century, François Baudouin, Jean Bodin, and others wrote elaborate manuals on how to read and use historical sources, ancient and modern. These included instructions on how to choose which historians to believe—a topic on which the ancient canons of the rhetorical tradition generally retained their authority. But they also included—in Baudouin's case— something more radical. Baudouin admitted that many historical texts had been lost, that some medieval chronicles were riddled with error. But he also insisted that a critical study of tradition could produce a coherent history of the whole known past. Modern scholars could draw on an imposing list of sources: literary texts like Cicero's letters, inscriptions and other material remains, the oral traditions mentioned both by Charlemagne's biographer, Einhard, and by European observers of the societies of the New World, derivative histories which preserved the gist of earlier texts now lost, and original documents held in the French royal archives. Any energetic student of

---

Valla, *La Donation de Constantin,* tr. J.-B. Giard (Paris, 1993), ix–xxi. On the hermeneutical uses of rhetoric see also K. Eden, *Hermeneutics and the Rhetorical Tradition* (New Haven and London, 1997). For the reception of Valla's work, see G. Antonazzi, *Lorenzo Valla e la polemica sulla Donazione di Costantino* (Rome, 1985), and R. K. Delph, "Valla Grammaticus, Agostino Steuco, and the Donation of Constantine," *Journal of the History of Ideas,* 57 (1996), 55–78.

history, Baudouin solemnly argued, must realize that "great and rich are the remains of ancient memory." Bodin—though far less sure-footed on philological questions than Baudouin—made clear that the reader must subject every historian to critical scrutiny, looking for possible sources of bias and omission.[22] Both men, in other words, saw history as a form of inquiry as well as a form of narrative: both offered arts of reading, as well

22. F. Baudouin, *De institutione historiae universae et eius cum iurisprudentia coniunctione prolegomenon libri ii,* in *Artis historicae penus,* ed. J. Wolf (Basel, 1579), I, 640–662, at 653: "Magnae et uberes sunt reliquiae veteris memoriae, si iis ipsi non defuerimus"; J. Bodin, *Methodus ad facilem historiarum cognitionem,* ibid., 35–78. On this literature see F. von Bezold, "Zur Entstehungsgeschichte der historischen Methodik," *Internationale Monatsschrift,* 8 (1914), reprinted in *Aus Mittelalter und Renaissance* (Leipzig and Berlin, 1918); L. Strauss, *The Political Philosophy of Hobbes,* tr. E. M. Sinclair (Oxford, 1936; repr. Chicago and London, 1952, 1963), chap. VI; J. L. Brown, *The Methodus ad facilem historiarum cognitionem of Jean Bodin: A Critical Study* (Washington, D.C., 1939); G. Spini, "I trattatisti dell'arte storica nella Controriforma italiana," *Quaderni di Belfagor,* 1 (1948), 109–136 (English translation in *The Late Italian Renaissance: 1525–1630,* ed. E. Cochrane [New York, 1970], 91–133); B. Reynolds, "Shifting Currents in Historical Criticism," *Journal of the History of Ideas,* 14 (1953), 471–492, reprinted in *Renaissance Essays,* ed. P. O. Kristeller and P. P. Wiener (New York, 1968), 115–136; J. G. A. Pocock, "The French Prelude to Modern Historiography," in *The Ancient Constitution and the Feudal Law* (Cambridge, 1957); J. Franklin, *Jean Bodin and the Sixteenth-Century Revolution in the Methodology of Law and History* (New York and London, 1963); D. R. Kelley, "François Baudouin's Conception of History," *Journal of the History of Ideas,* 25 (1964), 35–57; G. Cotroneo, *Jean Bodin teorico della storia* (Naples, 1966); G. Huppert, *The Idea of Perfect History: Historical Erudition and Historical Philosophy in Renaissance France* (Urbana, Chicago, and London, 1970); D. R. Kelley, *Foundations of Modern Historical Scholarship: Language, Law, and History in the French Renaissance* (New York and London, 1970); Cotroneo, *I trattatisti dell'ars historica* (Naples, 1971); E. Kessler, *Theoretiker humanistischer Geschichtsschreibung* (Munich, 1971); R. Landfester, *Historia magistra vitae* (Geneva, 1972); C.-G. Dubois, *La conception de l'histoire en France au xvie siècle* (Paris, 1977); E. Hassinger, *Empirisch-rationaler Historismus* (Bern and Munich, 1978); U. Muhlack, *Geschichtswissenschaft im Humanismus und in der Aufklärung: Die Vorgeschichte des Historismus* (Munich, 1991).

as writing, and showed that the modern reader must construct an account of the past by critical study of all the sources. True, not every learned student of ancient history took these points. Thomas Hobbes, the translator of Thucydides into English, thought it "a sign of too much opinion, and self-conceit, to be a follower in such an History, as has been already sufficiently achieved by others." He liked most to read, along with Homer and Virgil, "Xenophon, or some probable historie"—an author who met the moral and biographical criteria set down long before by Thucydides, Polybius, and Cicero. But others grasped and applied the new historical hermeneutics of the French theorists.[23] The study of history became one of the many areas in which traditional and innovative methods jostled and interfered with each other through the seventeenth century

Ranke himself cited Bodin at the outset of his discussion of Guicciardini's speeches: "Five years after Guicciardini's work first appeared, Jean Bodin described it in his *Methodus ad facilem historiarum cognitionem:* 'His zeal to discover the truth is remarkable. He is said to have taken letters, laws, and treaties from the original sources and copied them. Therefore he often uses terms like "He said these words"—or, if the original text is missing, "He spoke to this effect." ' Bodin's opinion is clear: the speeches in Guicciardini are genuine . . . And this opinion has remained the established one, though not without some contradiction, down to the present day."[24] Admittedly, Ranke

23. T. Hobbes, "A Discourse upon the Beginning of Tacitus," in *Three Discourses,* ed. N. B. Reynolds and A. W. Saxonhouse (Chicago and London, 1995), 39; J. Aubrey, *Brief Lives,* ed. O. Lawson Dick (London, 1949; repr. Ann Arbor, 1957), 154.

24. Ranke, *Zur Kritik neuerer Geschichtsschreiber,* 20–21: "Fünf Jahr, nachdem das Werk Guicciardini's zuerst erschienen, schrieb Johann Bodin im methodus

cited Bodin's opinion in order to refute it. But the fact that he quoted one of the first systematic treatises on how to read historical texts shows that he knew he was not entering uninhabited territory when he attacked the problem of Guiccardini's use of sources. Later, when Ranke set out to show his appreciation of the political subtlety of the rhetoric Guicciardini put in the mouths of his speakers, he quoted both Bodin and Bodin's reader, Michel de Montaigne.[25]

---

ad facilem historiae cognitionem cap. iv. von demselben: Est mirum in eo studium veritatis inquirendae. Fertur epistolas, decreta, foedera, ex ipsis fontibus hausisse et expressisse. Itaque frequenter occurrit illud: 'locutus est haec verba,' aut si ipsa verba defuerint: 'locutus est in hanc sententiam.' Man sieht, die Meynung Bodins ist: die Reden bey Guicciardini seyen ächt . . . Diese Meynung, obwohl nicht ohne einigen Widerspruch, hat sich jedoch bis auf den heutigen Tag erhalten." For another critical but revealing citation of Bodin see ibid., 73 and n. 1. Ranke's quotations from Bodin and Montaigne (for the latter see n. 25 below) had appeared earlier in the partial manuscript of *Zur Kritik neuerer Geschichtsschreiber* preserved in the Ranke Nachlass, Staatsbibliothek zu Berlin, Preussischer Kulturbesitz, Haus II, Fasz. 1, I

25. Ibid., 46–47: "Es ist wohl nie eine Zeit gewesen, welche in lebendiger Theilnahme an dem öffentlichen Leben, an jedem kleinsten Ereigniss die letzte Hälfte des 16. Jahrhunderts übertroffen. Allenthalben Selbstständigkeit, und doch durch die beyden Partheyen eine so enge Vereinigung, dass fast keine Geschichte geschrieben werden konnte, sie wäre denn allgemeine Weltgeschichte geworden. Da kamen denn die Discorse Guicciardini's, diese Betrachtungen jeder Begebenheit von allen Seiten zur rechten Stunde. 'Ubi quid in deliberationem cadit,' sagt Bodin, 'quod inexplicabile videatur, illic admirabilem in disserendo subtilitatem ostentat.' Man fühlte sogleich, dass diess die Hauptsache in dem Werk sey. 'La partie,' sagt Montaigne, 'de quoi il se semble vouloir prévaloir le plus, sont ses digressions et ses discours.' " ("There has perhaps never been a period when active participation in public life, in every minor event, was greater than in the second half of the sixteenth century. For all their independence, the two parties were so tightly connected that it was almost impossible to write a history, without its becoming a general world history. Guicciardini's speeches, which analyzed every event from all the angles, appeared at just the right time. 'When something very complex must be debated,' says Bodin, 'there above all he shows wonderful subtlety in the discussion.' It was clear at once

This late humanist tradition of historiographical debate, moreover, was far from dead in the Germany of the eighteenth and early nineteenth centuries.[26] The Halle theologian Johann Salomo Semler analyzed the sources for German medieval history in a widely read essay. The Göttingen scholar Johann Christoph Gatterer founded Germany's first historical seminar, where students learned to put the rules of higher and lower criticism into practice. And his colleague August Ludwig von Schlözer, who did exemplary work on the earliest Russian historians, also produced an impressive general program for the collection and analysis of historical sources.[27] The encyclopedically learned Marburg professor Ludwig Wachler brought out, not long before Ranke wrote, a heavily footnoted five-volume history of historical writing, a book which extended chronologically from the Renaissance to his own day, methodologically from sweeping narratives to antiquarian mono-

---

that this formed the most important feature of the work: 'The part of the work for which he seems most ambitious,' says Montaigne, 'consists of his digressions and his speeches.' ")

26. See esp. P. H. Reill, *The German Enlightenment and the Rise of Historicism* (Berkeley, 1975), and H. W. Blanke, "Aufklärungshistorie, Historismus, und historische Kritik. Eine Skizze," in *Von der Aufklärung zum Historismus,* ed. H. W. Blanke and J. Rüsen (Paderborn, 1984), 167–186, with the comment by W. Weber, 188–189, and Blanke's reply, 189–190.

27. "Schlözer über die Geschichtsverfassung (Schreiben über Mably an seinen deutschen Herausgeber)," in J. G. Heinzmann, *Litterarische Chronik* (Bern, 1785), I, 268–289, translated into English with useful commentary by H. D. Schmidt as "Schlözer on Historiography," *History and Theory,* 18 (1979), 37–51. See also Reill; N. Hammerstein, "Der Anteil des 18. Jahrhunderts in der Ausbildung der historischen Schulen des 19. Jahrhunderts," *Historische Forschung im 18. Jahrhundert,* ed. K. Hammer and J. Voss (Bonn, 1976), 432–450; G. Wirth, *Die Entwicklung der Alten Geschichte an der Philipps-Universität Marburg* (Marburg, 1977), 114–116, 141, 146–155; and the essays in *Aufklärung und Geschichte,* ed. H. E. Bödeker, G. Iggers, and J. Knudsen (Göttingen, 1986).

graphs, and geographically from Finland to Portugal. Ranke
admired it. Wachler did not anticipate Ranke's attack on Guicciardini's standing as a reliable and scholarly writer: "Guicciardini narrates in a properly serious and candid way, often as
an eyewitness and active participant, always with exact knowledge of the persons and conditions. Hence he can claim a high
degree of credibility." But he saw that Guicciardini had imposed his own view of situations and motives on his actors,
rather than allowing them to express their own views and per-
ceptions. And he praised Guicciardini, above all, because his
book so powerfully expressed the character of the epoch that
produced it: "When we set this work of history down, the
picture of the period has appeared to us in spirit in its out-
lines, drawn in a sharp and expressive way." Ranke, who saw
Guicciardini's responsiveness to his environment as crucial to
both his achievements and his defects, would certainly have
agreed—and could have found the core of part of his own critique and appreciation of Guicciardini, as well as some of the
received opinions he attacked, in Wachler.[28]

Ranke also knew other works of historical literature that
may, in a more general way, have stimulated him to see more

---

28. L. Wachler, *Geschichte der historischen Forschung und Kunst seit der Wieder-
herstellung der litterärischen Cultur in Europa*, I, pt. 1 (Göttingen, 1812), 174–
175: "Da er oft als Augenzeuge und thätiger Theilnehmer, stets mit genauer
Kenntniss der Personen und Verhältnisse, würdig ernst und freymüthig erzählt,
so kann er auf einen sehr hohen Grad von Glaubwürdigkeit Anspruch machen
. . . Das Bild des Zeitalters tritt in reinen Umrissen, scharf und ausdrucksvoll
gezeichnet, vor unser Gemüth, wenn wir dieses Geschichtsbuch aus der Hand
legen." For an appreciative discussion of Wachler, emphasizing his effort to set
past historians into their own historical contexts, see H. W. Blanke, *Historio-
graphiegeschichte als Historik*, Fundamenta Historica 3 (Stuttgart–Bad Canstatt,
1991), 193–204.

clearly than his predecessors had that Guicciardini's methods and goals had differed from his own. For example, he knew Giambattista Vico's *Scienza nuova,* which had put forward a complex, insightful program for a cultural history of the human race and treated traditional accounts of ancient history with sharp criticism a century before Ranke wrote. He cited the German translation of Vico, in passing, in his discussion of another Italian historian, Paolo Giovio.[29] Moreover, Ranke, as we have already seen, was far from the only young German historian to see that the history of the German lands, and that of the Middle Ages and early modern times more generally, must be reframed and rebuilt on a documentary foundation. All of them had learned at least part of their craft by reading the first classic of German-language historical literature, Johannes von Müller's history of Switzerland. This rested on massive documentary foundations, as befitted the work of an author who, so Ranke believed, thought that heaven itself would be an endless, untouched archive.[30]

Above all, one should bear in mind a simple fact that many students of Ranke have ignored. He addressed himself to the history of Italy during the Renaissance. This field had attracted many of the most erudite Italian scholars of the eighteenth century, a great age of manuscript-cataloguing, source-editing, and other forms of erudition.[31] At the very end of the century

---

29. Ranke, *Zur Kritik neuerer Geschichtsschreiber,* 76, n. 1.

30. Bernays, 334–336; on Ranke's appropriation of Müller see esp. L. Krieger, *Ranke: The Meaning of History* (Chicago and London, 1977), 81 and 366–367, n. 33.

31. See in general E. Cochrane, "The Settecento Medievalists," *Journal of the History of Ideas,* 19 (1958), 35–61; S. Bertelli, *Erudizione e storia in Ludovico Antonio Muratori* (Naples, 1960).

the rector of the University of Pisa, Angelo Fabroni, published learned lives of Cosimo and Lorenzo de' Medici and of Lorenzo's son Giovanni, who became Pope Leo X. Each of these books included a massive series of documentary endnotes. In his life of Lorenzo, Fabroni even adumbrated some of Ranke's most famous early statements about history. He insisted that the distinction of his work lay not in its solutions to disputed problems of historical interpretation but in its massive presentation of archival documents, which made the book itself a sort of virtual archive.[32] Ranke—as yet inexperienced in archival research—was more inclined to complain about the masses of other documents which, Fabroni admitted, he had had to omit, than to acknowledge his merits.[33] Neither Fabroni nor William

32. See A. Fabroni, *Laurentii Medicis Magnifici vita* (Pisa, 1784), "Lectori," I, vii–viii: "ea gloria contenti, quod in narrandis rebus incorrupta rerum gestarum monumenta secuti fuerimus. Ex his secundum operis volumen conflabitur; quodque eorum pleraque asserventur in Florentino tabulario, quod Mediceum vel *Segreteria Vecchia* appellari solet, quae nominavimus volumina, seu *Filze,* ad illud spectare existimabis" ("We will be content with the glory due us for having followed in our narrative of events the incorrupt records of them. The second volume of our work will consist of these. And since a great many of the volumes or *Filze* we have mentioned are preserved in the Florentine archive known as that of the Medici, or the Segreteria Vecchia, you will think you are actually seeing that"). See also his *Leonis X Pontificis Maximi vita* (Pisa, 1797).

33. At the end of his *Laurentii vita,* II, 399, after n. 227, Fabroni added a final caution: "Cave putes, lector humanissime, nos omnia monumenta, quae ad Laurentium pertinent, quaeque nos studiose collegimus, in hoc volumen retulisse. Innumera enim pene sunt, quae, dolenter sane, edere praetermisimus, ne nimium excresceret magnitudo voluminis. Utinam quae praestitimus, aequis iudicibus minime displiceant" ("You should not think, gentle reader, that we have included in this volume all the records relating to Lorenzo that we carefully gathered. With regret, we have had to omit countless documents, to prevent the volume from becoming too big. We hope that those we have provided may not provoke the displeasure of fair-minded judges"). In *Zur Kritik,* 173–174, Ranke insisted that even for Florence documents of foreign affairs were not

Roscoe, the amateur historiarn from Liverpool who continued his work on the Medici, read the souces with Ranke's critical eye. Nonetheless, their work presented him with much vital primary material and offered him what became his normal mode of presentation—the text followed by a long documentary appendix.[34]

More important still, the German historians who applied a critical method to the sources of medieval and early modern

---

available in adequate numbers (the situation for domestic ones was better). Of Fabroni he wrote: "Fabroni bekennt, es sey ihm nicht möglich gewesen, alle seine Urkunden aufzunehmen, als deren eine fast unzählbare Menge sey; und wenn er sich in seinem Lorenzo beschränkt hat, so hat er's im Leben Leo's X. noch mehr gethan. In Hinsicht auf den Zweck eines Biographen muss man diess billigen . . . Doch wem an der genauern Kenntniss dieser Dinge gelegen ist, der wird hiemit nicht befriedigt" ("Fabroni confesses that he could not include all of the almost countless sources at his disposal. If he accepted this limitation in his Lorenzo, he did so even more in his life of Leo X. With regard to a biographer's purposes, this is acceptable . . . But anyone to whom exact knowledge of these things really matters will feel most unsatisfied by it"). This seems ungracious—and certainly reflects Ranke's inexperience with the practical problems of providing documentation.

34. See W. Roscoe, *The Life and Pontificate of Leo the Tenth* (Liverpool, 1805), esp. his preface, I, [i]–xxxvii, at viii, where he anticipates Ranke by arguing that Giovio "had every opportunity of obtaining the most exact and authentic information on the subject of his history"; xi–xiii, on Fabroni, praising his use of "much original information"; xv, on literary matters, where Roscoe claims to have cited only original sources "as far as my opportunities would permit"; xvff., on his own use of "original documents" from the Florentine archives, the Vatican, and elsewhere. Roscoe warmly appreciated the Italian scholars who had explored this country before him. He thanked A. M. Bandini, author of the great catalogue of the manuscripts of the Laurenziana, for providing "several scarce and valuable documents, both printed and manuscript" (xviii–xix), J. Morelli for his help in Venice (xx–xxi), and an English friend who had made "several curious extracts" from the Parisian MSS of one of the papal diarists, Paris de Grassis (xxv–xxvi). The 218 extracts from sources at the end of his four volumes were heavily used by the more critical historians of the next generation. See also his *Life of Lorenzo de' Medici, Called the Magnificent* (Liverpool, 1795).

history imitated what German classical scholars had already done for the sources of ancient literary and political history.[35] From the 1760s onward German classicists like Christian Gottlob Heyne and Friedrich August Wolf worked through sleepless nights and sweaty days to tear down the idols of neoclassicism. They did not attack the cultural authority of the ancients. On the contrary, they insisted that the Greek spirit, as manifested in architecture and sculpture, poetry and religion, was absolutely fresh and creative, and had a unique moral and educational value for modern readers—especially German ones. But they also insisted that modern readers who hoped to grasp this spirit as it really had been must perform an act of iconoclasm before they could genuflect with proper reverence. Ancient scholars and historians had tried not to preserve but to adorn the remnants of older periods in the history of their civilizations. Accordingly, the modern student could not penetrate backward to the true freshness of Homer's epic or Rome's earliest society except by tearing away the veils that later writers had woven around them. The student of Greek epic, Wolf showed, must realize that the *Iliad* and the *Odyssey* had originally circulated in a radically different form: in the first instance, as songs rather than as fixed written texts. After suffering multiple changes in oral transmission, they underwent rearrangement and interpolation in the Athens of the sixth and fifth centuries B.C.E. The same Athenian statesmen who had the texts fixed in written form also added lines to them for political ends. Still later, the epics were edited even more

35. For a general argument along these lines see U. Muhlack, "Von der philologischen zur historischen Methode," *Theorie der Geschichte,* Beiträge zur Historik, V: *Historische Methode,* ed. C. Meier and J. Rüsen (Munich, 1988), 154–180.

heavily by the first professional scholars of Western history, the denizens of the Museum in the Hellenistic Greek city of Alexandria. These men had tried not to establish the original texts Homer wrote but to adjust the epics they inherited to fit their own, more modern standards in aesthetics and ethics. "The Homer that we hold in our hands now is not the one who flourished in the mouths of the Greeks of his own day, but one variously altered, interpolated, corrected, and emended from the time of Solon down to that of the Alexandrians."[36]

Niebuhr demolished the traditional story of Rome's foundation by Romulus and Remus, two youths nourished by a she-wolf, as handily as Wolf demolished the idea that Homer had written polished, classically coherent epics.[37] Both men, finally, insisted that their demolition jobs were only the prelude to a true appreciation of the ancient world. And both repeatedly argued that the critical reader had a duty to forget all prejudices, read the sources in historical order and context, and listen to the voice of history before trying to write about the past. The appearance of Wolf's text made writers as well as philologists think that scholarship was undergoing a revolution. Goethe and Herder, both Schlegels, and one Humboldt were fascinated by Wolf's and Niebuhr's discoveries—so fascinated, in fact, that they forgot that Wolf and Niebuhr, in their turn, were repeating work done long before by the critical humanists,

36. F. A. Wolf, *Prolegomena ad Homerum,* I (Halle, 1795), chap. XLIX: "Habemus nunc Homerum in manibus, non qui viguit in ore Graecorum suorum, sed inde a Solonis temporibus usque ad haec Alexandrina mutatum varie, interpolatum, castigatum et emendatum"; *Prolegomena to Homer {1795},* tr. A. Grafton, G. W. Most, and J. E. G. Zetzel (Princeton, 1985; rev. ed., 1988), 209 (slightly altered).
37. See Walther.

theologians, and philosophers of the sixteenth through the early eighteenth centuries.[38]

In this context, Ranke's assertion that he had not imitated or employed the method of Niebuhr and Gottfried Hermann deserves special scrutiny. The first assertion is called into question by a letter Ranke sent to Niebuhr in December 1824 to accompany copies of his *Histories*. Here the modern historian portrayed himself as the ancient historian's disciple. He made clear that he had read, studied, copied, and dissected Niebuhr's work with all the attention he would have brought to a primary source: "Your Excellency's *Roman History* was one of the first German historical works that I really studied. As early as my time [as a student] at the university I made notes on it and tried in every way I could to make it my own." Ranke explained that he had continued to use Niebuhr's work while teaching at the Gymnasium, and expressed the hope "that the present books may appear not wholly unworthy of your instruction, which I enjoyed without your knowing it."[39] Ranke could not imitate Niebuhr directly. He set out not to reinterpret a tradition, as Niebuhr did, but to identify the sources that would

38. See A. Grafton, *Defenders of the Text* (Cambridge, Mass., and London, 1991), chap. 9.

39. L. von Ranke, *Das Briefwerk,* ed. W. P. Fuchs (Hamburg, 1949), 69–70: "Ew. Exzellenz eigene Römische Geschichte ist eins der ersten deutschen historischen Werke, die ich eigentlich studiert habe. Schon auf der Universität habe ich dieselbe exzerpiert und mir auf alle Weise zu eigen zu machen gesucht . . . dass gegenwärtige Bücher des Unterrichts, den ich ohne Ihr Wissen von Ihnen genossen, nicht völlig unwürdig erscheinen mögen." Ranke really did read and make excerpts from Niebuhr's Roman history while at Leipzig, at a time when he was beginning to write historical essays and ponder methodological problems. See "Das Luther-Fragment von 1817," ed. E. Schweitzer, in Ranke, *Deutsche Geschichte im Zeitalter der Reformation,* ed. P. Joachimsen et al. (Munich, 1925–26), VI, 370–371, 375, 383–384.

enable him to replace tradition with history. But he could hardly have made it clearer that he owed at least part of his skeptical attitude toward received accounts and respected authorities to the man he called "the originator of a new form of criticism."[40] Admittedly, the letter must be read in context. Ranke wanted travel money to consult manuscripts in the library of the Alfieri family in Rome, to which Georg Heinrich Pertz had called attention. He hoped that Niebuhr, a political man as well as a scholar, could help.[41] Nonetheless, his debt seems clear enough that admirers as well as debunkers of Ranke have repeatedly acknowledged it—even though in doing so they have had to qualify his own testimony.[42]

Gottfried Hermann, the other older man whose influence Ranke denied, played at least as great a role in the historian's formation. When Ranke entered the University of Leipzig in 1814, he attended Hermann's lectures on Aeschylus and Pindar. Hermann—a brilliant, austere disciple of Kant—is now remembered for work of exceptional originality on Greek metrics and textual criticism. But he supposedly showed little interest in wider historical questions and little tolerance for scholars who did not share his priorities and views. In fact, as Ranke's notes on Hermann's lectures show, he taught his students a great deal about the pains and pleasures of historical criticism.[43]

40. Ranke, *Das Briefwerk,* 70: "der Urheber einer neuen Kritik."

41. See E. Vischer, "Niebuhr und Ranke," *Schweizerische Zeitschrift für Geschichte,* 39 (1989), 243–265; in the end, the Alfieri papers proved of no great value for Ranke's ends, but the relationship is fascinating, as Vischer shows, using newly found documents.

42. For an admirer, see C. Varrentrapp, "Briefe an Ranke . . .," *Historische Zeitschrift,* 105 (1910), 108; for a debunker, W. Weber, *Priester der Klio* (Bern and New York, 1984), 213.

43. For Ranke's own late recollections of Hermann and his other teachers at

Ranke's surviving notes on Hermann's course on Aeschylus' *Persae* begin on 26 May 1814, when the class was already three quarters of the way through the play. Almost immediately a historical question came up. The spirit of the Persian king Darius laments that his son Xerxes' defeat represents the worst calamity to befall the Persians since Zeus founded their royal line. "For Medos," he says, "was the first leader of the Persian army" (765); then he lists the others. Cyrus comes third. But Herodotus gave a divergent list of Persian kings (1.98). Who was to be trusted: the playwright or the historian? "Here," Hermann told his students, "we see the error of those who hold that Aeschylus is an accurate and certain historical source, because, they think, he is older than Herodotus. As a poet, he was at liberty to adapt everything, here as elsewhere, to his plot."[44] A long further discussion made it clear how hard it was to decide if Aeschylus's poetic Persian history coincided with the prose account of Herodotus or the divergent one of Xenophon; a second excursus described how historians of Persia had "tortured themselves" trying to make sense of the royal names in a slightly later verse.[45] The implications of these problems

---

Leipzig see his *Neue Briefe,* ed. B. Hoeft and H. Herzfeld (Hamburg, 1949), 476–477; here he speaks of "die geistvollen Interpretationen der Klassiker, z. B. des Pindar, welche der unsterbliche Hermann vortrug" (476) ("the sagacious interpretations of the classics, such as Pindar, which the immortal Hermann presented in his lectures"). See also Baur, 92–101.

44. Ranke-Nachlass, Staatsbibliothek zu Berlin, Preussischer Kulturbesitz (Haus II), 38 II C: "Kollegnachschriften aus Leipzig," 1: "Observationes Godofredi Hermanni ad Aeschyli Persas a v. 758 usque ad finem, a die XXVI mensis Maii ad diem XIV mensis Iulii MDCCCXIV," fol. 2 verso: "Hic frustra ii sunt, qui historicam fidem et certitudinem in Aeschylo quaerunt, cum, ut putant, antiquior sit ipso Herodoto: sed ut poetae ei licuit ut in omni re ita hic res ad consilium suum adtemperare."

45. Ibid., fol. 3 verso–4 recto.

of detail were clear: historical truths could be established only by critical, comparative study of the sources that attested to them, which might in turn yield surprising results.

Ranke also took notes on Hermann's lectures on Pindar's odes to the Greek Olympic victors, this time from the beginning. Here, especially in the introduction, Hermann not only discussed specific historical problems but also raised general questions about historical method—and, indeed, about the quality and extent of the knowledge one can hope to obtain about the past. He began by telling his students, depressingly, that "the monuments of Greek poetry that remain to us are the wreckage saved after a great shipwreck."[46] He evoked what he sadly but expressively described as "the history of Greek poetry that we do not have"—this in a section whose title he or his student later changed to read, even more pointedly, "On the difficulties which confront one who sets out to write the history of Greek poetry."[47] In the case of Pindar, Hermann made clear, the surviving works had been so radically altered in the course of transmission that one could not possibly hope to read exactly what Pindar wrote. The philologists of Hellenistic Alexandria had done their worst by way of deliberate editorial revision, making Pindar meet their own standards of taste and elegance. Only scholarship could scour away the false patina and reveal the real texts underneath: "Pindar's writings were edited in antiquity by Aristarchus and other grammarians of the Alexandrian school. They set out both to explain them and to cor-

46. Ibid., notebook 2, "Godofredi Hermanni Prof. Lips. Praelectiones in Pindarum," p. 3: "Quae nobis restant graecae poeseos monumenta, rudera sunt ex magno naufragio servata."

47. Ibid.: "Historia graecae poeseos quam non habemus," changed to "De difficultatibus quae se historiam graecae poeseos scripturo obiiciunt."

rect them so that they fitted the grammatical and ethical standards which these gentleman had made up for themselves. How they did this, we simply do not know, since a great portion of their commentaries has been lost. Hence we must not think that the text of these poems that we now have before us is what Pindar produced, but rather one into which the grammarians' corrections have been interpolated. We must, therefore, reconstruct the genuine texts and remove these inventions of the grammarians."[48] The surviving work was only a selection from the originals, made not by the poet or in his lifetime but by the Hellenistic scholar Aristophanes of Byzantium, centuries later. The oldest clearly identifiable stage in the transmission of the text reflected not what the poet had put down in the white heat of inspired composition, but the cold, calm scholarship carried out by the professional philologists of the Alexandrian Museum. And even this stage in the transmission of the text of Pindar could not be reconstructed completely, since the manuscripts, though they fell into two distinct families, all showed metrical errors so gross that they could not possibly stem from Pindar (or, presumably, his Alexandrian editors).[49] On Ranke—the young student, fresh from the Gymnasium, where he had learned to read the ancients as if they they wrote directly for him, and on the assumption that their works survived basically intact—these lectures must have had an explo-

48. Ibid., p. 13: "Pindari scripta in antiquitate et Aristarchus et alii scholae Alexandrinae grammatici tractarunt, ita ut tum ea explicarent, tum ad grammatices et ethices, quam sibi finxerant, praecepta corrigerent. Quod quomodo fecerint, non cognitum habemus, cum pleraque ex eorum commentariis interierint. Hinc quam nunc in manu habemus horum carminum recensionem, ea non putanda est ita esse a Pindaro instituta, sed Grammaticorum correctionibus interpolata. Genuina ergo eruenda sunt, eiicienda haec Grammaticorum figmenta."

49. Ibid., 13, 16.

sive impact. Ranke learned from listening to his professor of Greek, as well as from reading Sir Walter Scott, to prefer bare facts and historical sources to derivative later narratives, however well they read.

Hermann's considerations were not wholly original. Much though he disliked his rival Hellenist, August Böckh, he had learned a good deal from the brand-new first volume of Böckh's edition of Pindar (1811), which provided fresh information about the textual tradition as well as stimulation and irritation. Hermann told his pupils that Böckh had used the manuscripts of Pindar in an exemplary, critical way, after making a systematic study of their relations to one another—and thus touched on what would become central tenets of Ranke's historical method.[50] More generally, Hermann clearly modeled his brief

50. Ibid., pp. 15ff. Before criticizing Böckh's views on Pindaric metrics, Hermann praised his approach to the manuscript tradition (ibid., 16): "non potest negari, Bockhium primum ex editoribus veram viam esse ingressum. Recte enim intellexit diversas esse codicum familias, quarum alia magis, alia minus interpolata sit, neque his aequum pretium concedendum esse a Critico, id quod novos, quorum erat ei copia, codices conferens confirmavit. Multo magis tamen a prioribus metri ratione differt" ("No one can deny that Böckh is the first editor of Pindar to have proceeded in the right way. For he correctly grasped that the manuscripts belong to different families, some of which have suffered more interpolation and some less, and that the critic cannot attach equal worth to these. By collating new manuscripts, to a number of which he had access, he confirmed this. But he differs much more from the earlier editors in his metrics"). Some humanists had studied the genealogy of manuscripts of classical and legal texts in the fifteenth and sixteenth centuries, and German scholars had seen the need to carry out a systematic recension of the manuscripts of the New Testament in the eighteenth century. Wolf, borrowing from the theologians, emphasized in his *Prolegomena ad Homerum* that systematic recension of the manuscripts must precede any effort to edit a text. But this approach, which remains fundamental to textual criticism, was still taking shape in the early nineteenth century, and Böckh's work had considerable novelty. For the history of systematic recension see S. Timpanaro, *La genesi del metodo del Lachmann*, new ed., repr. with corrections (Padua, 1985). Böckh's discussion of the thirty-seven

history of the text of Pindar on the big history of the text of Homer that Wolf, Böckh's teacher, had reconstructed in his *Prolegomena* two decades before.[51] As Ranke's disciples imitated his criticism of the Renaissance historians, so Hermann imitated what Wolf had done to Homer and the Homeric tradition. But Hermann's impact matters more than his sources. He showed the young Ranke how to think as a historical critic: he cautioned him to view traditions and texts with suspicion and to reason about the age and value of sources. That Ranke would ask such questions in his own later work was almost foreordained—however much the old Ranke, romantically recalling his all too well-spent youth, refused to admit the point. Like Wolf—and Niebuhr—he could not refrain from asserting his claims to that originality which all desired—even at the price of censoring his memories of the tradition he came from.[52]

Ranke innovated in many ways. He combined narrative with analytical history, on the grand scale. He dramatized the process of criticism as powerfully as the events it enabled him to reconstruct. And he set the stage for new research projects and forms of exposition—many of which he himself devised and

---

manuscripts of Pindar he used, as well as of the Byzantine scholars whose efforts to correct the text he deplored, appears in *Pindari opera quae supersunt* (Leipzig, 1811–1825), I, vii–xxvii.

51. In Ranke's second notebook, Hermann's introduction bears the title "Prolegomena" (p. 3). Böckh touched only briefly on the early history of the Pindaric text (*Pindari opera*, I, ix).

52. See Walther's interesting analysis of Niebuhr, 319–320; he in turn draws on W. Lepenies, "Fast ein Poet. Johann Joachim Winckelmanns Begründung der Kunstgeschichte," in *Autoren und Wissenschaftler im 18. Jahrhundert* (Munich and Vienna, 1988), 91–120. Ranke's efforts to think his way through to a pedagogy more appropriate for creating patriotism in young Germans also led him to evince bitter impatience with the domination of the Gymnasium by philologists: see "Luther-Fragment," ed. Schweitzer, 374.

carried out. Nothing quite like his *Geschichten* had appeared before. But he and his first book did not represent the beginnings of documented, critical history. If not in 1824, when? If not Ranke, who? Like so many genealogies, that of the footnote turns out to have more branches and twists than one might have expected. The next one leads away from historicism and back into the Enlightenment, away from the hard-pressed teacher begging for books and travel grants and into the well-stocked libraries of several eighteenth-century gentlemen.

CHAPTER FOUR

Footnotes and Philosophie:
An Enlightenment Interlude

✳ Evidently Ranke did not officiate at the marriage of eloquent and erudite history. The time is ripe, then, for a new hypothesis: the combination of narrative and reflection probably established itself in historiography well before the nineteenth century—or Ranke—dawned. True, this thesis may seem paradoxical at first sight. One of the most eminent and influential historians of the eighteenth century, Voltaire, repeatedly made clear his distaste for scholarly details. In preparing the segments of his *Age of Louis XIV* that would deal with the king's private life, Voltaire told the Abbé Dubos, "I have the memoirs of M. Dangeau in forty volumes from which I have extracted forty pages." He was writing history on the grand scale, painting "frescoes of the great events of the time" and trying

> to trace the onward march of the human mind in philosophy, oratory, poetry and criticism; to show the progress of painting, sculpture, and music; of jewelry, tapestry making, glassblowing, gold-cloth weaving and watchmaking. As I do this I want to depict only the geniuses that have excelled in these under-

takings. God preserve me from devoting 300 pages to the story of Gassendi!

To the philosopher who composed this innovative essay on cultural history and its political background, technical scholarship naturally seemed little more than an interruption to his proper studies: "Woe to details! Posterity neglects them all; they are a kind of vermin that undermines large works."[1] A penetrating historical critic who treated his sources with a well-informed lack of deference, Voltaire nonetheless notoriously despised the "empty, sterile science of facts and dates."[2]

Voltaire both reflected and set intellectual fashion. In 1768, when S. A. Tissot published his elaborate study *The Health of Scholars,* for example, he felt it necessary to defend himself in his preface for having "retained the citations even though they daily undergo even sterner banishment from French writing"; only those authors who had written works which were absolutely complete and in need of no further development by their successors, he explained, had a right to forgo citations. In his own case, since he expected his readers to continue attacking the same problems, he felt it necesssary to indicate the sources he had used. After all, he argued, he found "nothing evil" in showing the authors he had drawn on "the honor he owed them,

1. Voltaire to Dubos, 30 October 1738; tr. J. Barzun in *The Varieties of History,* ed. F. Stern (New York, 1973), 38–40 (for the original, see Voltaire, *Complete Works,* ed. T. Besterman, 89 [Geneva and Toronto, 1969], 344–345). See G. G. Iggers, "The European Context of Eighteenth-Century German Enlightenment Historiography," *Aufklärung und Geschichte,* ed. H. E. Bödeker et al. (Göttingen, 1986), 225–245, esp. 229.

2. Voltaire to Maffei, 1744, as quoted in K. Pomian, *Collectionneurs, amateurs et curieux. Paris, Venise: xvie-xviiie siècle* (Paris, 1987), 198: "cette science vague et stérile des faits et des dates."

with some words set at the margin, where they hurt nobody in any way."[3] Tissot's defensive tone reveals as much as the content of his preface. The dry, humble footnote seems ill at ease in the glamorous company of the eighteenth century's new theories about the relation between climate and constitution, the evolution of material and artistic culture, and the sequence of stages in the development of human society.

In fact, however, in the last generation it has become clear that the eighteenth century harbored more than one kind of historiography. Social and cultural history flourished alongside political and military narratives. Fiction and history intersected, before Ranke was born or thought of, and not all their contacts took the form of collisions. The new taste for reading about the details of family life and relationships that inspired both readers and writers of the English novel expressed itself, as Mark Phillips has shown, not only in new kinds of analytical history but also in new forms of documentary publication.[4]

3. S. A. Tissot, Vorrede, in *Von der Gesundheit der Gelehrten,* tr. J. R. Füesslin (Zurich, 1768), sig. []8() recto-verso: "Die Citationen habe ich beybehalten, weil sie mir nützlich scheinen, obgleich sie täglich mehr aus den französischen Schriften verbannt werden. Schriftsteller die ihren Gegenstand erschöpfen, und ihren Nachfolgern nichts mehr zu sagen übrig lassen, können derselben entbehren; ihre Werke sind vollendete Gebäude, an die man niemals mehr Hand legen wird; zum Unglück ist das mein Fall nicht, so wenig als vieler andern ihrer, und dennzumahl, dünkt mir, soll man citiren, damit man denen welche die nämliche Arbeit einmal für die hand nehmen wollen, die Entdeckung der Quellen erleichtere, woraus sie schöpfen können. In Werken die der Erfolg meiner eigenen Bermerkungen sind, habe ich es nicht gethan, allein wenn man sich anderer ihrer bedient, so find ich nichts böses darinn, wenn man ihnen durch einige unten an der Seite hingesetzte Worte wo sie niemandem nichts schaden, dieserwegen die schuldige Ehre beweiset."

4. M. S. Phillips, "Reconsiderations on History and Antiquarianism: Arnaldo Momigliano and the Historiography of Eighteenth-Century England," *Journal*

Erudite collectors of texts and iconoclastic critics of historical tradition coexisted, sometimes contentiously, but sometimes quite happily, with the philosophical students of social and cultural development: some individuals—like William Robertson—played both roles at once. Some kinds of information—like the unsettlingly long chronologies of Egyptian, Chinese, and Indian history that circulated widely in the eighteenth century, apparently calling the short chronology of the Bible into question—attracted the attention of erudite antiquaries and disrespectful *philosophes* alike. Some antiquaries used sharp philosophical chisels to shape—or demolish—the multiple and contradictory accounts of ancient history; some *philosophes,* as we will see, enjoyed displaying their mastery of the tools of erudition.[5] It seems only reasonable, then, to examine this lively scene of historical exchange and debate for signs of new methods in the documentation, as well as the composition, of history. Scholars have already cut paths into the sources, down which the student can travel with some ease. Momigliano, for example, argued in a pioneering essay that Edward Gibbon, with whom I began this inquiry, fused existing traditions to create a modern, critical history of the ancient world. The *Decline and Fall* combined the irony and broad viewpoint of the *philosophes* with the minute erudition of the antiquaries, the crabbed, Latin-writing, pedantic students of the ancient and medieval worlds whom many *philosophes* loved to ridicule. Gibbon wrote the high classic language of traditional historiography, but he addressed himself to the dusty details of

---

of the History of Ideas, 57 (1996), 297–316 (a thoughtful essay, which, however, takes too narrow a view of the antiquarian tradition).

    5. See C. Grell, *L'histoire entre érudition et philosophie* (Paris, 1993).

the sources as well as to the lurid lives of emperors. The bottoms of his pages swarm with references to the literature of erudition, tantalizingly precise and yet frustratingly uninformative to the modern reader. He regularly referred to the heroes of early modern scholarship: the erudite Maffei and Muratori, the reliable Mosheim and Tillemont, and the learned but overheated Lipsius. These short passages in small type may reveal the grand fusion of two kinds of history.[6]

Only Gibbon, moreover, could have brought it about. In his youth he studied, unhappily, at Oxford, where at age sixteen he converted to Catholicism. Sent by his father to live with a Calvinist minister at Lausanne, he not only recovered from this uncharacteristic outbreak of piety but improved his Latin, began to study Greek, and thoroughly mastered French literature and the French language—which he both wrote and spoke, fluently and elegantly. He thus knew at first hand the French standards of taste and elegance that dominated the literature of the Enlightenment. Later still—or so, at least, he firmly maintained—his period as a sociable, if hardly heroic, volunteer officer gave him the military experience a classical historian needed. Above all, however, Gibbon loved erudition. In his teens, as he obsessively studied the chronology of the ancient world, "the Dynasties of Assyria and Egypt were my top and cricket-ball: and my sleep has been disturbed by the difficulty of reconciling the Septuagint with the Hebrew computation."[7] On returning from the Continent to England, he set out to show in an essay that "all the faculties of the mind may be

6. See above all A. Momigliano, "Gibbon's Contribution to Historical Method," *Contributo alla storia degli studi classici* (Rome, 1955), 195–211.

7. E. Gibbon, *Memoirs of My Life,* ed. G. A. Bonnard (New York, 1966), 43.

exercised and displayed by [the] study of ancient litterature"—an iconoclastic thesis, especially in France, where "the learning and language of Greece and Rome were neglected by a philosophic age."[8] Years before Gibbon undertook to write the *Decline and Fall,* he had read his way into the most technical scholarly literature of the previous three centuries. Numerous remarks in his journal, alternatively caustic and admiring, trace his progress through the byways of modern discussions of such thorny subjects as ancient chronology and geography.[9] Gibbon's efforts to explain Rome's fall were for the most part rather conventional. But his ability to combine massive knowledge of the older scholarly tradition with the high style of eighteenth-century letters still excites admiration. And only this ability enabled him to create what seemed, in his day, the radically unlikely synthesis of philosophical and erudite history. The argument is temptingly neat, and sheds, as we will see, a penetrating light on Gibbon's historical position. But the historical footnote certainly did not originate with Gibbon, or even in his generation.

Consider just one of Gibbon's most famous polemical writings—*A Vindication of Some Passages in the Fifteenth and Sixteenth Chapters of the History of the Decline and Fall of the Roman Empire* (1779). A Mr. Davis of Balliol College, now forgotten except by readers of the *Decline and Fall,* had had the effrontery to attack not only Gibbon's text, but his footnotes—which amounted, in this context, to his honor:

8. Ibid., 99.
9. *Gibbon's Journal to January 28th, 1761,* ed. D. M. Low (New York, n.d.), 22–23, 42, 44, 81, 87, 95, 104, 105, 108–109, 123–125, 163, 166–169, 173, 181–182, 187, 197–198.

The remarkable mode of quotation, which Mr. Gibbon adopts, must immediately strike every one who turns to his notes. He sometimes only mentions the author, perhaps the book, and often leaves the reader the toil of finding out, or rather guessing at the passage. The policy, however, is not without its design and use. By endeavouring to deprive us of the means of comparing him with the authorities he cites, he flattered himself, no doubt, that he might safely have recourse to *misrepresentation.*[10]

Davis accused Gibbon of every sin in the footnote-writer's catechism: heaping up without distinction citations to authorities who actually disagreed, partial quotation designed to suppress inconvenient facts or theses, reliance on secondary sources not cited, and plagiarism. Gibbon's method of citation seemed to him designed above all "as a good artifice . . . to escape detection."[11]

Gibbon had no trouble replying to what he rightly described as a "rude and illiberal" attack. Turning Davis' concern with petty details into an indication of social inferiority, Gibbon invited his opponent to call at his house "any afternoon when I am *not* at home." "My servant," Gibbon promised, "shall shew him my library, which he will find tolerably well furnished with the useful authors, ancient as well as modern, ecclesiastical as well as profane, who have *directly* supplied me with the materials of my History." But he also replied with detailed argu-

10. H. E. Davis, BA, *An Examination of the Fifteenth and Sixteenth Chapters of Mr Gibbon's History of the Decline and Fall of the Roman Empire* (London, 1778), ii, quoted in Gibbon, *Miscellaneous Works,* ed. John, Lord Sheffield (London, 1814), IV, 523 (Gibbon's emphasis). Gibbon says in his *Memoirs of My Life* that Davis "presumed to attack, not the faith, but the good faith, of the historian"; ed. G. Bonnard, 160.

11. Davis, *Examination,* 230 n.

ments of his own. Gibbon examined and counted the 383 notes he had appended to chapters 15 and 16, pointing out that they contained hundreds of precise citations. He insisted that when he had borrowed evidence from earlier scholars, he had "explicitly acknowledged my obligation." And he showed that the vast majority of Davis' criticisms in fact rested on errors of Davis's own. The ignorant critic had failed to confirm Gibbon's references, for example, because he checked them in differently paginated editions, or did not know the whole texts from which they came. Gibbon even acknowledged that no learned apparatus can be complete. All 383 of his footnotes, he admitted, had not made fully explicit the grounds by which he used and combined his sources. Many of the texts he cited, as he pointed out with an honesty that deserves respect, had to be "softened" if they were to be made to agree far enough to yield a coherent narrative or a plausible analysis of a political institution or a social development. Only an expert reader—not a Davis— could actually work backward from the citations and arguments to the thought and research that had produced them.[12]

What matters here is not the reduction of a fool to rubble or the glory of Gibbon's prose, but the single point that the adversaries had in common. Both assumed—without arguing the point—that a serious work of history must have notes. Both evidently agreed that these notes must lead the reader to the original sources and represent them accurately. And both implicitly accepted that the apparatus provided the diagnostic test of a historian's critical expertise. These shared assumptions reveal much about Gibbon's stance and method. Evidently, the

12. For Davis' not very effective response see *A Reply to Mr. Gibbon's Vindication* (London, 1779).

footnote had already become part of historians' standard operating procedure, before the great English historians of the Enlightenment made it theirs. That helps to explain why a German reviewer of volume III of the *Decline and Fall,* writing from the new and advanced University of Göttingen, hailed Gibbon not as the creator but as a skilled practitioner of historical criticism. Gibbon, he said, had drawn his information from the best sources, with good criticism, and explained them with sound reasoning. From a German viewpoint at least, Gibbon appeared to be the master of an existing craft rather than the inventor of a new one.[13]

Further confirmation comes from one of the most illustrious documents ever to concern itself with the humble problem of the footnote: David Hume's letter of 8 April 1776 to the publisher William Strahan. Strahan had brought out the first volume of the *Decline and Fall* and was currently printing Hume's own *History of England.* The philosopher declared himself "very much taken with Mr Gibbon's Roman History" and "glad to hear of its success." He also asked that "a Copy of my new Edition shoud be sent to Mr Gibbon, as wishing that a Gentleman, whom I so highly value, shoud peruse me in the form the least imperfect, to which I can bring my work"—clear evidence of his esteem for Gibbon's learning and acuity. But Hume also put forward some technical complaints, which he hoped Gibbon might take into account in preparing the second edition of his work, chiefly in order to make it more accessible to the reader:

> He ought certainly to print the Number of the Chapter at the head of the Margin, and it would be better if something of the

13. *Göttingische Gelehrte Anzeigen,* 18 October 1783, 1704.

Contents coud also be added. One is also plagued with his Notes, according to the present Method of printing the Book: When a note is announced, you turn to the End of the Volume; and there you often find nothing but the Reference to an Authority: All these Authorities ought only to be printed at the Margin or the Bottom of the Page.[14]

This text reveals much. It reminds us, first of all, that Gibbon's footnotes began as endnotes, and only reached what we now think of as their traditionally prominent position on Gibbon's page after Hume complained. But it also confirms that the technical, documentary side of Gibbon's footnoting did not represent a radical innovation in exposition or format. Hume did not see the notion that citations should identify the sources of statements in a historical text as radically new. Instead, he urged that such notes should occupy a convenient position, at the foot of the page or in the margin. He himself, after all, had learned a decade or so earlier to support his statements with references, when Horace Walpole and others criticized him for his failure to do so in his *History of England*.[15] Hume did not ask that Gibbon's longer notes, the ones that amounted to a partly satirical commentary, move as well, though that was the solution Gibbon adopted. Perhaps Hume thought that the need to find the satirical comments after the text proper actually enhanced their impact. At all events, here too Gibbon's method emerges not as wholly radical but as part of an ongoing enterprise—though his own mixture of references and commentaries proved unique.

Gibbon—like Hume and his fellow philosophic historian

14. *The Letters of David Hume*, ed. J. Y. T. Greig (Oxford, 1932), II, 313.
15. F. Palmeri, "The Satiric Footnotes of Swift and Gibbon," *The Eighteenth Century*, 31 (1990), 245–262 at 246. See also Chapter 7 below.

William Robertson—pioneered in writing double, critical narratives in English. But these inventive English and Scottish authors had colleagues on the Continent.[16] Consider a writer far less philosophic—and even in Germany far less famous—than Gibbon, the Osnabrück notable Justus Möser. Like Gibbon, Möser was a man of broad culture, who spoke French as well as he did German; unlike Gibbon, Möser enjoyed the most up-to-date education of his time, which he obtained at the University of Göttingen. There Möser studied law, and learned from the erudite tradition of jurisprudence that flourished in the Holy Roman Empire from the late sixteenth to the late eighteenth century how to base a description of a social or legal transaction on a solid mass of sources, cited in detail.[17] The highly technical questions of public law and royal genealogy that occupied students of the constitution of the Holy Roman Empire required them to know, compare, and cite historical and legal texts. Taught at an early age to value "the testimonies of ancient writers" more than "the varied and clever genealogical arguments of more recent writers, which rest on conjecture alone, and use the mere agreement of certain names, as if it provided a solid foundation for their demonstration," future bureaucrats were trained to base their historical arguments on long series of "probationes," direct quotations from primary sources, meticulously arranged.[18]

16. On the increasingly systematic use of documentation in eighteenth-century English historiography see D. Hay, *Annalists and Historians* (London, 1977), 175–181.

17. See on this tradition N. Hammerstein's classic *Jus und Historie* (Göttingen, 1972).

18. *Dissertatio genealogica de familia Augusta Franconica quam sub praesidio Io.*

Möser dedicated his life both as civil servant and as historian to the ecclesiastical principality of Osnabrück. Gradually he formed the conviction that the old-fashioned institutions of this old-fashioned corner of the Holy Roman Empire worked for its inhabitants in a way that innovations could not: history had fitted them to the land, the population, and the traditions of the community. In his own account he set out to show society and institutions taking shape, to help the reader watch historical processes *in vitro*. Like Gibbon, but from a totally different point of view, he combined the erudition of traditional humanism with the philosophical history and political thought of Saint-Evremond and Montesquieu.[19] Möser worked through a vast mass of materials, including ancient, medieval, and modern histories and the sources collected and printed by learned antiquaries in the sixteenth and seventeenth centuries. He copied out large extracts from the sources, some of which he hoped to publish.

Möser was no cutting-edge historical critic. He took positions on questions of provenance and authenticity with reluctance, since he normally had no opportunity to assess the material and script, as opposed to the textual contents, of prob-

---

Davidis Koeleri P.P. publice disceptandam proponit Carolus Gustavus Furer de Haimendorf et VVolkersdorf ad d. xxv. Septembris a. MDCCXXII (Altdorf, 1722), Praefatio, sig. [*4] recto: "Plus enim apud nos valent tot antiquorum scriptorum testimonia . . . quam variae et ingeniosae [ed. ingeniosa] recentiorum autorum deductiones genealogicae, quae nudis innituntur coniecturis, et solam convenientiam quorundam nominum pro solido fundamento demonstrationis adhibent." The work consists of a series of genealogical tables with sixty-six pages of documentary "probationes."

19. See in general J. Knudsen, *Justus Möser and the German Enlightenment* (Cambridge, 1986).

lematic documents. His own reproductions of texts were often marred by carelessness in detail. And at times he made fun of his own propensity to combine materials of the most wildly different natures and provenances in his massive notes. In these he responded not only to the primary sources, but also to the sprawling historical literature of the seventeenth century, every encounter with which set him haring off down another scholarly alley. "Yesterday," Möser wrote to Thomas Abbt in June 1765,

> I quoted a Hebrew word in a note—and I cannot even read the language. Isn't that pedantic? And yet I couldn't leave it out. In fact, after I had gone through the *Geographia sacra* of Bochart, I was even tempted to make a hundred notes about it and to correct him in Hebrew and Aramaic—I, who do not even know the alphabet.[20]

For all Möser's self-mockery, he set out, even more systematically than Gibbon, to write a double story. Like a good lawyer, Möser provided virtually every statement of fact in his history with a footnote, not an endnote, in which sources were cited and divergent opinions laid out and assessed. Ten years before Gibbon brought out the first, endnoted volume of the *Decline and Fall,* Möser had already finished printing the first, prelim-

---

20. Möser to Abbt, 26 June 1765; Möser, *Briefwechsel,* ed. W. F. Sheldon et al. (Hanover, 1992), 365: "Allein, wie wird man das alles in einer ossnabrück-ischen Geschichte vertragen? Doch es sind 12 Bogen Einleitung, und ich kann mir nicht helfen. Gestern führte ich in einer Note ein hebräisch Wort an und kann doch diese Sprache nicht lesen. Ist das nicht pedantisch? Und doch konnte ich es nicht lassen; ja, ich war sogar in der Versuchung, nachdem ich des Bochart Geographiam sacram durchgelesen hatte, einhundert Anmerkungen darüber zu machen und ihm im Hebräischen und Arabischen zurecht zu weisen, ich, der die Buchstaben nicht kenne." The seventeenth-century polymath Samuel Bochart wrote with great erudition on biblical geography and chronology.

inary, spectacularly documented edition of his *Osnabrückische Geschichte*. The early twentieth-century historian of historiography Eduard Fueter—ever more willing to notice exceptional individual achievements than to abandon the traditional categories they challenged—found Möser's achievement surprisingly modern, even radical, in method and presentation (though highly conservative in content). Möser, he admitted, did not try to conceal, but strove to reveal, the sources from which he worked.[21] Footnotes, in short, were written by eighteenth-century historians who lived and worked in very different worlds, societies, and even libraries. The need for clearly presented historical documentation established itself, paradoxically, in the age of the *philosophes,* who despised pedantry as a form of secular superstition.

If the Enlightenment saw footnotes proliferate, the intellectuals of the nineteenth century did not view them with the unmixed admiration and affection one might expect. Hegel, for example, clearly rebelled against the idea that a philosopher's text should use footnotes to exemplify and carry on a dialectical argument. In fact, he fled them like the plague, as if they were the outward signs of an infectious erudition that he feared he might catch. He appreciated a predecessor, like Dietrich Tiedemann, who provided "valuable extracts" from rare books. But he appreciated even more the chance to point out that another one, Wilhelm Gottlieb Tennemann, had used his extensive footnotes only to shoot a scholarly own goal: "With great honesty Tennemann puts the passage from Aristotle under his text,

---

21. See E. Fueter, *Geschichte der neueren Historiographie* (Munich and Berlin, 1911), 393–397 at 396–397, and, for a detailed analysis of his working method, P. Schmidt, *Studien über Justus Möser als Historiker* (Göppingen, 1975).

so that the original and the translation often contradict one another."[22] In this rhetorical way as in many others, Hegel wished to distance himself from Kant, the most oppressive and challenging of his predecessors, who had made masterly use of footnotes to give material form to his inner ambiguities. Kant, as Wolfert von Rahden has shown, deliberately confined all suggestions that reason might have had a historical origin or might undergo a further development to the murky region below the superstructure of his texts.[23]

Even in more philological fields, the intellectual landscape of nineteenth-century positivism was not always adorned by intellectual flower beds swarming with colorfully blooming footnotes. A recent, intelligent essay points out that in modern American classical scholarship, footnotes often serve to prove the author's membership in a guild rather than to illuminate or support a particular point. Citations are heaped up, without much regard to their origins or compatibility, in order to make the text above them seem to rest on solid pilings. The author, no doubt rightly, connects this practice with the authority long enjoyed by German philology in America, and lays particular weight on the habit of citing Ulrich von Wilamowitz-Möllendorff, the student of Greek literature and religion whose editions and analyses of texts remain deeply influential decades after his death.[24]

Stephen Nimis rightly argues that many of these references

22. G. W. F. Hegel, *Vorlesungen über die Geschichte der Philosophie,* I: *Sämmtliche Werke, Jubiläumsausgabe,* XVII (Stuttgart–Bad Canstatt, 1965), 147–148: "Dabei ist Tennemann so aufrichtig, die Stelle aus dem Aristoteles unter den Text zu setzen, so dass Original und Uebersetzung sich oft widersprechen."

23. On Kant see W. von Rahden, "Sprachpsychonauten," *Sprachwissenschaften im 18. Jahrhundert* (Munich, 1993), 111–141 at 118–127.

24. S. Nimis, "Fussnoten: das Fundament der Wissenschaft," *Arethusa,* 17 (1984), 105–134.

play no substantive role in the arguments they supposedly support. But he nowhere mentions the curious fact that Wilamowitz himself had little use for the footnote that exhaustively cited secondary works on a given topic; when he could, he preferred to write a straightforward, uninterrupted text. Though he often quoted primary sources lavishly, both in his text and in notes, he assumed that his readers knew the literature of philology well enough to supply the references he presupposed. This is not altogether surprising. One of the rare teachers of philology whom the aristocratic Wilamowitz actually admired in his days as a student was Jacob Bernays. And Bernays, though himself an expert on the history of scholarship and a lavish composer of erudite appendices to his short, eloquent texts, had little love for the literary appurtenances of erudition. He described the detailed endnotes that filled three quarters of one of his books as a *Giftschrank* ("poison cupboard"), denying any desire to comply with the request of distinguished and sympathetic colleagues for a more detailed presentation. Neither his warm friend the Roman historian Theodor Mommsen nor the distinguished classicist and musicologist Otto Jahn could persuade Bernays to clutter his text with notes of the normal kind. "If [Jahn] thinks, as Mommsen does, that all the detail from the notes should have been woven directly into the text, and that the citations should cover the lower halves of the pages, in the normal fashion, in rebuttal I can say only that this is not my way, that the whole thing would thus have taken on a really horrifying appearance of erudition. I did not envisage a public with strong enough lungs to plow through twenty gatherings of that kind at one go."[25] Even on the central stages of nine-

25. Bernays to Paul Heyse, 9 March 1855, quoted by H. I. Bach, *Jacob Bernays* (Tübingen, 1974), 128 ("Giftschrank"); Bernays to Friedrich Ritschl,

teenth-century positivism, in short, the footnote played at best an equivocal role. Some of the most learned nineteenth-century scholars harbored literary ambitions that did not exhaust themselves in exhaustive display of what they had read. The sins of twentieth-century epigoni should not be projected backward onto nineteenth-century heroes—who, after all, committed quite enough sins of their own.

These facts may not seem altogether puzzling or surprising, in the light of the evidence that Ranke himself wrote footnotes reluctantly. They will seem less puzzling still if we step back for a moment from the historical tradition, to examine the wide range of other roles played by footnotes in the literary culture of Enlightenment Europe. For in that age of polite conversation, when philosophers loved to present the most abstruse problems of Newtonian physics at a level accessible to the gentle—especially the gentle female—reader, the footnote enjoyed surprising popularity as a literary device. From Rabelais and Cervantes on, as Walter Rehm showed long ago, the tendency of many writers to support every sentence in their own texts and illustrate every sentence in those of others with some sort of gloss or reference has provided a fruitful source of satirical pleasure.[26]

---

29 July 1855, quoted ibid., 130, n. 23: "Was Jahns Wunsch nach mehr Detail angeht, so kann ich nicht 'simpliciter' darauf antworten. Meint er, mit Mommsen, dass alles Detail der Noten gleich in den Text hätte verwebt werden und die Citate, nach der gewöhnlichen Manier, die untere Hälfte der Seiten bedecken sollen: so kann ich dagegen nur sagen, dass dieses nicht meine Weise ist, dass das Ganze dadurch ein viel zu abschreckend gelehrtes Ansehen bekommen hätte und dass ich mir ein kurzathmigeres Publicum gedacht habe als dasjenige sein dürfte, welches im Stande wäre, 20 Bogen solcher Art in einer Tour durchzuackern."

26. W. Rehm, "Jean Pauls vergnügtes Notenleben oder Notenmacher und Notenleser," *Späte Studien* (Bern and Munich, 1964), 7–96.

In the eighteenth century, literary footnotes burgeoned and propagated like branches and leaves in a William Morris wallpaper.[27] Even in Enlightened France, footnotes adorned some best-selling—if hardly respectable—texts. The garret-dwellers of Paris's Grub Street, the poor devils of literature, used the appurtenances of historical learning to pretend that their pornographic novels about randy royals were actually sober "secret histories" of court life, based on genuine letters, clandestine memoirs or other unimpeachable sources. Thus the compiler of *Anecdotes about Mme. la comtesse du Barry,* which appeared in 1775, claimed to have called his work "anecdotes" in order that he could include in the text "a multitude of details which would have sullied the majesty of a history." Otherwise, he would have been forced "to omit, or to relegate to notes," such "spicy" facts. Louis-Sébastien Mercier used elaborate, preachy footnotes to show that his best-seller *The Year 2440,* which went through some twenty-five editions, was meant as a "massive indictment" of the France of 1771.[28]

In England, tradition and philosophy, erudition and philology, solid learning and its counterfeit double met in sharp conflicts that were waged on the bottom margins of some of the most brilliant pages of eighteenth-century literature. England's professional textual scholars included some of the most up-to-date intellectuals of the day—like Richard Bentley, Master of Trinity College, Cambridge, specialist in Latin poetry and scientific ally and correspondent of Isaac Newton. Their attitude

27. See in general H. Stang, *Einleitung—Fussnote—Kommentar* (Bielefeld, 1992).

28. See R. C. Darnton, *The Forbidden Best-Sellers of Pre-Revolutionary France* (New York, 1995), 76–77, 115–136, 139, 337–389 (where parts of the *Anecdotes* are translated [for the preface, see 337–338]); for specimens of Mercier's work in English translation, see ibid., 300–336.

toward traditional texts was anything but reverential. Bentley professed that "reason and the case in point," not the wording of older printed editions or even that of manuscripts, should determine how one printed and explained the text of an ancient writer. He set out, accordingly, to rewrite the Latin poems of Horace and Manilius to meet his own standards of logic and consistency. He planned to do the same, more shockingly still, to the Greek text of the New Testament, which he claimed he could restore to the state it had been in at the time of the Council of Nicea, in the fourth century C.E. And he took even more radical steps with a modern classic of the English language, Milton's *Paradise Lost.* This, he insisted, the blind poet's amanuensis had corrupted as he took it down, while a later "editor" had added further mistakes and interpolated foolish verses of his own composition. Milton, unable to check their work, had never been read as he had meant to be—until Bentley's critical edition of his work restored the lost, never-written original text.[29]

Bentley's lordly approach to literary classics won him some splendid enemies—notably the amiably vicious wits who briefly came together in 1714 in the Scriblerus Club, and who for years before and after had fun turning Bentley's own methods against him. Jonathan Swift, who took the side of the Ancients against the Modern Bentley, ridiculed his opponent in

29. For this version of the context I am most indebted to J. Levine, *Doctor Woodward's Shield* (Berkeley, 1977), and *Humanism and History* (Ithaca, N.Y., and London, 1987). R. C. Jebb's *Bentley* (London, 1882) remains an excellent introduction to Bentley's scholarship; see also S. Timpanaro, *La genesi del metodo del Lachmann,* 3rd ed. (Padua, 1985), C. O. Brink, *English Classical Scholarship* (Cambridge, 1986), and L. D. Reynolds and N. G. Wilson, *Scribes and Scholars,* 3rd ed. (Oxford, 1991).

his *Battle of the Books* in 1710. Swift wielded a varied set of weapons, including the satirical view of modern science that would also inspire *Gulliver's Travels.* He represented Bentley as the quintessence of modern folly, unable to treat the new ideas he espoused with critical distance: when Bentley tries, in the *Battle,* to attack two ancient chiefs, he is "cruelly obstructed by his own unhappy Weight, and tendency towards his Center; a Quality, to which, those of the *Modern* Party are extreme subject; For, being lightheaded, they have in Speculation, a wonderful Agility, and conceive nothing too high for them to mount; but in reducing to Practice, discover a mighty Pressure about their Posteriors and their Heels."[30] But Swift also showed his mastery of the details of Bentley's philological career when he mocked "THE *Guardian* of the *Regal Library*" for his *"Humanity"* (Bentley refused to let a young man, Charles Boyle, keep a manuscript from the Royal Library, of which he was keeper, as long as he wished. The young man in turn mentioned in print that Bentley had refused his request "pro singulari sua humanitate").[31] And Swift showed that he knew the minutiae of philological technique when he left gaps in his own text, filling them with asterisks and describing them, in the margins, as "hiatus in MS."[32]

But Bentley's most effective assailant and parodist was Alexander Pope, whose translation of Homer he mocked. As a committed neoclassicist, Pope resented the belief of Bentley and his friends that the moderns knew better than the ancients

---

30. J. Swift, *A Tale of a Tub. To which is added The Battle of the Books and the Mechanical Operation of the Spirit,* ed. A. C. Guthkelch and D. Nichol Smith, 2nd ed. (Oxford, 1958), 225.
31. Ibid., 224 and n. 2.
32. Ibid., 244, 247, 248, 250.

on many points. As an English poet, he was infuriated by a
mere scholar's daring to rewrite the central poetic text of the
English canon. As an editor of Shakespeare, he was enraged
that more modern, professional editors, like Lewis Theobald,
who took Bentley as their model, questioned his competence
to establish and explicate the text. Pope was appalled by the
rise of Grub Street and the fact that so many pretenders to
learning had ventured to comment on and criticize his work.
A scholar in his own right, Pope not only mocked the antiquaries but mastered some of their skills. Though he ridiculed
the critics who spent dusty hours in libraries collating variant
versions of texts, he also argued in some detail that their emendations could not improve the irremediably corrupt transmitted text of Shakespeare.[33] Pope's fury against both real and
pseudo-scholars expressed itself in many forms—but above all,
and most memorably, in footnotes. In his epic attack on the
monstrous Dullness of his age, the *Variorum Dunciad,* Pope
commented at length on both the excellences of his own works
and the immense, irremediable stupidity of his opponents. He
used the footnote throughout as the hockey-masked villain in
an American horror film uses a chain saw: to dismember his
opponents, leaving their gory limbs scattered across the landscape.

The particular sort of footnote Pope chose as his favorite
satirical medium had been fashionable just before his day. Between the fifteenth and the seventeenth centuries, classical
scholars bent on correcting every error, explicating every literary device, and identifying every thing or custom that
cropped up in a classical text had mounted every major piece
of Greek or Latin prose or verse in a baroque setting of exegesis

33. S. Jarvis, *Scholars and Gentlemen* (Oxford, 1995), 51–62.

and debate. Polemics raged, glosses spread, a thick moss of modern, secondary literature grew over the broken columns of Greek and Roman literature. It rapidly became hard for a single scholar to find—let alone afford—the main commentaries on the central texts. By the late fifteenth century the poems of Virgil were already ringed with a band of text wider than the original, printed in illegibly small type, in which commentators ancient and modern, literal and allegorical debated the meaning and application of his texts. Propertius, Martial, Ovid, and Livy soon had their multiple commentaries and handy, large-sized editions to read them in as well. These sixteenth- and early seventeenth-century editions "with the commentaries of various critics"—"cum notis variorum"—became the model, between 1650 and 1730, for a raft of editions of lesser authors, from Petronius to Phaedrus, in all of which the voices of the arguing commentators threatened to drown the thin classic monotone of the original text.[34]

This model of literary scholarship Pope employed not to imitate but to demolish his opponents. From the start of the *Dunciad* every feature of the work and its supposed author becomes the object of a heavily documented debate: "We purposed," says Martin Scriblerus in his preface to the reader,

> to begin with his [Pope's] Life, Parentage and Education: But as to these, even his contemporaries do exceedingly differ. One saith, he was educated at home; another, that he was bred at St. *Omer's* by Jesuits; a third, not at St. *Omer's,* but at *Oxford;* a fourth, that he had no University education at all. Those who allow him to be bred at home, differ as much concerning his Tutor . . . Nor has an author been wanting to give our Poet

34. For a case study see A. Grafton, "Petronius and Neo-Latin Satire: The Reception of the *Cena Trimalchionis," Journal of the Warburg and Courtauld Institutes,* 53 (1990), 117–129.

such a father as *Apuleius* hath to *Plato, Iamblicus* to *Pythagoras,*
and divers to *Homer,* namely a *Daemon:* For thus Mr. *Gildon:*
"Certain it is, that his original is not from *Adam,* but the devil:
and that he wanteth nothing but horns and tail to be the exact
resemblance of his infernal Father."[35]

Every statement has its footnote to the work of one of Pope's
opponents; just as almost every line of Pope's text has its note,
in which information is supplied, the dull scribblers of London's Grub Street are ridiculed, or—best of all—Pope's enemy
Bentley appears, idiotically trying to rewrite Pope's own poetry
by conjectural emendation. In a curious way, the book even
turned into a variorum edition in the normal sense. Pope invited friends to contribute their own parodies of learning to
the commentary. These became as staccato in form and riven
with contradictions in content as any real anthology of commentaries on Petronius or Virgil.[36]

The very title of Pope's poem, *Dunciad,* becomes the first
pretext for a debate, the fictional participants in which range
themselves, naturally, as commentators, on the bottom of the
page. "It may be well disputed," remarks Theobald, "whether
this be a right Reading? Ought it not rather to be spelled
Dunceiad, as the Etymology evidently demands?" "I have a just
value," replies Scriblerus, "for the Letter E, and the same affection for the Name of this Poem, as the forecited Critic for that

35. Pope, *The Dunciad Variorum, with the Prolegomena of Scriblerus. Reproduced
in Facsimile from the First Issue of the Original Edition of 1729,* ed. R. K. Root
(Princeton, 1929), 2.

36. On 28 June 1728 Pope wrote to Swift that the poem "will be attended
with *Proeme, Prolegomena, Testimonia Scriptorum, Index Authorum,* and Notes *Variorum.* As to the latter, I desire you to read over the text, and make a few in any
way you like best." Quoted in Root's Introduction, ibid., 12.

of his Author; yet cannot it induce me to agree with those who would add yet another *e* to it; and call it the *Dunceiade;* which being a French and foreign Termination, is no way proper to a word entirely English, and Vernacular." The pedantry of critics comes in for mockery at once: if Bentley had cited *ratio,* "reason," as his authority for emending Horace, Scriblerus insisted on following what he described as the manuscript of the *Dunciad,* "mov'd thereto by Authority, at all times with Criticks equal if not superior to Reason. In which method of proceeding, I can never enough praise my very good Friend, the exact *Mr. Tho. Hearne;* who, if any word occur which to him and all mankind is evidently wrong, yet keeps he it in the Text with due reverence, and only remarks in the Margin, *sic M.S.*"[37] Paradoxically, the learned textual critic thus found himself playing the role of an ignorant dunce, which academic satirists of an earlier age had reserved for the opponents of humanistic learning and textual criticism—like the priest described by Erasmus, who insisted on saying "mumpsimus" instead of the correct "sumpsimus" because he had said it that way for twenty years.[38]

When Pope invited Swift to add some of his own notes to the *Variorum,* he wrote that these might take a variety of forms, "whether dry raillery, upon the style and way of commenting of trivial critics; or humorous, upon the authors in the poem; or historical, of persons, places, times; or explanatory; or collecting the parallel passsages of the ancients."[39] In fact the notes range in content from the myths and classical parallels to which

37. *The Dunciad Variorum,* pt. II, 1.

38. *Opus Epistolarum Des. Erasmi Roterodami,* ed. P. S. Allen et al. (Oxford, 1906–1958), II, 323; cf. Jarvis, chap. 1.

39. Pope to Swift, 28 June 1728, quoted by Root, Introduction, 12.

Pope alluded to the London literary scene he savaged. But hatred of pedantry regularly appears as a central theme. Displays of unnecessary antiquarian learning identify such actors as the well-named Cloacina: "The *Roman* Goddess of the Commonshores."[40] A whole appendix, "Virgilius restauratus," is given over to a ludicrous series of notes in Latin, evidently written some years before by Pope's friend Dr. John Arbuthnot. These show Bentley arbitrarily altering the most familiar lines in Virgil. Aeneas, *fato profugus,* "exiled by fate," becomes *flatu profugus,* "exiled by the blowing of the winds of Aeolus, as follows."[41] Clearly, not only Pope and his collaborators but their intended readers knew the procedures and paraphernalia of scholarly annotation well enough to savor detailed, technically adept parodies of them. By 1729, then, when the first version of the *Dunciad variorum* appeared, the footnote had become a Europe-wide fashion, as likely to appeal to a wit in a London coffee-house as to a subrektor in a Wittenberg Gymnasium. A large and appreciative public could decode its learned symbols.

German readers seem to have found footnotes particularly appealing. The universities and learned academies, courts and schools of the Holy Roman Empire offered shelter throughout the seventeenth and early eighteenth centuries to a lumbering, ultimately doomed breed of learned dinosaurs, the polyhistors. These men insisted, in the teeth of the Cartesian and Baconian modernism that flourished in France and England, that the cosmopolitan scholar must still take all knowledge as his uni-

40. *The Dunciad Variorum,* pt. II, 30.
41. Ibid., 99: "*Flatu,* ventorum Aeoli, ut sequitur." On the date and authorship of these notes see A. Pope et al., *Memoirs of the Extraordinary Life, Works, and Discoveries of Martinus Scriblerus,* ed. C. Kerby-Miller (New Haven and London, 1950), 267–269.

versal province. The polyhistors' ideal of universal learning was both mocked and pursued in the age of Enlightenment. At the beginning of the century the modernist scholar Johann Burckhard Mencke, editor of the Leipzig *Acta eruditorum,* a pioneering scientific journal, mercilessly displayed and satirized their social ineptitude and scholarly credulousness in his orations *On the Charlatanry of the Learned.*[42] At the other end of the Enlightenment, the popular writer Jean Paul Richter made his own work of the 1780s and after into a tapestry of divertingly varied erudition. He devoted a life of hard work to excerpting, retelling, citing and alluding to the most bizarre details he could find in the most bizarre collections he could turn up. His favorite books bore titles which sound like baroque self-parodies: Pancirolli's *De rebus inventis et deperditis,* Happel's *Relationes curiosae,* Hofmann's *Mikroskopische Belustigungen,* and Vulpius' *Curiositäten der physisch-artistisch-historischen Vor- und Nachwelt.*[43] Jean Paul claimed to be so proud of the notebooks and indexes that filled his library that he would not exchange them for a collection of 200,000 volumes; Ranke probably recognized him as an older soul brother.[44] He recycled this material endlessly, parodying it, alluding to it, both enjoying and satirizing learning, in work after work. Thus the footnote came, not for the last time, to play a comic role, and at the heart of the work of a major writer.

No wonder, then, that footnotes not only enabled German

42. J. B. Mencke, *De charlataneria eruditorum declamationes duae* (Leipzig, 1715) = *On the Charlatanry of the Learned,* tr. F. E. Litz, ed. H. L. Mencken (New York, 1937).

43. Rehm, 43.

44. Ibid., 51. See also W. Schmidt-Biggemann, *Maschine und Teufel* (Freiburg and Munich, 1975), 104–111.

writers to produce satires, but became the object of them in their own right—as when Gottlieb Wilhelm Rabener, in 1743, published *Hinkmars von Repkow Noten ohne Text.*[45] This dissertation, which consists entirely of footnotes, begins with the author's frank confession that he is out for fame and fortune. Nowadays, he argues, one wins these not by writing one's own text but by commenting on those of others. Hence he has set out to eliminate the middleman: to write his own footnotes, and become famous through them, without waiting for a text to tie them to. After all, the footnote had clearly become the royal road to fame, even for those who did not deserve it: "People, of whom one would swear, that Nature had made them fit for any calling other than that of the scholar; people who, without thinking themselves, explicate the thoughts of the ancients and other famous men; such people make themselves great and fearful, and with what? With notes!"[46] The book amused its readers, yet reality surpassed fantasy, as Lichtenberg remarked: "Rabener's *Notes without a Text* arouse laughter, but Lavater went much further. He gave us notes to which the text must serve as a commentary. That is the real language of seers, which one understands only after the events they announce have taken place."[47]

45. See in general W. Martens, "Von Thomasius bis Lichtenberg: Zur Gelehrtensatire der Aufklärung," *Lessing Yearbook,* 10 (1978) 7–34.

46. G. W. Rabener, *Satiren,* III (Bern, 1776), 6: "Leute, von denen man schwören sollte, dass sie Natur zu nichts weniger, als zu Gelehrten, geschaffen hätte; Leute, welche, ohne selbst zu denken, die Gedanken der Alten und anderer berühmten Männer erklären; solche Leute sind es, die sich gross und furchtbar machen; und wodurch? Durch Noten!" Rabener also remarks: "hingegen getraue ich mir, durch hundert Exempel zu behaupten, dass man durch kein Mittel in der Welt leichter zur gehörigen Autorgrösse gelangen kann, als durch die Beschäfftigung, die Schriften anderer Männer durch Noten zu vermehren, und zu verbessern."

47. Rehm, 12 and n. 7: "Man lacht über Rabeners Noten ohne Text, aber

Footnotes, in short, spread rapidly in eighteenth-century historiography in part because they were already trendy in fiction. The literary food chain already included prominent, sharptoothed annotators as well as soft, juicy authors, and commentary was already seen as an established literary genre susceptible of artistic effort and comic effect. But history is not only literature—as Wachler already emphasized, almost two centuries ago, when he called his work a *Geschichte der historischen Forschung und Kunst (History of Historical Research and of the Historical Art)*. The rise of the footnote in the age of Gibbon and Möser must have something to do with developments inside the historical tradition as well as with a fondness for them outside it: with the rise, or acceptance, or revival of the view that historians not only tell stories but cite evidence. The trail from Ranke leads still farther back: into the stately urban palaces of great Renaissance lawyers and collectors, and perhaps all the way to the ancient world itself. Though distinctively modern in its final form, the footnote—as we shall see—has some surprisingly ancient prototypes.

Lavater ist in der That noch viel weiter gegangen, der hat uns Noten gegeben, wozu der Text der Commentar seyn muss. Dass ist die wahre Sprache der Seher, die man erst versteht, wenn sich die Begebenheiten ereignet haben, die sie verkündigen." One satire on footnotes and much else that provoked discussion in Lichtenberg's circle (cf. letter 2452 in his correspondence) was J. F. Lamprecht's wildly funny *Der Stundenrufer zu Ternate* (1739). For the later history of the footnote in literature see Stang.

CHAPTER FIVE

Back to the Future, 1: De Thou Documents the Details

✳ One commonly received tenet about the history of historiography has remained basically unquestioned in this investigation. Most students of historiography have agreed with Ranke and his followers, assuming that historians who wrote in the grand narrative tradition did not carry out research, much less base their narratives on systematically chosen and analyzed sources. Gibbon, Möser, von Müller, and other eighteenth-century writers formed a partial exception to this rule, to be sure. But they violated the old rules of historical writing in many other ways as well. They insisted on the need to combine systematic, extended analysis of social, political, and religious conditions with the narrative of high events. They considered demographic growth and economic well-being as significant as battles and more so than speeches. They even took a strong interest in the low details of private life. It is tempting simply to assume that they invented critical as well as cultural history and leave the matter at that.

One could, of course, criticize Ranke and his followers for appropriating and taking credit for this segment of their critical method, as other nineteenth-century intellectuals did for so many other eighteenth-century discoveries and principles. Or one could defend the founder of Ranke & Company at the expense of later generations of managers. The old master, unlike some of his disciples, admitted that ancient history had been carried on in a critical way throughout the eighteenth century. He admired the Dutch savant Louis de Beaufort, who demolished the traditional story of Rome's origins, as well as Gibbon, who created the first modern story of Rome's fall.[1]

In fact, however, the historical tradition developed on lines considerably more twisted and complex than these simple formulas would suggest. The Historical School itself was not of one mind about the historical tradition. Unlike his followers, Ranke did not argue, even when in the radically critical mood that accompanied his debut, that all premodern historians had been uncritical. As we have already seen, he acknowledged Gibbon as a colleague. More important, he also acknowledged— even insisted—that some Renaissance writers had been what Guicciardini so decidedly was not: "urkundlich" (historians who worked from eyewitness testimony or documentary evidence, and thus could serve as reliable sources for a critical later historian to draw on). Ranke attacked Guicciardini, but he praised another Italian historian of the first half of the sixteenth century, Paolo Giovio—once again arguing against Jean Bodin as he did so. Giovio's Latin rhetoric had been all too polished,

---

1. L. von Ranke, *Aus Werke und Nachlass,* ed. W. P. Fuchs et al. (Munich and Vienna, 1964–1975), IV, 226–231 ("Einleitung: Die Historiographie seit Machiavelli," from Ranke's course on Römische Geschichte in the Sommersemester 1852; cf. 360, 365). The "Einleitung" reveals nicely that Ranke already saw how hard it would be to make the development of the discipline of ancient history follow the normal scheme, in which the Historical School triumphantly emerged from the Napoleonic Wars.

and he had passed over in silence the bad deeds of his friends.
But he had had a remarkable knowledge of topography. Moreover, he had lived in the Vatican itself, a prominent node on
every political network of his time; and he had taken the opportunity to intercept and interpret hundreds of messages.
Giovio had thus had access to much first-hand reportage, oral
and written, about the events he described.[2] Even more enthu-
siastic was Ranke's analysis of the Milanese historian Bernar-
dino Corio.[3] Ranke could not believe the story that the seventeenth-century German editor Johannes Georgius Graevius
had refused to include Corio's work in his enormous *Thesaurus*
of writings on Italian history because it swarmed with errors:
"Graevius cannot possibly have meant to condemn the last
books. In them he is a splendid source for important historical
events; he includes many documents, word for word."[4] Here—
in contrast to his treatment of Guicciardini—Ranke closely
followed the older standard treatment of historiography by
Ludwig Wachler, who had already noted that Corio worked
extensively in archives and that in the latter part of his work,
"he reports the most insignificant circumstances with extreme
precision and the all-embracing conscientiousness of a serious
researcher. Many reports are produced here from sources for the
first time, and many narratives of others are carefully corrected."[5]

2. Ranke, *Zur Kritik neuerer Geschichtschreiber* (Leipzig and Berlin, 1824), 68–
78. On Giovio's use of first-hand information in his histories, see T. C. Price
Zimmermann, *Paolo Giovio* (Princeton, 1995).

3. On Corio see E. Cochrane, *Historians and Historiography in the Italian Renaissance* (Chicago and London, 1981), 117–118.

4. Ranke, *Zur Kritik,* 94: "Unmöglich aber kann Grävius hiemit die letzten
Bücher gemeint haben, wo er die vorzüglichste Urkunde wichtiger Geschichten
ist, wo er viele Denkmale wörtlich aufnimmt."

5. L. Wachler, *Geschichte der historischen Forschung und Kunst,* I, pt. 1 (Göttin-

In fact, the Latin-writing humanist historians of Renaissance Italy used procedures that varied from context to context and developed, to some extent, over time. Leonardo Bruni, for example, derived most of the narrative in his massive *Histories of the Florentine People* from the Italian chroniclers of the fourteenth century, whose works he rewrote in classical form. He removed much of their glittering local color and violent detail as he subjected their sometimes chaotic stories of riot and assassination to the aesthetic discipline of classical Latin. As chancellor of the Florentine Republic Bruni had full access to the city's archives, but he cited relatively few identifiable documents from them.[6] In the later fifteenth century, however, as Gary Ianziti has shown, the same officials who compiled official correspondence often wrote, or assembled the materials for, official histories. Giovanni Simonetta's history of the Sforzas, for example, amounted to "a creative act of reelaboration and synthesis," based on the archival files he tended.[7] Historians who came from outside their subject's bureacracy depended on the services of an "instructor"—a local official who would assemble the relevant documents for them, either in their original form or woven into a bare factual narrative.[8] The influential historian

gen, 1812), 135–136 at 136: "Die kleinlichsten Umstände sind auf das genaueste und mit der Alles untersuchenden Gewissenhaftigkeit eines ernsten Forschers angegeben; viele Nachrichten sind hier zuerst aus Urkunden beygebracht, viele Erzählungen Anderer mit Sorgfalt berichtigt."

6. See E. Santini, "Leonardo Bruni Aretino e i suoi 'Historiarum Florentini Populi Libri XII,' " *Annali della Scuola Normale Superiore di Pisa,* cl. di filosofia e filologia, 22 (1910); Cochrane, 5; and above all M. Phillips, "Machiavelli, Guicciardini, and the Tradition of Vernacular Historiography in Florence," *American Historical Review,* 84 (1979) 86–105.

7. G. Ianziti, "A Humanist Historian and His Sources: Giovanni Simonetta, Secretary to the Sforzas," *Renaissance Quarterly,* 34 (1981), 491–516 at 515.

8. R. Valentini, "De gestis et vita di A. Campano. A proposito di storia della storiografia," *Bollettino della R. Deputazione di Storia patria per l'Umbria,* 27

Giannantonio Campano, who broke the restraints of Latinity to produce a dazzlingly colorful account of the brilliant deeds and terrifying death of the condottiere Fortebraccio Baglioni, cited both the public archives of Perugia and the family archives of the Baglioni to prove his hero's noble descent. He introduced a letter of Fortebraccio's into his text, translated from the original Italian. And he regularly registered the points where his sources or informants disagreed on a given point.[9]

References to archival documents, as Ianziti has shown, often reveal less a disinterested search for truth than a deliberate effort to create a favorable impression about the historian's employer. The documents themselves embodied elements of propaganda and ideology, and the "commentaries" based on them often manipulated men and events as willfully as had their ancient model, Caesar's *Commentaries*.[10] Campano, however, clearly saw the historian's duty to report fully and honestly

(1924), 153–196 at 165–176; G. Ianziti, *Humanistic Historiography under the Sforzas: Politics and Propaganda in Fifteenth-Century Milan* (Oxford, 1988). For examples of the sort of rough "commentary" that humanist historians often relied on, see P. Paltroni, *Commentari della vita et gesti dell'illustrissimo Federico Duca d'Urbino,* ed. W. Tommasoli (Urbino, 1966). See further Valentini and a much more famous work, Vespasiano da Bisticci, *Vite di uomini illustri del secolo xv* (Florence, 1938). In his preliminary "discorso" Vespasiano said that he wrote "in the form of a short commentary" ("per via d'uno breve commentario"). He hoped that his work would preserve the fame of the virtuous men it commemorated, but also suggested that it could provide the necessary material for anyone who might care to write the same lives in Latin (11).

9. G. Campano, *Braccii Perusini Vita et gesta,* ed. R. Valentini, *Rerum italicarum scriptores,* n.s. 19.4 (Bologna, 1929), 5–6, 24, 68, 77, 139, 140, 193. He recognized that not all such disagreements could be resolved: see e.g. 75: "Utra fama sit verior, ne illi quidem satis conveniunt, qui interfuere" ("Not even those who were present entirely agree as to which report is truer than the other").

10. Ianziti, *Humanistic Historiography*.

as more than a Ciceronian commonplace to be rehearsed in a grandiose preface and ignored thereafter.[11] When Campano set out to correct the text of the Roman historian Livy for the Roman printer Ulrich Han, for example, he made clear that the errors that disfigured the text resulted from the malpractice of the scribes "who think that what they do not understand is excessive, or what they do not clearly perceive is obscure, or that what the author deliberately inverted is a corruption. Turning themselves from scribes to correctors, the less they understand, the more they apply their own judgment."[12] Campano, in short, knew all the forms of havoc that ignorance and presumption could wreak with a historical tradition. It seems only reasonable to accept that he was sincere when he said that he could not write the life of the commander Piccinino because "I would have to address all my inquiries to those who followed that leader as they took part in war and peace alike. You can hardly doubt that they would want to direct their efforts chiefly to praising his victories and excusing his defeats. This was the chief reason that restrained me from trying to write anything."[13] Under some of the smoothly classical texts of human-

11. G. Campano, *Opera* (Venice, 1495), II, fol. xxxvi verso = *Epistolae et poemata,* ed. J. B. Mencke (Leipzig, 1707), 251–253.

12. Ibid., I, fol. lxiii verso = 549: "Inde librariorum coorti errores, dum aut, quod ipsi non capiunt, nimium esse, aut quod non cernunt, obscurum, aut quod inversum est studio auctoris, depravatum putant, et de librariis emendatores facti ibi plus adhibent iudicii, ubi minus intelligunt." Campano's edition of Livy, with this prefatory letter to Iacopo Ammannati, was first published in summer 1470 (Goff L-237).

13. Ibid., II, fol. xxiiii recto = 163: "Sed erant omnia ab iis perquirenda, qui Ducem illum secuti pace belloque interfuissent, quorum studia non dubitas fuisse futura et ad extollendas victorias et extenuandas calamitates propensiora. Haec ratio maxime omnium me, ut nihil susciperem scribendum, detinuit." Cf. his repeated claim that he could not make progress with his life of Federico da

ist history, with their gleaming marble facades of unfootnoted Latin and their elegantly arched niches in which medieval Italian and modern French orators incongruously spouted Ciceronian periods, lay massive foundations carved from the historical granite of archival documentation and detailed, pertinacious interviewing. The Renaissance even saw some anticipations of the nineteenth-century historians' excessive faith in documents. Tristano Calco, a Milanese historian who loved to explore archives, believed everything he found there, including such spurious sources as the confessions extracted from the Templars by torture.[14]

Some Renaissance historians even anticipated the provision of footnotes for historical narratives—though their example, if Ranke knew them, could hardly have reassured him. Between 1597 and 1607, for example, the English Catholic Richard White of Basingstoke published his eleven books of *Historiarum libri . . . cum notis antiquitatum Britannicarum* at Douai. In the dedicatory letter to Archduke Albert of Austria that led off his first volume, White made clear that his country's history—at least in its early centuries—was a special case that required special literary measures to be taken. Ancient writers, like the elder Pliny, had celebrated ancient Britain. But they had not provided a continuous narrative of its history. "Therefore," White explained,

---

Montefeltre until he received information from "instructores" at the Urbino court, "sine quibus historia nulla, auctor vanus esset" ("without which the history would be nonexistent and its author unreliable") (ibid., II, fol. lxx recto = 497; cf. fol. II, lxx verso = 500–501). On this point I follow Valentini rather than the important revisionist account by Ianziti, *Humanistic Historiography,* 54–58: his emphasis on propaganda, though undoubtedly well-taken in general, seems exaggerated in Campano's case, and he takes no account of the rich collateral documentation on Campano's sense of history.

14. F. Chabod, *Lezioni di metodo storico* (Bari, 1969), chap. 3.

as bees take honey from different flowers, so we must take materials from all sorts of different authors and, once they have been systematically collected, store them away, as it were, in the proper combs. It is easy to see how hard this job of selecting a few bits from the many sources carefully read was for a man who is immensely busy with both private and public tasks.[15]

White acknowledged the technical difficulties involved in establishing by conjecture the truth about events that had taken place so long ago.[16] But his ingenuity and learning did not fail him at this literary impasse. Instead, he devised a form of historical narrative that enabled him to acknowledge the diversity of the sources he had used, to quote them for the reader's benefit, and to refute his critics: a text with endnotes. Book 1 of his history, for example, extends from page 7 to page 26 of his first volume: just 20 pages of exposition about England's origins. The 38 endnotes—printed cues to which occur both in the margins and within the text of White's work—fill almost five times as much space, from page 27 to page 124, and offer a flood of primary sources to support the florid and unconvincing narrative in the text.

Unfortunately, White's choice of sources to cite sheds little credit on his historical insight. As he told the reader, England's origins had become the object of a heated debate some generations before his own time. The Italian humanist Polydore Virgil had audaciously (and correctly) demolished the medieval

15. R. White, *Historiarum libri . . . cum notis antiquitatum Britannicarum* ("Arras" [Douai], 1597), 3–4: "satis admirari nequeo, Princeps illustrissime, nullum extare librum antiquitus ea de re scriptum; sed oportere nos, tanquam apes ex variis floribus mel carpunt, ita de diversis auctoribus carpere [ed. capere] passim sententias easque simul ad unum collectas velut in alveos recondere. Qui labor admodum pauca seligendi ex multis perlectis, quantus fuerit homini publicis privatisque negotiis occupatissimo, intelligi facile potest."

16. Ibid., 5.

legendary history of England, which made the Britons descend from the Trojan prince Brutus, who fled his city after it fell to the Greeks. English scholars sprang up at once, of course, to defend the honor of such standard accounts of national origins as the fantastic histories of Geoffrey of Monmouth. And they found support above all in one particularly elaborate and provocative set of ancient works: the twenty-four ancient histories and related texts published by the Dominican Annius of Viterbo in 1498, with an elaborate commentary. These texts bore the names of exotic and venerable authors like the Babylonian priest Berosus and the Egyptian priest Manetho. They and their commentator supported one another's credibility with an elaborate network of interlocking cross references. They attacked the histories of the ancient Greeks, like that of Herodotus, with well-aimed scorn and a mass of conflicting, precise details. And they incorporated, as the Greeks did not, the twisted tendrils of medieval genealogical legend that traced the nations and royal families of northern Europe back to aristocratic Trojan ancestors sent into exile by the Greeks. These were essential to English (and French) national pride—as well as to the iconography of court festivals and public pageants. Annius' book reached an immense public and remained standard for a century and more.[17] White, in particular, found in it both the source for many of his notes and the model for his presentation of his results. Like the friar, White used an intolerable deal of com-

17. See T. D. Kendrick, *British Antiquity* (London, 1950), J. D. Alsop, "William Fleetwood and Elizabethan Historical Scholarship," *Sixteenth Century Journal*, 25 (1994), 155–176 at 157–169, and, for another case of northern reception of Annius' texts and ideas, M. Wifstrand Schiebe, *Annius von Viterbo und die schwedische Historiographie des 16. und 17. Jahrhunderts* (Uppsala, 1992). See more generally M. Tanner, *The Last Descendant of Aeneas* (New Haven and London, 1993). On Annius himself see above all W. Stephens, Jr., *Giants in Those Days* (Lincoln, 1989).

mentary to support a shilling's worth of text. His work had only one defect—but a fatal one. Annius had in fact forged his most alluring histories: paradoxically, his edition of these purportedly ancient texts, rather than White's re-use of them a century later, represents the first historical narrative by a modern writer to support its assertions with a separate commentary. And White's apparently sober, critical history and antiquities of England, his elegant, modern-looking concoction, sinks on inspection into nothing more than a reheated version of Annius' casserole, in which a few new ingredients made no fundamental difference to the taste and certainly could not extend the long-expired sell-by date. Though White admitted that many scholars of high reputation had attacked Annius' texts as forgeries, he made no serious effort to examine their arguments. Instead he emphasized the large number of Annius' defenders and borrowed a half-hearted refutation of the critics from one of them.[18]

18. See White, 105–106, at 106: "[many cite and praise Berosus (e.g. John Caius, a famous medical man and philologist who had used the text in the course of his effort to prove Cambridge University older than Oxford)] et ceteri numero plures, quam sunt ii, qui reprehendunt. Itaque Iacobus Middendorpius lib. 1. Academiarum. Et si non mediocrem, inquit, controversiam esse scio inter scriptores de illo Beroso, qui nunc circumfertur, dum quidam eum non modo recipiunt, sed tuentur etiam atque propugnant, quidam vero gravissimis argumentis refellunt, ego tamen mediam viam puto seligendam, ut Berosus de rebus indifferentibus loquens toleretur. Quia enim fuit olim ille liber in omnium fere gentium doctorumque hominum bibliothecis: et superioribus temporibus, quando passim omnes bibliothecae a viris litterarum studiosissimis excussae fuerunt; neque tamen usque alius, quam iste repertus est, nec adhuc verior aliquis, quod mihi quidem constare potuit, Berosus productus: videtur hic ferendus esse donec integritati pristinae restituatur" ("... and others, more numerous than those who criticize him. Therefore Jacob Middendorp said, in book I of his book on Academies: 'I know that writers disagree about the Berosus now in circulation. Some not only accept him, but defend him in a powerful and polemical way, while others use very serious arguments to refute him. I,

Even as some of the English were trying to fill modern footnotes with old stories, however, French historians were trying to write a genuinely new kind of history—one that really did rest on a sound, critical foundation. As we have already seen, the avalanche of printed historical and ethnographic publications that sent the readers and librarians of the fifteenth and early sixteenth centuries skidding into abysses of confusion and despair also stimulated a considerable amount of thought about how to read history selectively and critically. By the middle years of the sixteenth century, philologically-trained jurists like François Baudouin and Jean Bodin, whom we have already met, had learned to reflect on the sources and methods of the writers they studied. Their works remained central to the culture of erudition, and continued to be epitomized and contested until deep into the eighteenth century. Writers of history—especially the great humanist historians, who often had a legal training and sometimes enjoyed direct access to historical actors and documents—came from the same world as these readers. Not surprisingly, their practices as researchers became increasingly systematic and self-critical; they tried to write the sort of history that they knew they should prefer to read.[19]

---

however, think one should choose a middle way, so that Berosus may be tolerated when speaking of things indifferent. That book was at one time to be found in the libraries of almost all races and scholars. And in earlier times, when scholars examined all libraries everywhere, they found no other Berosus but this one. So far as I have been able to establish, no other or truer Berosus has been brought to light. I think that this one should be accepted until he is restored to his original purity"). White here paraphrased J. Middendorpius, *Academiarum orbis Christiani libri duo* (Cologne, 1572), 14–18 at 16. Middendorpius, who emphasized that he had cited the "nomina et libros" ("names and books") of all his sources (sig. *8 recto), may well have served White as a partial model.

19. On the theorists see e.g. J. Franklin, *Jean Bodin and the Sixteenth-Century Revolution in the Methodology of Law and History* (New York and London, 1963); U. Muhlack, *Geschichtswissenschaft im Humanismus und in der Aufklärung* (Munich,

Consider the case of Jacques-Auguste de Thou, the brilliant lawyer and Latinist who wrote what may be the longest historical narrative ever undertaken—at least before the 1930s, when a famous Harvard graduate and beggar named Joe Gould, who became something of a celebrity in the old Greenwich Village, undertook a still longer *Oral History of the World.*[20] De Thou prepared himself for the task of writing the history of Europe in his own day, from 1544 to 1607, with study in France and Italy, travel to foreign courts, and long years of intense work in the Parisian Parlement, or sovereign court. He produced an admirable piece of Latin prose—one so pure and eloquent that German visitors to Paris were astonished to find that its creator could only write Latin, not speak it as they did. But he did far more. From when de Thou started compiling information—perhaps as early as 1572—he set himself to produce a history as accurate as it was eloquent. The task mattered deeply. Like Bodin, de Thou had watched the French polity fall apart in the Wars of Religion. Unlike Bodin, he continued to believe that French Catholics bore as much of the blame as the Protestants, or more, for the religious wars—not to mention the massacre of St Bartholomew. An honest, impartial narrative, de Thou decided, would serve as a foundation for social and political peace. It would demonstrate the guilt of powerful Catholic malefactors like the Guise and the innocence and nobility of scholarly Protestants like his close friend Joseph Scaliger. More to the point, it would prove that religious tolerance and austerity in public life could bring together what intoler-

---

1991). On one late Renaissance reader who applied their prescriptions, see L. Jardine and A. Grafton, " 'Studied for Action': How Gabriel Harvey Read His Livy," *Past and Present,* 129 (1990), 30–78.

20. Sadly, Gould's work existed only in his own imagination: J. Mitchell, *Up in the Old Hotel* (New York, 1992), 52–70, 623–716.

ance and venality had torn apart. De Thou, like many high French lawyers, was a Gallican, who firmly believed in Catholicism, but also in the general autonomy of the French church. He felt certain that the truth, fairly presented, would prove impossible to deny, and would both heal the state and save the church. He was wrong, of course; his book did not unite France, create tolerance, or eliminate the sale of office to incompetents, and in the seventeenth century the Jesuits and dévots he loathed would dominate the French church. But the book did win him a reputation for strenuous honesty and heroic independence, which lasted deep into the Enlightenment—when his Latin historical works received the exceptional compliment of a monumental entombment in seven volumes, each of them too heavy to lift.[21]

The historical de Thou was far more flexible than the monumental hero of stone that his panegyrists liked to sculpt. Samuel Kinser and Alfred Soman have shown, in complementary ways, that the content of his massive, stately, solid-looking Latin books was in fact unstable. De Thou's works perpetually changed shape and tone, not as a whole but in almost every detail. The author, for all his high position, had a raw youth's sensitivity to every blast of cold political or intellectual air, and many of these came his way. From Rome the mails brought private assurance of several cardinals' good will—and public denunciations of his freedom of speech, his attacks on immoral popes and praises of moral Protestants (one of whom he had described not as dying, but as "passing into a better life"). The Congregation of the Index threatened condemnation. From

---

21. On the larger context of de Thou's enterprise see above all C. Vivanti, *Lotta politica e pace religiosa in Francia fra Cinque e Seicento* (Turin, 1963).

England, the unsinkable aircraft carrier of European Protestantism, the airwaves crackled with hostile messages. James VI and I took sharp exception to de Thou's treatment of his mother, Mary Queen of Scots—especially since it seemed to depend on the earlier narrative by James's boyhood nemesis, the Scottish humanist George Buchanan, who had succeeded in making him swallow a great deal of Latin but had failed to force down more unpalatable lessons about the limits on royal power and the rights of subjects. Caught in the liberal's ever uncomfortable *via media,* de Thou temporized and trimmed, excising potentially offensive passages and changing verbs and adjectives that might offend. He gratefully accepted and drew on materials compiled by Robert Cotton to modify his treatment of events in England. Later he used William Camden's *Annals of the Reign of Queen Elizabeth* in the same way. He even tried to placate the Roman censors. De Thou was no Giordano Bruno, willing to burn to preserve his right to say what he liked about life, the universe, and everything.[22]

Yet one should not exaggerate de Thou's willingness to compromise. He was not a modern academic, tenured and safe, writing for a public that could be numbered on the fingers of one hand, but a statesman exposed to everything from invective to assassination. Nonetheless he stuck to what he considered his most important guns. His changes did not alter the basic character of his text—which was indeed honored in 1609, five

---

22. See S. Kinser, *The Works of Jacques-Auguste de Thou* (The Hague, 1966); A. Soman, "The London Edition of de Thou's *History:* A Critique of Some Well-Documented Legends," *Renaissance Quarterly,* 24 (1971), 1–12; A. Soman, *De Thou and the Index* (Geneva, 1972). For de Thou's relations with Cotton and Camden, see H. R. Trevor-Roper, *Queen Elizabeth's First Historian* (Neale Lecture, 1971), and K. Sharpe, *Sir Robert Cotton, 1586–1631* (Oxford, 1979), chap. 3.

years after its first appearance, by being placed on the Index, and never won James's full approval. De Thou's *Histories* were a social as well as an individual product, the result of collaborative effort and multiple pressures rather than a reproduction of the author's original manuscript (which remains in part unpublished). But de Thou's participation in a literary system of challenge and response should hardly be held against him by those who inhabit a very different one. Though he was no martyr, he was also no traitor to his principles. Every edition of his book continued his fight against religious intolerance, arguing in the teeth of many higher authorities that forcible conversion could not produce good Catholics (or Christians of any sort).

De Thou retained confidence in his material, moreover, not only because it matched his prejudices but also because he had obtained it in a particular way. As soon as the first part of his book appeared in a tentative edition, de Thou sent copies of it across Latin Europe, to scholars everywhere from Prague to Edinburgh. He did so in the hope of confirming and supplementing the facts he had already assembled. Where he had left holes in his narrative or saw the prospect of new ones, he begged for help; where he had made mistakes, he asked for correction. Scholars of every party weighed in.[23] Henry Savile sent a life of the Hungarian scholar and bishop Andreas Dudith, with whom he had lived for six months as a young man. Christophe Dupuy and Paolo Sarpi filled in the lives and works of Italian humanists for whom de Thou lacked information. Just about everyone forwarded corrections of details, ranging from names and dates

---

23. Much of the relevant correspondence is preserved in the Bibliothèque Nationale (hereafter BN), Paris; here I use MS Dupuy 632, the materials in which were published in J.-A. de Thou, *Historiarum sui temporis libri cxxxviii*, 7 vols. (London, 1733), VII.

to major points of interpretation.[24] Joseph Scaliger, who had traveled in Scotland in the 1560s, redated the death of Rizzio and the birth of James VI.[25] The famous botanist Charles de l'Escluse, who found de Thou's "lovely present" so thrilling that he could not wait to have it bound before reading it, corrected his underestimate of the scientific prowess of the naturalist Guillaume Rondelet. Camden forwarded not only corrections of topographical details but a draft of his *Annals,* avowedly based on state papers, as the solidest of all supports for de Thou's treatment of English history. Others suggested changes in everything from de Thou's account of the laws of the Holy Roman Empire to his discussion of the love lives of the Hapsburg kings of Spain.[26]

The dossier, much of which survives in manuscript, shows that de Thou and his correspondents shared a belief in the authority of first-hand testimony. When de l'Escluse corrected de Thou on Rondelet, for example, he explained that he had worked with the man for more than two years, collecting specimens of marine life for him on the shore after storms and watching him dissect them; when he did the same about Hapsburg hanky-panky, he argued that he had seen the little spiral stairway down which a Habsburg prince had fallen on the way to visit a young woman.[27] And when de Thou refused to accept

24. For Savile on Dudith see BN, Paris, MS Dupuy 632, fol. 105 recto-verso, and R. Goulding, "Henry Savile and the Tychonic World System," *Journal of the Warburg and Courtauld Institutes,* 58 (1995) 152–179.
25. BN, Paris, MS Dupuy 632, fol. 57 recto.
26. Cf. Trevor-Roper, 12, who eloquently evokes de Thou's "seminar": "he drew the whole Republic of Letters into his orbit. But what professor has ever ruled such a seminar as his? Hugo Grotius and Paolo Sarpi and Francis Bacon were all members of it."
27. BN, Paris, MS Dupuy 632, fols. 78 verso, 82 verso–83 recto.

corrections, he did so on the same grounds. He could not accept James's version of the death of Darnley, for example, precisely because he had eyewitness reports that contradicted it. So far as possible, de Thou placed no obstacles except his Latin style between his evidence and his reader. When he received detailed lives of scholars from his friends, for example, he simply incorporated them into his text. He thus made the book a repository of reliable evidence about the history of culture.

In a contemporary history, first-hand testimony naturally predominated. But de Thou had other resources as well. He built his vast library, for example, as a public basis for his own and others' research.[28] And he used the state papers to which his official positions gave him access. Long before Ranke or Gibbon, critical history—the sort of history whose author agonized about a mistake of a few months in chronology, as well as about the ascription of motives and the identification of causes—had come into being. De Thou was not the only writer of this kind: Camden, who relied on Robert Cotton's great collections of manuscripts as well as eyewitness testimony for his own history of England in the age of Elizabeth, provides a remarkable parallel.[29]

De Thou did not convince everyone that his enterprise made sense. The Augsburg patrician and polymath Markus (or Marx) Welser, a stalwart Catholic, wrote to refuse help, using terms that sound as strikingly modern as de Thou's own practice:

28. See K. Garber, "Paris, die Hauptstadt des europäischen Späthumanismus. Jacques Auguste de Thou und das Cabinet Dupuy," *Res publica litteraria. Die Institutionen der Gelehrsamkeit in der frühen Neuzeit,* ed. S. Neumeister and C. Wiedemann (Wiesbaden, 1987), I, 71–92; A. Coron, " 'Ut prosint aliis': Jacques Auguste de Thou et sa bibliothèque," *Histoire des bibliothèques françaises,* II: *Les bibliothèques sous l'Ancien Régime,* ed. C. Jolly (Paris, 1988), 101–125.

29. See Trevor-Roper and, for Cotton's library, Sharpe, chap. 2, and C. G. C. Tite, *The Manuscript Library of Sir Robert Cotton* (London, 1994).

As to the censure you request: your text will certainly enjoy a magnificent reputation with posterity. So far as the events are concerned, I shall not serve as your editor. It's far too hard for any human being to rid himself of passions and keep the truth always in his sights. Take the history of Charles V and Francis I—a Frenchman and a German will always tell it differently. And the one will never persuade the other of what he himself thinks is true and would guarantee at any price. The same holds true for the rest—especially when you're concerned with counsels, with the rights of provinces, with the causes of wars, with the private lives of princes, and above all with the problem of religion. Truth lies at the bottom of the well; we drink water from the surface in its place, especially when relying on the testimony of others to scoop it up.[30]

The indictment sounds plausible enough—as do the similar ones of Ranke. In fact, however, it was motivated by religious prejudice, not methodological sophistication. In private Welser railed against what he saw as de Thou's preference for the French over the Germans and for Protestants over Catholics.[31]

30. Welser to de Thou, 23 October 1604, BN, Paris, MS Dupuy 632, fol. 74 recto: "De censura quod petis: magna est futura scriptionis ad omnem posteritatem sine controversia commendatio: de rebus, Palaemon ego non sedeo. Nimis quam difficile homini nato affectus exuere et semper recte ad veritatis scopum collineare. Caroli et Francisci exempli caussa historiam, qui non aliter Gallus aliter Germanus narret? Nec unquam alter alteri quod verissimum esse ipse credat et quovis pignore contendat, tamen persuadeat. Iam in ceteris eadem est ratio, ubi praesertim ad consilia, ad iura provinciarum, ad bellorum caussas, ad privatam principum vitam et multo maxime ad caussam religionis ventum. Veritas fere imo puteo latet, nos summam saepe pro ea aquam libamus, aliena praesertim fide, tanquam haustris usi." On Welser's own scholarship see P. Joachimsen, "Marx Welser als bayerischer Geschichtschreiber [1904/05]," *Gesammelte Aufsätze,* ed. N. Hammerstein (Aalen, 1970–1983), II, 577–612; R. J. W. Evans, "Rantzau and Welser: Aspects of Later German Humanism," *History of European Ideas,* 5 (1984), 257–272.

31. See the evidence in de Thou, *Historiarium sui temporis libri cxxxviii,* VII, pt. 6, 9–11.

Most scholars who lacked an institutional or denominational impetus to attack de Thou, Catholics as well as Protestants, accepted his good faith and praised his objectivity.

The reason is simple enough. De Thou did not annotate his history. But he made his correspondence—which reached across the learned Latin world—into a running collaborative commentary on his text. He repeatedly proved his earnest desire for authoritative information, his willingness to accept (polite) correction, and his unwillingness to suppress inconvenient facts. Rather like the modern scholar who addresses the limited audience that really matters in a code that the larger public cannot break, de Thou provided the Republic of Letters with a critical apparatus that proved the reliability, the *fides,* of his unannotated text. Moreover, his library became a way station where all the vastly erudite travelers of the Republic of Letters stopped on their way from Hamburg to Madrid or London to Rome in order to read the newest books and swap the newest gossip. In this museum created to show how late Renaissance history at its best had been written, where the librarians, the learned brothers Dupuy, pointed morals and adorned tales about scholars and scholarship, everyone could see how de Thou had worked. It was only natural, then, that when Thomas Carte and Samuel Buckley printed what remains the best edition of the *Histories* in 1733, they added what survived of the correspondence that had accompanied its creation. These files of letters supplied the gloss with which de Thou had refused to encrust his eloquent prose. The presence of this apparatus—as well as de Thou's evident independence, good faith, and sympathy for Protestants—ensured his reputation deep into the nineteenth century.[32] Wachler, in his history of historiography,

32. See Soman, "The London Edition," who shows that this apparatus does

treated de Thou as an incomparable master, whose careful use of authentic materials he celebrated.[33] Ranke admired him unreservedly.[34] A model for self-critical narrative history, for a story about high politics based on archive-grubbing and source-criticism, existed before Ranke or Gibbon was born or thought of. Neither de Thou's methods nor his dilemmas, moreover, were unique. Half a century before him, Giovio sent draft books of his histories to the imperial court for correction—only to find that the entourage of Charles V considered him a Francophile, while the French saw him as an imperialist. Only the patronage of an exceptionally intelligent and enlightened ruler, Cosimo I, Grand Duke of Tuscany, enabled him to try in practice for the dangerous impartiality he and other historians prized in theory.[35] De Thou, in short, had solid resources to draw on in the existing traditions of historical practice.

The only thing de Thou refused to do was, quite simply, to add the notes that would have given all contemporary readers access to the information he stored up for later visitors to his workshop. In fact, he fulminated, in untranslatable Latin, against Melchior Goldast, who festooned a pirated edition of the *Histories* with "political" glosses. And his reasons are not far to seek. For all the critical effort that went into the foundations of de Thou's work, he wanted its superstructure to remain classical. He must have thought that footnotes would spoil its crisp Greco-Roman colonnades and roofline. But he may also have had more in mind. For both the literary and the

---

not straightforwardly present all of the texts, but alters the documents to create a particular picture of de Thou.

33. L. Wachler, *Geschichte der historischen Forschung und Kunst,* I, pt. 2 (Göttingen, 1813), 679–685 at 682–683.

34. See Ranke, *Aus Werk und Nachlass,* 4, 112 and n. b.

35. Zimmermann, 238–243.

intellectual problems associated with footnotes were much discussed in de Thou's immediate circle—which consisted, after
all, of Roman lawyers, practitioners of a discipline in which
the tradition of full and precise citation, or "allegation," came
into being in the ancient world itself.

Another erudite lawyer, Etienne Pasquier, who did pioneering work on the history of the French language and of legal
and political institutions, published as his *summa* a great set of
Recherches de la France. Pasquier wrote in French, not Latin, and
compiled a miscellany rather than a narrative. Nevertheless, he
admitted in the revised edition of 1596 that friends to whom
he had shown the text complained "that at every turn I used
some old author to confirm my statement." Some pointed out
that earlier writers had copied their sources "without wasting
time on such confirmations, which somehow reveal more of the
shadowy life of the schools than of the light of history." In the
course of time, they argued, which "refined works, like gold,"
his writings would "supply their own authority," as those of
the ancients had. Others praised his precise references but found
his habit of full citation at once pedantic and bordering on
plagiarism: "but they thought it too pernickety to insert these
passages in full; this was to swell my own work at the expense
of others. Doing this involved a combination of superstition
and superfluity; the best solution would have been to remove
this excess matter."[36]

36. E. Pasquier, *Les Recherches de la France* (Paris, 1596), fol. 2 recto: "Mais
estimoient chose d'une curiosité trop grande, d'inserer tout au long les passages,
et que c'estoit enfler mon oeuvre mal à propos aux despens d'autruy; Qu'en ce
faisant il y avoit de la superstition et superfluité tout ensemble, et que le plus
expedient eust esté de retrancher cest excez." For Pasquier see G. Huppert, *The
Idea of Perfect History* (Urbana, Chicago, and London, 1970); D. Kelley, *Foundations of Modern Historical Scholarship* (New York and London, 1970); N.

A second set of critics were cleverer than the first: they identified a genuine paradox in the modern routine of documentation, which claims to require that one prove both that each sentence is original and that it has a source. But the first set impressed Pasquier even more, especially since—as he pointed out in a proleptic use of the terminology of Astérix and Obélix—"our ancestors the Gauls did it this way." He had to agree that the provision of documentation was more likely to provoke dissent than assent from a modern reader. Cited documents necessarily suggested that a problem could be solved in ways other than that chosen by the historian.[37] Pasquier still felt proud that he had brought many French antiquities to light for the first time in the *Recherches*. But he found it depressing that so many of his readers had cited the texts he discovered without giving him any credit.[38] Not for the last time, footnotes and plagiarism embraced one another uneasily. Nonetheless, Pasquier decided to keep his "proofs," and even to translate the Latin ones into French, since "otherwise anyone who read these antiquities and did not know Latin would have been a second Tantalus, standing in the midst of water but unable to drink from it."[39]

Struever, "Pasquier's *Recherches de la France:* The Exemplarity of His Medieval Sources," *History and Theory,* 27 (1988), 51–59; and *Etienne Pasquier et ses Recherches de la France,* Cahiers V.-L. Saulnier, 8 (Paris, 1991). On this passage see Huppert, 33–34, and S. Bann, *The Invention of History* (Manchester and New York, 1990).

37. Pasquier, *Recherches,* fol. 2 recto-verso. "Aussi discourant avec un stile nud et simple, l'ancienneté, le lecteur en croiroit ce qu'il voudroit: au contraire alleguant les passages, c'estoit apprester matiere à un esprit de contradiction, de les induire d'autre façon que vous ne faictes, et par ce moyen vous exposer à la reformation, voire aux calomnies d'autruy."

38. Ibid., fol. 2 verso.

39. Ibid., fol. 3 recto: "Autrement celuy qui n'eust sceu le latin, lisant ces

Neither Pasquier's problem nor his solution to it was unique. Across the channel, in England, the playwright Ben Jonson also faced problems of historical authority in 1605 when he published the quarto edition of his play about the fall of Tiberius' onetime favorite, *Sejanus*. Jonson's work dealt with a subject that was politically dangerous, especially since it was first performed in 1603, only two years after the Earl of Essex made his abortive attempt at a coup d'état. The style and even the factual content of his play, which drew heavily on the *Annals* of Tacitus, probably also seemed suspicious. The followers of Essex, like other political adventurers of the late Renaissance, had quoted Tacitus to justify their manipulations and rebellion.[40] More generally, for at least a generation, many European intellectuals had agreed with the arguments forcefully advanced by Marc-Antoine Muret and Justus Lipsius: the imperial court portrayed by Tacitus, that Caligari-like hall of shadows, where informers overheard every honorable word and brave rebels fell under the sawtoothed wheels of the imperial machine, resembled the dangerous courts of their own time.[41] Two decades later, when the Dutchman Isaac Dorislaus lectured on Tacitus at Cambridge, a number of his remarks were taken down and formally reported to Archbishop Laud, and he him-

---

anciennetez eust esté un autre Tantale, au meilieu des eauës sans en pouvoir boire."

40. See in general A. Patterson, *Censorship and Interpretation* (Madison, 1984), 49–58, as well as J. Barish's introduction to his edition of *Sejanus* (New Haven and London, 1965).

41. See e.g. G. Oestreich, *Geist und Gestalt des frühmodernen Staates* (Berlin, 1969), chaps. 2–3; P. Burke, "Tacitism," *Tacitus*, ed. T. A. Dorey (New York, 1969), 149–171; J. H. M. Salmon, "Cicero and Tacitus in Sixteenth-Century France," *American Historical Review*, 85 (1980) 307–331; M. Stolleis, *Arcana imperii und Ratio status* (Göttingen, 1980); W. Kühlmann, *Gelehrtenrepublik und Fürstenstaat* (Tübingen, 1982).

self was silenced.[42] No wonder that the Privy Council found it necessary to examine Jonson in 1603, or that he found it necessary to defend his work when he printed it two years later.

Jonson built a sturdy fence of authorities to protect his vulnerable text. He wreathed its margins with long lists of precise references to classical histories and modern treatises. In these he had found not only the details of Sejanus' career, but also the wording of many of the political speeches and religious rituals he depicted.[43] Jonson's extremely precise references to "Tacit. Lips. edit. 4°" and "Bar. Brisson *de form. lib.* I" showed, he thought, that he had not invented anything seditious in composing his work.[44] So seriously did Jonson take his annotations that he defended them in detail in his preface against the charge of "affectation." He pointed out that he had gone so far as "to name what Edition I follow'd" for Tacitus and Dio, in citing both of whom he had used page numbers: "For the rest, as *Sueton. Seneca* &c. the Chapter doth sufficiently direct, or the Edition is not varied."[45]

Modern scholars have speculated about Jonson's intentions in glossing his own play. Some have argued that in supplying ancient authorities for statements that might seem politically dangerous, he hoped to allay the authorities' suspicions.[46] But this seems unlikely. As Annabel Patterson rightly points out,

42. *Tacitus: The Classical Heritage,* ed. R. Mellor (New York and London, 1995), 118–121.

43. See E. B. Tribble, *Margins and Marginality* (Charlottesville and London, 1993), 146–157. Plate 20, on p. 153, reproduces a page from the quarto edition.

44. The marginalia are reproduced in *Ben Jonson,* ed. C. H. Herford and P. Simpson (Oxford, 1925–1952), IV, 472–485; for a comment on their accuracy see p. 273. Barish shows that Jonson, quite naturally, imposed a highly personal interpretation on his sources.

45. *Ben Jonson,* ed. Herford and Simpson, IV, 351.

46. Patterson, 51; Tribble, 154–155.

Jonson made clear at every point the relation between his own text and the charged, complex, and notoriously obscure ancient model. References to Tacitus, however precise, could hardly deflect the idea that Jonson had current conditions in mind—especially since his preface and his very first marginal gloss referred explicitly to Lipsius' edition of Tacitus, which in turn began with a vigorous argument for the Roman historian's immediacy and relevance.[47]

If Jonson's political motives remain elusive, it does seem possible to locate the technical models for his scholarly practice. In *Sejanus* as in some of his masques, Jonson filled his text with the details of Roman rituals and customs. These he took, often word for word, from the heavily documented treatises of continental humanists like Lipsius and Bartolomé Brisson. His versions of Roman history, similarly, often amounted to translations not of the original Roman texts, but of Lipsius' notes

---

47. For some of Lipsius' writing on Tacitus see *Tacitus: The Classical Heritage,* ed. Mellor, 41–50. On Lipsius' Tacitean scholarship see M. W. Croll, *Style, Rhetoric, and Rhythm,* ed. J. M. Patrick et al. (Princeton, 1966); A. D. Momigliano, "The First Political Commentary on Tacitus," *Journal of Roman Studies,* 37 (1947) 91–101 = *Contributo alla storia degli studi classici* (Rome, 1955), 38–59; J. Ruysschaert, *Juste Lipse et les Annales de Tacite* (Louvain, 1949); A. D. Momigliano, review of Ruysschaert, *Journal of Roman Studies,* 39 (1949), 190–192; C. O. Brink, "Justus Lipsius and the Text of Tacitus," ibid., 41 (1951), 32–51; F. R. D. Goodyear, *The Annals of Tacitus,* I (Cambridge, 1972), 8–10; J. Ruysschaert, "Juste Lipse, éditeur de Tacite," *Studi urbinati,* 53 (1979), 47–61; M. Morford, *Stoics and Neostoics* (Princeton, 1991); Morford, "Tacitean *Prudentia* in the Doctrines of Justus Lipsius," in *Tacitus and the Tacitean Tradition,* ed. T. J. Luce and A. J. Woodman (Princeton, 1993), 129–151. On its reception and amplification by others see J. H. M. Salmon, "Stoicism and Roman Example: Seneca and Tacitus in Jacobean England," *Journal of the History of Ideas,* 50 (1989), 199–225, and D. Womersley, "Sir Henry Savile's Translation of Tacitus and the Political Interpretation of Elizabethan Texts," *Review of English Studies,* 42 (1991), 313–342.

on and summaries of them.[48] Perhaps Jonson hoped to produce a critical history play by uniting narrative with the philological and antiquarian scholarship on which he drew so heavily.

Both Pasquier and Jonson recorded and answered powerful literary objections to precise citation of the sources of their histories. Their shared difficulty shows that historians had to leap a high literary hurdle in order to create a modern form for their work, but the way both writers solved it also suggests an explanation for their new ability to do so. Writing a self-consciously critical narrative, as de Thou already did, is not the same as letting the reader have a look through one's study window and a dig in one's filing cabinets, which de Thou refused to do. Pasquier and Jonson, by contrast, insisted that they had a duty to cite their sources. And they wrote within, or in response to, a different historiographical tradition—a learned, rather than an eloquent tradition, usually known as "antiquarianism." Did this other form of "precritical" history have something to offer to the "critical" history that took root and flourished in the eighteenth and nineteenth centuries? Did the antiquaries also play a part in the coming of the footnote?

48. For Jonson's use of Lipsius see E. M. T. Duffy, "Ben Jonson's Debt to Renaissance Scholarship in *Sejanus* and *Catiline*," *Modern Language Review,* 42 (1947), 24–30; D. Boughner, "Jonson's Use of Lipsius in *Sejanus,*" *Modern Language Notes,* 73 (1958), 247–255; A. A. N. McCrea, "Neostoicism in England: The Impact of Justus Lipsius' Neostoic Synthesis on English Political Thinking, 1586–1652" (Ph.D. diss., Queen's University, Ontario), esp. II, chap. 5; R. C. Evans, *Habits of Mind: Evidence and Effects of Ben Jonson's Reading* (Lewisburg, London, and Cranbury, 1995). For Jonson's use of the antiquarian tradition more generally see the classic studies of D. J. Gordon, collected in *The Renaissance Imagination,* ed. S. Orgel (Berkeley, Los Angeles, and London, 1975).

CHAPTER SIX

Back to the Future, 2: The Antlike Industry of Ecclesiastical Historians and Antiquaries

✳ History, as should by now be clear, has taken many forms for a long time. In the ancient world a variety of historical genres took shape, in some of which methods of research and discussions of evidence played prominent roles. Some of these lasted over the centuries, finding new practitioners and new life in early modern Europe. A number of clues connect these forms of argument and exposition, which took place in the text, with those that later took place underneath it. Some French historians of the nineteenth century, for example, claimed as heatedly as any German that they practiced a science. But they insisted that its intellectual roots lay not in the new universities across the Rhine but in the Renaissance law school of Jacques Cujas at Valence and in the St. Germain des Pres of the Benedictine antiquaries Jean Mabillon and Bernard de Montfaucon, which had been active centers of critical source study in the sixteenth and seventeenth centuries respectively.[1] This tradition

1. See Fustel de Coulanges' presentation of the *Revue historique,* in F. Hartog, *Le xixe siècle et l'histoire* (Paris, 1988), 359: "L'érudition n'est pas a créer en France;

must also have its place in any history of the origins of modern history.

Consider, for example, the German Jesuit Athanasius Kircher, who adorned his order's central college in Rome for decades and who, like so many seventeenth-century scholars, wrote more books than his modern counterparts can hope to read. He lived in an age of polymaths whose literary works filled multivolumed Latin folios truffled with quotations in Greek, Arabic, Hebrew, and Aramaic; whose preferred language for writing occasional poetry was as likely to be biblical Hebrew as classical Greek; and whose favorite subject was in many cases a frighteningly complex combination of classical philology and mathematical astronomy.[2] Still, Kircher stood out for the multiplicity of his interests. As a young man he taught mathematics, ethics, and Oriental languages at Würzburg: as a middle-aged one he excavated obelisks, explored volcanoes, and reconstructed the voyage of Noah's Ark. Throughout his life, as Thomas Leinkauf has shown, he treated all of these pursuits as integrally related parts of a single effort to understand the physical and human history of the world.[3]

---

elle y existe et depuis longtemps" ("Learning does not need to be created in France; it has existed here for a very long time").

2. A. Grafton, "The World of the Polyhistors: Humanism and Erudition," *Central European History,* 18 (1985) 31–47.

3. T. Leinkauf's *Mundus combinatus* (Berlin, 1993) is the first systematic (and largely successful) analysis of Kircher's thought. For his career and context see also the survey by D. Pastine, *La nascita dell'idolatria* (Florence, 1978), *Athanasius Kircher und seine Beziehungen zum gelehrten Europa seiner Zeit,* ed. J. Fletcher (Wiesbaden, 1988), P. Findlen, *Possessing Nature* (Chicago and London, 1994), and, above all, R. J. W. Evans, *The Making of the Habsburg Monarchy, 1550–1700* (Oxford, 1979).

In 1677 Kircher brought out at Amsterdam a magnificently illustrated work on the sacred and profane antiquities, natural and human wonders of China.[4] The book covered many subjects, from comparative religion to physical geography. But it started with a historical essay and ended with a fold-out plate different from anything we have seen so far. Kircher began the work by publishing, in facsimile and in translations into more than one European language, an inscription from a ninth-century stone monument which had turned up in 1625 in a Christian graveyard in Sian. The bilingual text of the stele explained in Chinese and in Syriac the theology and the history of the Nestorian Christians—Christians who had scattered through Asia in the fifth century C.E. and after, and whose existence Western scholars and churchmen had generally forgotten (though their predecessors had known about them in the Middle Ages). The new text created a sensation, provoking widespread controversy when Kircher discussed it in his *Prodromus coptus* of 1636. Protestant critics like Georg Hornius dismissed the stele as "a pure invention of the Jesuits."[5]

Kircher found himself confronted, in other words, by a document whose historical solidity he thought incontestable, but which he could not see, and by bitter opponents, whose carping voices he wanted to silence. He attacked the problem systematically. In a long chapter, he reproduced, one after another, the

4. A. Kircher, *China monumentis qua sacris qua profanis necnon variis naturae et artis spectaculis aliarumque rerum memorabilium argumentis illustrata* (Amsterdam, 1677; repr. Frankfurt a. M., 1966).

5. Ibid., 1. For the context and the debate see the useful account in D. Mungello, *Curious Land*, Studia Leibnitiana, Supplementband 25 (Wiesbaden and Stuttgart, 1985), 164–172.

accounts in which the Jesuits Álvaro Semedo and Martinus Martini had already discussed the stone. Then he printed a long letter from another Jesuit, Michael Boim, with a long introduction:

> In addition to these texts [wrote Kircher] Father Michael Boim provided me with an account of this monument more precise than the rest. He corrected all its defects in copying it from a Chinese manuscript in my collection. Then he completed, in my presence, a new and meticulous translation of the whole inscription, word by word, beginning from the work of his colleague Andreas Don Sin, who was born in China and knows the language extremely well. He wished to attest to all this in the following letter to the reader, in which he described precisely the whole sequence of events and everything of importance connected with this sort of monument. I decided, with his assent, to place this text before the translation, as a splendid testimony to the true history, to preserve the memory of the matter forever. And I had the stone monument engraved, following the "autographum" brought from China, which is preserved to this day in my museum, with all its true marks and letters, both Chinese and Chaldean [Syriac], and a commentary.[6]

6. Kircher, *China,* 7: "His demum accessit *P. Michael Boimus,* qui exactam prae omnibus huius Monumenti relationem mihi attulit, omnes defectus in eo describendo, ex manuscripto Sinensi, quod penes me habeo, emendavit, novam denuo minutamque totius Tabulae interpretationem verbotenus factam opera socii sui Andreae Don Sin ex ipsa China oriundi, nec non linguae nativae peritissimi orditus, me praesente confecit; quae quidem omnia testata voluit, sequenti *epistola ad lectorem* data, qua totius rei seriem et quicquid tandem circa huiusmodi Monumentum consideratione dignum occurrit, exacte descripsit, quamque veluti luculentum veritatis testimonium huic interpretationi, ipso annuente, ad aeternam rei memoriam praefigendam censui; lapideum vero Monumentum iuxta Autographum ex China allatum, quod in Musaeo meo in hunc

Boim's letter was signed at the end by its author and by two
Chinese associates, whom Kircher described as "both eyewitnesses of the monument and the ones who copied this inscription from the original."[7] Much more detail and much more
corroboration followed, including a word-for-word Latin translation of the text, with annotation. At all points Kircher took
special care to establish locations, identities, and provenances.
The facsimile of the inscription that appeared at the end of the
book, for example, gave the place and date of the stele's discovery and stated explicitly that Matthaeus the Chinese "copied
this inscription from the original with his own hand . . . at
Rome in 1664."[8] Kircher did not subject his material to a
completely systematic critical examination. Even when the primary sources he reproduced contradicted each other, he simply
copied them and left his reader to worry about the discrepan-
cies.[9] But he took care to document everything as best he could.
The discovery, the transcription, and the translation of the
monument were all recorded, not in his words but in those of
his sources, even though that resulted in a text constantly in-
terrupted by section breaks and pocked throughout with dif-

---

usque diem superstes est, genuinis suis notis et characteribus [tam] Sinicis,
quam Chaldaeis, Scholiis etiam additis, incidendum curavi. *Epistola* dicta *P.
Michaelis Boimi* sequitur." The "autographum" brought from China was presumably a rubbing like or identical to Vatican Library Borg. or. 151, fasc. 2d, for
which see H. Goodman, "Paper Obelisks: East Asia in the Vatican Vaults," in
Rome Reborn, ed. A. Grafton (Washington, D.C., Vatican City, New Haven, and
London, 1993), plate 186.

7. Kircher, *China,* 10: "Oculati inspectores Monumenti nec non huius Tabulae ex Prototypo descriptores."

8. "Hanc Tabulam propria manu ex autographo descripsit Matthaeus Sina
Oriundus ex Siganfu Romae A° 1664."

9. Mungello, *Curious Land,* 171–172—but he exaggerates, and sometimes
misinterprets Kircher's text.

ferent languages and alphabets. Kircher offered a model of historical work very different from de Thou's—one characterized by an encyclopedic willingness to accommodate the incongruous and the alien, one that allowed many voices to speak, and many alphabets to appear, on the same page. Above all, he showed more interest in establishing the facts than in weaving them into an eloquent story. The hospitable smile of the south German churchman replaced the steely, cold correctness of the French lawyer. Just as Kircher's museum gave traveling gentlemen and intellectuals the chance to experience, at a safe distance, the wonders of nature he himself glimpsed close up in the volcanoes he explored, so his books gave his readers a chance to experience—almost at first hand—the shock of direct contact with the physically solid evidence of distant stone inscriptions.

Kircher's ability to collect and edit this material—like his ability to read and explicate the Syriac part of the monument's text—reflected his position as a member of an aggressive, modern, worldwide religious order. The Jesuits boasted a uniquely cosmopolitan range of skills and experience and a highly developed system of communication. Kircher stood waist-deep in the rapidly moving river of systematic reportage about foreign lands and languages that ran through the colleges and libraries of his order. He enjoyed a level of information about other societies that no one in Europe—even the well-traveled and omnivorous Poggio Bracciolini or Pope Pius II—could have imagined a century before.[10]

10. On Kircher's museum see P. Findlen, *Possessing Nature* (Chicago and London, 1994). For his larger intellectual position see Goodman and U. Eco, *The Search for the Perfect Language,* tr. J. Fentress (Oxford and Cambridge, Mass., 1995), 158–159.

Yet Kircher's spectacularly modern book on China belonged to a traditional historical genre. In form, in concern for documentation and provenance, and—it must be admitted—in credulity, the *China* closely resembled many older and now better-known compilations, like the classic history of the early church by the learned, uncritical Eusebius (fourth century C.E.) or the enormous, erudite *Annales* of the late sixteenth-century scholar Cesare Baronio. Throughout the history of the Christian church, scholars had compiled documents of diverse kinds, anxiously offered guarantees of their authenticity, and woven what were called "ecclesiastical histories" from them. The age-old rules of this well-established scholarly game dictated the form that Kircher's *China* took. Even Kircher's vivid plates had their counterpart in the physically magnificent study of the early Christian monuments of the catacombs that Antonio Bosio, the "Columbus of the Catacombs," had published, some years before Kircher's *China* came out, under the title *Roma sotterranea—Underground Rome.*[11] In trying to come to terms with a brand-new document, in short, Kircher could fall back on an existing, well-established historical genre, with its own norms and practices.

The heavily documented form of history to which Kircher's work belonged predates the origins of Christianity, and should probably be referred to by a less restrictive term than "ecclesiastical." Its origins are old enough to be obscure. They may lie in the Persian Empire, whose rulers liked to publish edicts, some of which were reproduced in historical works by their

11. G. Wataghin Cantino, "Roma Sotterranea: Appunti sulle origini dell'Archeologia Cristiana," *Ricerche di storia dell'arte*, 10 (1980), 5–14; H. Gamrath, *Roma sancta renovata* (Rome, 1987).

subjects—such as the Jews. The tradition took on its first clear shape in the Hellenistic world during the third and second centuries B.C.E., when the intellectuals of Mesopotamia, Egypt, and Israel found themselves the subjects of Greek-speaking, foreign powers—first Alexander of Macedon and his successors, then the Romans. The shared language of empire under Alexander's successors and of culture under the Romans—Greek—enabled representatives of many religions and traditions to speak to one another directly for the first time. They naturally saw one another as rivals, and those who had lost the wars hoped (like their academic counterparts today) to avenge in the archive their defeats on the battlefield. It became a matter of urgency to show that one came from an old state, which possessed a venerable religion, as well as a long-standing political, social, and scholarly tradition, its history duly recorded on a long series of documents, preferably inscribed in stone. In the third century B.C.E., the Egyptian priest Manetho and the Chaldean priest Berossus translated into Greek accounts of Egyptian history and Babylonian myth and history as well. These accounts emphasized the antiquity of their races and traditions.

By the second century B.C.E. at the latest, the Jews had followed suit. The first full-scale specimen of this genre to survive is perhaps the so-called Letter of Aristeas, a text which explained the origins of the Greek translation of the Hebrew Bible, the Septuagint. The author inserted directly into the narrative a number of what look like official documents—for example, the memorandums in which the librarian of Alexandria, Demetrius of Phalerum, and the king of Egypt, Ptolemy Philadelphus, discussed the need to acquire a Greek text of the Hebrew Bible for their great library. This fascinating book—like the documents it includes—has the defect of being a forgery, but also the compensating virtues of brevity and clarity.[12] It exemplifies the main lines along which the genre would grow.

From the first, ecclesiastical historians wrote as controversialists and believers: as Jews seeking to prove the Torah older than Homer or as Christians determined to prove the priority of a doctrine or an institution. The genre's ends determined its form: not the neat, classical prose of the political historians, but a mixture of technical arguments and supporting documents, the latter quoted verbatim in the text proper. Documents performed two functions, each vital: they supported the theses put forward by the author and they gave the reader a distinct, vivid sense of what it had meant to be a faithful Jew or a Christian in a distant and more difficult world.

Ecclesiastical history on the grand scale—like that produced by Eusebius—required new working conditions. The historian, instead of traveling the Mediterranean world to interview participants in a great war, had to scour the world of books for accounts of martyrs' deaths and heretics' ideas. Eusebius himself worked in the largest of early Christian libraries, in Caesarea. Here he drew on thousands of well-catalogued volumes collected by the earlier Christian scholar Origen and his own teacher Pamphilus, who energetically developed the library. He also made his own collections of the letters of Origen and the "martyrdoms of the ancients."[13] Eusebius excerpted these materials lavishly, and for the most part accurately, in his *Ecclesi-*

12. See *Lettre d'Aristée à Philocrate,* ed. A. Pelletier (Paris, 1962); W. Speyer, *Die literarische Fälschung im heidnischen und christlichen Altertum* (Munich, 1971).

13. H. Y. Gamble, *Books and Readers in the Early Church* (New Haven and London, 1995), 154–160.

astical History.[14] But disagreements between Eusebius' preliminary paraphrases of the texts he cited and the actual documents suggest that secretaries played a major part in the day-to-day work of compilation and composition.[15] A new form of history had taken shape—one avowedly based on erudite research, and sometimes so large in scale as to require collaboration.

This sort of history was preserved by Bede and others in the Middle Ages. It revived in the Renaissance, when Lorenzo Valla gave it a characteristically individual turn in his *Declamation on the Donation of Constantine.* This diatribe explicitly quoted any number of documents, if only in order to show how ridiculous they were. Valla grafted the ecclesiastical historian's careful citation of documents onto the classical form of a polemical oration, with riotous results.[16] The methods of church historians varied radically from period to period. Eugene Rice has shown, in an exemplary study, how the life and works of St. Jerome were treated over the centuries. In late antiquity and the Middle Ages, admirers equipped the saint with a pet lion, a wonder-working name and relics, and a host of spurious works. History served and supported spiritual needs. In the Renaissance, Trithemius, Erasmus, and others suppressed the lion,

---

14. See F. Winkelmann, "Probleme der Zitate in den Werken der oströmischen Kirchenhistoriker," *Das Korpus der Griechischen Christlichen Schriftsteller: Historie, Gegenwart, Zukunft,* ed. J. Irmscher and K. Treu, Texte und Untersuchungen 120 (Berlin, 1977), 195–207, summarized (so far as Eusebius is concerned) in Winkelmann, *Euseb von Kaisarea* (Berlin, 1991), 111–112.

15. T. D. Barnes, *Constantine and Eusebius* (Cambridge, Mass., and London, 1981), 141. Cf. also B. Gustafsson, "Eusebius' Principles in Handling His Sources, as Found in His 'Church History,' Books I–VII," *Studia Patristica,* IV, Texte und Untersuchungen, 79 (Berlin, 1961), 429–441.

16. On Valla's use of rhetorical categories for analytical purposes see C. Ginzburg, "Aristotele, la storia, la prova," *Quaderni storici,* 29 (1994), 5–17 at 12–14; cf. Chapter 3 above.

exposed the fakes, and tried to set Jerome back into a richly reconstructed historical context—though most of the artists of the time, and many others, ignored them, seeing no need "to distinguish respect for the scholar from veneration for the saint."[17] In all its forms, however, ecclesiastical history remained large in scale and tightly connected to the compiling and study of documents.

The Reformation, finally, transformed church history, vastly increasing the scale of intellectual and financial investment in the discipline. This movement confronted the Catholic church with a radical challenge, as historical as it was theological in nature. From Luther on, Protestant theologians and polemicists charged that the church had become corrupt in head and members during the Middle Ages. In doctrines and institutions, laws and customs, rituals and prayers, they argued, the authorities had eliminated or distorted the heritage of the early church in order to exploit for profit the superstitious mass of the laity. One of the Reformers' early sympathizers, Ulrich von Hutten, printed an edition of Valla's *Declamation.* Luther, though himself less concerned with history than with theology, read the treatise with fascinated incredulity, horrified that the church had replaced the articles of the true Christian faith with lies. Valla's attack on tradition helped to inspire Luther's radical appeal *To the Christian Nobility of the German Nation.*[18] Luther's friend and partner Philipp Melanchthon gave their views new currency in the heavily documented captions he wrote for Lucas Cranach's *Passional Christi und Antichristi,* a short picture book

17. E. F. Rice, Jr., *Saint Jerome in the Renaissance* (Baltimore and London, 1985), quotation at 113.
18. See G. Antonazzi, *Lorenzo Valla e la polemica sulla donazione di Costantino* (Rome, 1985), 161–164, 189–190.

which juxtaposed the life of Christ with that of Antichrist (the pope). This graphic exposure of the conflicts between the Word of God and the canon law, which included the Donation of Constantine, went through many editions and inspired a vast range of antipapal images.[19] In it the footnote melded with the comic book, to the temporary enrichment of both.

Catholic intellectuals and reformers also turned to history. Leo X and Clement VII replied to Hutten's edition of Valla by commissioning Giulio Romano to paint spectacular frescoes of the baptism and Donation of Constantine for the Sala di Costantino in the Vatican. These made full use of the most up-to-date archaeological information of the period to confirm the historical reality of Constantine's gift of lands and power to the church.[20] Ignatius Loyola enjoined on his followers in the Jesuit order the duty to defend the innovations of the medieval church, from invocation of saints to creation of images, as evidence of the continued intervention of God in the history of His people. The past had become polemic. And the polemic involved more than the truth about events in the distant past. It also involved every aspect of the daily life of Christians in the present. Catholic scholars, as Simon Ditchfield has shown, devoted themselves to minute investigation of the lives of individual saints on a scale never seen before. They did so not from abstract curiosity but in order to solve concrete problems of liturgical practice. They had to verify—or falsify—the existence and deeds of saints who had been venerated for decades

19. L. Cranach and P. Melanchthon, *Passional Christi und Antichristi* (Wittenberg, 1521); see B. Scribner, *For the Sake of Simple Folk* (Cambridge, 1981; rev. ed. Cambridge, 1994), 149–157.

20. See Antonazzi, 161–162, and A. Chastel, *The Sack of Rome, 1527*, tr. B. Archer Brombert (Princeton, 1983).

or centuries in particular communities. By doing so they could produce reliable breviaries and liturgies for priests in every diocese. Local traditions were sometimes destroyed, but more often supported, by this exacting process of research and criticism. Like the Protestant turn to the past, in short, Catholic historiography of the church was motivated by powerful and precise religious needs.[21]

Vast learned compilations—above all the full-scale Protestant treatment given in the Magdeburg *Centuries* of church history by Melanchthon's irritable enemy Flacius Illyricus, and the *Annales* of the Catholic Cesare Baronio—joined Eusebius' *Church History* on the dark oak shelves of scholarly libraries.[22] True, Flacius condemned Eusebius' church history, and those of all Eusebius' imitators.[23] They concentrated on the wonder-

21. S. Ditchfield, *Liturgy, Sanctity, and History in Tridentine Italy* (Cambridge, 1995).

22. The importance of ecclesiastical history as a mode of scholarly research and writing was established by A. Momigliano, in "Pagan and Christian Historiography in the Fourth Century A.D.," *Terzo contributo alla storia degli studi classici e del mondo antico* (Rome, 1966), I, 87–109 at 99–101; Momigliano emphasized the differences, as well as the similarities, between Christian ecclesiastical historiography and the Hellenistic-Jewish literature that preceded it. For further discussion of the development of church history see H. Zimmermann, *Ecclesia als Objekt der Historiographie,* Österreichische Akademie der Wissenschaften, Phil.-hist, Klasse, Sitzungsberichte 235, 4 (Vienna, 1960); *Historische Kritik in der Theologie,* ed. G. Schwaiger (Göttingen, 1979); E. Cochrane, *Historians and Historiography in the Italian Renaissance* (Chicago and London, 1981), chap. 16; Momigliano, *The Classical Foundations of Modern Historiography* (Berkeley, 1990), chap. 6; B. Neveu, *Erudition et religion aux xviie et xviiie siècles* (Paris, 1994).

23. On Flacius' work see above all H. Scheible, *Die Entstehung der Magdeburger Zenturien,* Schriften des Vereins für Reformationsgeschichte 183 (Gütersloh, 1966); a useful short account in English, with good documentation, is given by O. K. Olson, "Matthias Flacius Illyricus," *Shapers of Religious Tradition in Germany, Switzerland, and Poland, 1560–1600,* ed. J. Raitt (New Haven and London, 1981), 1–17.

ful deeds of individuals instead of reconstructing the history of church doctrines and institutions. By contrast, Flacius proposed to show "not only what doctrines existed in the church in particular centuries, but also what ceremonies and songs, though briefly, for all of these things are closely connected to one another."[24] In method, however, Flacius followed Eusebius closely, envisioning his task, as his ancient predecessor had, as one of research in written documents. By the early 1550s, when he began collecting texts written by the Waldensians and other pre-Reformation heretics, he saw that a full history of the church would require the work of a whole historical institute. At first he hoped to find funding for a group of four: two readers who would collect, excerpt, and organize the sources, a writer who could put the results into eloquent Latin, and a scribe.[25]

24. Flacius Illyricus to Philo Lotharius, 9 September 1555; Vienna, Österreichische Nationalbibliothek, MS 9737b, fols. 14 verso–15 recto: "Scribis ceremonialia et cantiones Ecclesiasticas nihil ad nos. Nos vero omnino cupimus ostendere non tantum qualis doctrina singulis seculis in Ecclesia fuerit, sed etiam quales ceremoniae et cantiones, tametsi breviter, nam illa omnia inter sese cohaerent connexaque sunt."

25. Flacius to Schuibermair, 1 October 1553, Vienna, Österreichische Nationalbibliothek, MS 9737b, fol. 3 recto: "Erunt enim necessarii ut minimum floreni vel taleri 500 annuatim in sexennium, quibus alantur quatuor homines, unus qui stylo valeat et ea, quae scribenda erunt, scriptione complectatur, duo, qui tantum in inquisitione materiarum seu lectione occupentur, illique scriptori materias iam paratas suppeditent, et quartus, qui in describendo aliisque vilioribus ministeriis huic conatui inserviat" ("We will need at least 500 florens or talers a year for six years, to support four men. One of them must be a good stylist, who will set down in prose what needs to be written. Two will concern themselves only with the investigation or reading of the sources, and will supply the writer with his materials, all prepared for him. And the fourth will serve the project as a copyist and by carrying out other tasks of little importance"). See also Flacius' *Consultatio de conscribenda accurata historia ecclesiae,* in K. Schottenloher, *Pfalzgraf Ottheinrich und das Buch* (Münster i. W., 1927), 147–157 at 154.

But over time Flacius came to see that many kinds of evidence were directly relevant to his project. With his assistants, he collected and catalogued trial records and oral testimonies, popular prophecies and printed broadsheets, as well as theological treatises and histories.[26] By the time Flacius' team had actually assembled the first weighty volume of the *Centuries* for publication, seven young students were at work making the notes for the two young Masters of Arts and the scribe who produced the final text. A group of "inspectors" then checked every passage systematically. This enterprise proved costly—suspiciously costly. Flacius and his friends soon found themselves fully occupied defending themselves against attacks from their fellow Protestants. Justus Menius and others claimed that Flacius had kept most of the money he collected for the work for himself, paying the collaborators starvation wages, and that his procedures for collecting sources included not only note-taking of the normal kind, but also cutting pages from manuscripts with the legendary *culter flacianus* (the "Flacian knife" became proverbial).[27] Church history, in other words, spawned the first

26. For one study in Flacius' research methods, see K. Schottenloher, "Handschriftenschätze zu Regensburg im Dienste der Zenturiatoren," *Zentralblatt für Bibliothekswesen,* 34 (1917), 65–82. Flacius and his secretary Marx Wagner compiled a very detailed guide to the sources, the *Catalogus testium veritatis* (Basel, 1566). On this see now T. Haye, "Der Catalogus testium veritatis des Matthias Flacius Illyricus—Eine Einführung in die Literatur des Mittelalters," *Archiv für Reformationsgeschichte,* 83 (1992), 31–47, emphasizing Flacius' efforts to rely on the oldest available sources and to pose and solve questions of authorship and authenticity.

27. See *De ecclesiastica historia quae Magdeburgi contexitur narratio, contra Menium et scholasticorum Wittebergensium epistolas. A gubernatoribus et operariis eius historiae edita Magdeburgi. Cum responsione scholasticorum Witebergensium ad eandem* (Wittenberg, 1558) and Flacius Illyricus et al., *Ecclesiastica historia* (Basel, 1560–74), I, sig. β2 recto.

grant-supported historical research institute—and the first charges that the grant money had been wasted. Through the 1560s, as historians set out to produce polemical histories of the Reformation in France, England, and elsewhere, formal and informal networks carried the details of contemporary martyrs' lives, views, and doctrines to the writers, like John Foxe, who shaped them into modern equivalents of the acts of the ancient martyrs.[28]

Catholic church historians also collaborated to collect and exchange the masses of information they needed. Masses of data were gathered for the canonization proceedings, which began again in 1588 after a lapse of sixty-three years, as the Catholic church set out to mobilize its spiritual forces to combat Protestantism and convert the heathen. By canon law, these proceedings required the mobilization and scrutiny of vast quantities of eyewitness information. So did many other forms of inquiry about the past—especially the large-scale research in church history undertaken to refute Flacius, whose anti-Catholic *Centuries* urgently required refutation.[29] Baronio, though he liked to emphasize how hard he worked and to claim sole authorship for his *Annales,* drew help from networks of scholars in Rome and elsewhere. By the middle of the seventeenth century, the Italian members of one order, the Oratory, had created something like a peninsula-wide research institute for church history.[30]

Political historians prized pragmatic insight and high style

28. See B. Gregory, "The Anathema of Compromise: Christian Martyrdom in Early Modern Europe" (Ph.D. diss., Princeton University, 1996).

29. J. L. de Orella y Unzue, *Respuestas católicas a las Centurias de Magedeburgo (1559–1588)* (Madrid, 1976).

30. Ditchfield, chaps. 10–12.

above all, even when they insisted on systematic collection and collation of all the evidence. Ecclesiastical historians prized learning. Janus Nicius Erythraeus shuddered, as he wrote his life of Baronio, in awe not at Baronio's piety but at the sheer excess of energy with which he had "collected an immense and varied mass of materials, scattered through an almost infinite number of books, mastered it all mentally, arrived at a judgment about each point and finally committed it to writing in a learned and precise way."[31] This assessment accurately reflected Baronio's view of his own work. In the preface to his *Annales* he insisted that he had spent thirty years on research, beginning as a mere youth, in the Vatican and other libraries. He assured the reader that he had quoted the exact words of his sources, however unattractive, rather than paraphrase them, and that he had named them explicitly in marginal glosses.[32]

Protestant scholars expended comparable energy on the gigantic tasks of searching for and publishing the sources that could prove that their supposed innovations were in fact restorations. Matthew Parker, an erudite Anglican Archbishop of Canterbury, sent agents up and down the British Isles in search of the manuscript remains of the medieval English church, in Anglo-Saxon and in Latin: this head of the Church of England pillaged cathedral libraries as ruthlessly as any invader. Unlike many great patrons and collectors, Parker evidently read through the treasures he assembled, marking his progress

31. J. N. Erythraeus, *Pinacotheca imaginum illustrium* (Leipzig, 1692), I, 88–89: "ut infinitam vim rerum ac varietatem, per infinitos pene libros dissipatam atque dispersam, colligeret, intelligentia comprehenderet, de unaquaque earum judicaret, ac denique literis docte accurateque mandarit."

32. C. Baronio, *Annales ecclesiastici*, I (Antwerp, 1589), Praefatio, 1–7 at 4 and 6. See S. Zen, *Baronio storico* (Naples, 1994), esp. chaps. I–II.

through the margins of his precious manuscripts with his legendary red chalk. He printed some of the new texts, and saw to it that many other manuscripts were lodged in the library of Corpus Christi College, Cambridge. Parker's secretary, John Joscelyn, described his program eloquently:

> Besides he was verie carefull and not without some charges to seeke out the monumentes off foremer tymes to knowe the religion off thancient fatheres and those especiallye which were off the Englishe churche. Therfore in seekinge vpp the cronicles off the Brittones and Inglishe Saxons which laye hidden euery wheare contemned and buried in forgetfullnes and throwgh the ignoraunce off the Languages not wel understanded, his owen especially and his mens diligence wanted not. And to the ende that these antiquities might last longe and be carefullye kept he caused them being broughte into one place to be well bounde and trymly couered. And yet not so contented he indeuored to sett out in printe certaine off those aunciente monumentes whearoff he knew very fewe examples to be extante and which he thoughte woulde be most profitable for the posterytye to instructe them in the faythe and religion off the elders.[33]

Complex, delicate networks of annotation identified matters of historical or theological interest in Parker's manuscripts, and later supplied the matter for the long printed glosses that adorned the works he wrote or "inspired." These documents amply confirm Joscelyn's account.[34]

33. J. Joscelyn, *The Life off the 70. Archbishopp of Canterbury presentlye Sittinge* (London, 1574), sig. C1, quoted in M. McKisack, *Medieval History in the Tudor Age* (Oxford, 1971), 39. For Parker's program see in general ibid., chap. 2, and A. J. Frantzen, *Desire for Origins* (New Brunswick and London, 1990), 43–46.

34. See the erudite if sometimes ill-tempered Sandars Lectures of R. I. Page, *Matthew Parker and His Books* (Kalamazoo, 1993).

Heavy documentation did not confer—or imply—strict objectivity. Parker, for example, employed expert scribes to "improve" his manuscripts by filling in their lacunae with new leaves, their contents written in facsimiles of the original script. When he published Bishop Asser's ninth-century life of King Alfred, he tacitly changed the spelling and even the nonclassical wording of the manuscript, now lost. He interpolated passages from another source, which he wrongly ascribed to Asser, into the text. And he actually had the whole work printed in Anglo-Saxon rather than Latin type, in homage to "the venerable antiquity of the original manuscript"—even though the manuscript itself was written in a normal Latin book-hand, Carolingian minuscule, while the special type he used imitated a script used only for the vernacular language. He thus succeeded in creating what looked and felt like a genuine antique—but only at the expense of misrepresenting his actual source.[35] Other Protestant scholars working on more recent materials performed similar forms of cosmetic surgery—as Foxe did, for example, when he omitted evidence that might reveal that the martyrs he celebrated had held views which did not accord with Protestant doctrine.[36]

Catholic scholars also manipulated their evidence—some-

35. S. Hagedorn, "Matthew Parker and Asser's *Aelfredi Regis Res Gestae*," *Princeton University Library Chronicle*, 51 (1989), 74–90.

36. Much work remains to be done on Foxe's use of his sources. For varying perspectives see J. A. F. Thomson, "John Foxe and Some Sources for Lollard History: Notes for a Critical Appraisal," *Studies in Church History*, II, ed. G. J. Cuming (Edinburgh, 1965), 251–257; P. Collinson, "Truth and Legend: The Veracity of John Foxe's Book of Martyrs," *Britain and the Netherlands*, VIII, ed. A. C. Duke and C. A. Tamse (Zutphen, 1985), 31–54; T. Freeman, "Notes on a Source for John Foxe's Account of the Marian Persecution in Kent and Sussex," *Historical Research*, 67 (1994), 203–211; Gregory.

times very forcibly. The opening of the Roman catacombs, for example, created not only new views of early Christian life and art, but a spiritual gold rush. Powerful rulers and rich cities throughout the Catholic world competed to obtain the bones of martyrs for their churches. The Roman scholars in charge of the catacombs complied. They assembled bones into skeletons and assigned them names, assuming without much argument that the inscriptions found near them confirmed their status as martyrs as well as their identities. Official documents, adorned with seals, confirmed each find. Retired officers of the pope's Swiss Guard made a profession of obtaining these. Triumphal processions, staged with vast pomp and great expense, installed the tangible relics of early Christianity in churches throughout the Catholic world. Church history came alive, after a fashion, in a Dance of Death, inspiring worshippers and scholars everywhere—at some expense in standards of verification.[37] The connection between the recovery of primary evidence about the early church and the reform of devotional life in modern times could hardly have been clearer.

In the seventeenth century, finally, the age of primitive accumulation of ecclesiastical learning gradually gave way to one of analysis and investment. Catholic scholars waged *bella diplomatica*—"wars over documents"—as Bollandists and Benedictines systematically debated about which archival documents were genuine, which Catholic institutions had a historical foundation, and which saints had actually lived.

---

37. H. Achermann, *Die Katakombenheiligen und ihre Translationen in der schweizerischen Quart des Bistums Konstanz,* Beiträge zur Geschichte Nidwaldens 38 (Stans, 1979); T. Johnson, "Holy Fabrications: The Catacomb Saints and the Counter-Reformation in Bavaria," *Journal of Ecclesiastical History,* 47 (1996), 274–297.

These conflicts spawned a whole range of modern technical disciplines, from paleography to sphragistics.[38] Gibbon knew this world of modern monastic learning intimately, contentedly relying upon its products even though he did not try to emulate the deep original documentary research of its creators. He recalled with characteristic irony that in the 1760s, when he worked in the great Parisian libraries,

> the view of so many Manuscripts of different ages and characters induced me to consult the two great Benedictine Works, the *Diplomatica* of Mabillon, and the *Palaeographica* of Montfaucon. I studied the theory, without attaining the practise of the art: nor should I complain of the intricacy of Greek abbreviations and Gothic alphabets since every day, in a familiar language, I am at a loss to decypher the Hieroglyphics of a female note.[39]

Ecclesiastical history, in other words, provided much of the substance and the model of learned research which the Enlightened historians fused with elegant narrative. Whether they learned from the great Catholic editor and compiler Ludovico Antonio Muratori or the Protestant historian of the early church J. L. Mosheim, enlightened historians like Gibbon revealed themselves as the incongruous disciples of the very holy fathers whom they loved to mock. No one did more than Sebastian le Nain de Tillemont—the seventeenth-century Jansenist who piled up and analyzed all the documents that shed

38. See D. Knowles, *Great Historical Enterprises: Problems in Monastic History* (Edinburgh, 1963), chaps. 1–2; G. Schwaiger, ed., *Historische Kritik in der Theologie* (Göttingen, 1980); B. Barret-Kriegel, *Les historiens et la monarchie* (Paris, 1988), II, pt. 2, and III, pt. 1.

39. E. Gibbon, *Memoirs of My Life*, ed. G. A. Bonnard (New York, 1969), 131.

light on the history of the Roman Empire and the church—to assemble the raw materials from which Gibbon reared the great neoclassical country house and witty gazebos of the *Decline and Fall.*[40] Gibbon found it "much better" to study the history of the later emperors "in so learned and exact a compilation than in the originals, who have neither method, acuracy, eloquence, or Chronology."[41] Even Eusebius, for whom he had little respect, provided him with such vital materials as the list of all the inhabitants of Alexandria "entitled to receive the distribution of corn"—as well as with his famous joke about Origen and literal interpretation.[42]

The literature of ecclesiastical history had more to teach than the simple need for documentation, moreover: it explicitly insisted on the importance of repositories and the supreme value of the primary source. Already in antiquity some historians had discovered the pleasures of the archive.[43] Josephus, the Jewish leader who went over to the Romans during the terrible Roman-Jewish war of C.E. 70 and spent the rest of his life writing

40. On the Jansenist erudition of the seventeenth century see Neveu; on Tillemont see Neveu's classic earlier study, *Un historien à l'école de Port-Royal* (The Hague, 1966).

41. *Gibbon's Journal to January 28th, 1763,* ed. D. M. Low (New York, n.d.), 163.

42. E. Gibbon, *The History of the Decline and Fall of the Roman Empire,* chap. 10; ed. D. Womersley (London, 1994), I, 294; chap. 15, n. 96: "Eusebius, I.vi.8. Before the fame of Origen had excited envy and persecution, this extraordinary action was rather admired than censured." Gibbon refers to Eusebius, *Historia ecclesiastica* 6.8.1–2, where Origen is censured for taking Jesus in too literal a sense. Cf. Chapter 1 above, n. 7.

43. For a useful review of the development and use of ancient archives see *Reallexikon für Antike und Christentum,* s.v. Archiv, by K. Gross; on Greek archives cf., however, R. Thomas, *Literacy and Orality in Ancient Greece* (Cambridge, 1992), chap. 7. On Roman archives see *La mémoire perdue: à la recherche des archives oubliées, publiques et privées, de Rome,* ed. C. Nicolet (Paris, 1994).

the history of his people, used numerous archival documents
to show that the Greek scholar Apion and the Egyptian Manetho had slandered the Jews. Some of these texts Josephus
simply read, already translated, in earlier Greek works now lost.
Others, however, he claimed to have found in the archives of
real cities. More than once he cited Tyrian documents which
reached back a thousand years before his time.[44] Josephus made
clear to every reader that these documents deserved belief because they were preserved by priests, rather than mere historians, in public places. He also argued, cleverly, that a document written by an enemy of the Jews which nonetheless
sustained Jewish claims deserved particular credence and respect.[45] The Christian Eusebius, though less articulate about
his method, also claimed to use materials from official collections and in foreign languages—like the notorious correspondence between Jesus and King Abgar of Edessa, which he supposedly found in the archives of that city.[46] The power of these
claims—and the scholarly reasoning that underpinned them—
should not be underestimated, even if the curious nature of the
documents that Jewish and Christian scholars cited so profusely
has sometimes made their discipline seem a source of critical
problems rather than of methods for solving them. Annius of
Viterbo—whom we met in the last chapter, happily forging
the lost historians of the ancient world—learned from Josephus
to claim that his writers deserved more credence than the

44. See Josephus, *Contra Apionem* 1.73, 106–127, and *Antiquitates* 8.50–55
and elsewhere. The nature of these archives has been much discussed: see e.g.
F. Millar, "The Phoenician Cities: A Case Study in Hellenization," *Proceedings of
the Cambridge Philological Society* (1983), 55–71 at 63–64; J. Van Seters, *In Search
of History* (New Haven and London, 1983), 195–199.

45. Josephus, *Contra Apionem* 1.6–18, 28–29, 69–74, 143.

46. Eusebius, *Ecclesiastical History* 1.13.5–21. Eusebius remarks that "there
is nothing like hearing" the original texts themselves.

Greeks because they were priests who had kept official records over the centuries. Kircher's bravura publication of new Chinese documents fits cosily into this millennial tradition—and illustrates its weaknesses as well as its strengths. Chapters 15 and 16 of the *Decline and Fall* show how intimately Gibbon knew both—the former as embodied in Eusebius, the latter in Mosheim.

Kircher also worked within a second learned tradition that emphasized the explicit citation and analysis of historical evidence. In the 1640s, he excavated a fallen obelisk in the Appian Way outside Rome. This, he held, was only one of many Egyptian relics that contained the traces of an ancient natural philosophy and metaphysics. These still had profound truths to offer the modern, Christian intellectual. He devised an elaborate interpretation of the hieroglyphic inscriptions on the obelisk, one largely based on his reading of the forged Egyptian dialogues in Greek ascribed to the legendary Hermes Trismegistus. The references to these and other texts Kircher supplied, in precise, clipped marginal glosses (he quoted works in many languages within the text as well).[47] Kircher insisted that he had used only the oldest and most genuine sources to reconstruct and reconnect the links of the broken chain of Egyptian wisdom.[48]

In practice, Kircher did not cite all relevant ancient texts or

47. A. Kircher, *Obeliscus Pamphilius* (Rome, 1650), esp. book V, 391–560; cf. his *Prodromus Coptus sive Aegyptiacus* (Rome, 1636), *Oedipus Aegyptiacus* (Rome, 1652–54), and *Sphinx Mystagoga* (Amsterdam, 1676).

48. Kircher, *Obeliscus Pamphilius,* 391: "Lector vero ipso facto comperiet: Non me solis coniecturis, ut quidam sibi imaginari possent, indulsisse, sed ex veterum probatissimorum authorum monumentis, doctrinam hanc Aegyptiorum depromptam, ita, ni fallor, me feliciter combinasse, ita successu temporum dissipatam connexuisse; ut vel inde catenam illam hieroglyphici contextus hucusque desideratam restituisse videamur."

give full accounts of all the modern arguments he denied. To use the dialogues of Hermes Trismegistus as sources for the wisdom of ancient Egypt, he had to refute the thesis of the Calvinist scholar Isaac Casaubon and others that the texts in question were late Greek forgeries. The chapter Kircher dedicated to this question began with a powerful defense of tradition against certain iconoclasts who, he said, hoped to build themselves great reputations by destroying the credit of texts long considered genuine. But he neither presented Casaubon's argument in detail nor dealt with the massive linguistic documentation Casaubon had compiled to show that the texts in question could not be the antiques Kircher thought them.[49]

But Kircher produced an apparatus more dramatic than any imaginable set of glosses. He reassembled the obelisk's shattered inscriptions, determining that not a single piece had been

49. Ibid., 35–44. See esp. 35: "Ita quibusdam ingeniis a natura comparatum est, ut iis potissimum rebus, quae longo seculorum ordine a quibusvis doctissimis authoribus in pretio et aestimatione fuerunt, suamque authoritatem solidissima doctrina hucusque sine violentia sustinuerunt, expungendis, infringendis, penitusque abolendis operam impendant; quo quidem nihil aliud pro scopo habere videntur, nisi ut doctrinam tot insignium graviumque virorum aestimatione partam prorsus aboleant, aliosque hoc pacto omnium praeteritorum temporum scriptores coecos fuisse, se vero solos Aristarchos illud *autos epha* sollicitius ambientes, insolenti sane et intolerabili ostentatione, mundo vendi-tent" ("Some minds are so constituted by nature that they spend all their efforts on expunging, attacking, and wholly abolishing the very things which all the most learned authors have esteemed from time immemorial, and whose authority they have supported with wholesome learning, and up to now without violence. They seem to have no other goal in this than to abolish entirely a doctrine supported by so many outstanding and serious men. And they convince the world that other writers were blind with regard to past time, and they are the only Aristarchuses. They make heavy use of that well-known phrase 'he said it,' showing an arrogant and unbearable ostentation"). For the criticisms Kircher did not rebut see A. Grafton, *Defenders of the Text* (Cambridge, Mass., and London, 1991), chaps. 5–6.

lost, and had them reproduced in whole and in part in his book. Unfortunately, Kircher, like many antiquaries, saw visual evidence through a veil of verbal testimonies. The artists he used found it impossible to reproduce Egyptian images without introducing Western conventions that distorted them. Worse still, Kircher himself sometimes based his interpretations on faulty older images of Roman obelisks, rather than on the monuments themselves. His quotations of visual evidence, accordingly, hardly served as a preventive against errors in reporting the data—much less against errors in analyzing them.[50] Nonetheless, Kircher's books were always visually stunning; and this time he managed to place the monument itself on public view. In the center of that elliptical symphony in orange and yellow, the Piazza Navona, the Roman crowds still swirl around Bernini's fountain, with its statues of the four rivers of the world. The figures bear the obelisk Kircher had dug up. Inscriptions below the shaft in elegantly cut Latin make clear how erudite passers-by should interpret this "Hermetic obelisk." Even Kircher's splendid Egyptological folios must yield in beauty to the setting he helped to create for the original document: it makes perhaps the most impressive, and certainly the most bewitching, *pièce justificative* placed on display to support the bold theses of Renaissance archaeology.[51]

Like Kircher's Sinology, his Egyptology fell within the

50. See H. Whitehouse, "Towards a Kind of Egyptology: The Graphic Documentation of Ancient Egypt, 1587–1666," in *Documentary Culture: Florence and Rome from Grand-Duke Ferdinand I to Pope Alexander VII,* ed. E. Cropper et al. (Bologna, 1992), 62–79; for the context see F. Haskell, *History and Its Images* (New Haven and London, 1994).

51. See E. Iversen, *The Myth of Egypt and Its Hieroglyphs in European Tradition* (Copenhagen, 1963; repr. Princeton, 1993) and *Obelisks in Exile, I: The Obelisks of Rome* (Copenhagen, 1968).

boundaries of a recognizable historical tradition. For critical, document-based history was by no means confined to the world of Jewish and Christian polemicists, Benedictines and Jesuits. By the fifth century B.C.E. at the latest, Greek intellectuals had begun not only to write narrative histories of great events, but also to produce historical monographs in which they discussed technical problems. Roman scholars followed suit in the first century B.C.E. and after. Such scholars, traditionally known as antiquaries, attacked an immense range of subjects. They tried to establish the precise dates on which major historical events had happened. They reconstructed the religious practices and political institutions, public rituals and private lives of their ancestors. Men like Varro, who wrote on the whole *Life of the Roman People* he belonged to, were the intellectual ancestors of those legendarily broad-gauged social and cultural historians who flourished in twentieth-century Strasbourg and Paris, Marc Bloch and Lucien Febvre.[52]

It is not easy to say what ancient antiquarian books looked

---

52. The classic survey of this literature is still A. Momigliano, "Ancient History and the Antiquarian," *Contributo alla storia degli studi classici* (Rome, 1955); see also his treatment of this material in his *Classical Foundations of Modern Historiography* (Berkeley, Los Angeles, and London, 1990), chap. 3. For recent discussions see Cochrane, *Historians and Historiography,* chap. 15; H. Wrede, "Die Entstehung der Archäologie und das Einsetzen der neuzeitlichen Geschichtsbetrachtung," *Geschichtsdiskurs,* ed. W. Küttler, J. Rüsen, and E. Schulin, II: *Anfänge modernen historischen Denkens* (Frankfurt a. M., 1994), 95–119; W. Weber, "Zur Bedeutung des Antiquarianismus für die Entwicklung der modernen Geschichtswissenschaft," ibid., 120–135; M. Daly Davis, *Archäologie der Antike* (Wolfenbüttel, 1992); *L'Anticomanie: La collection d'antiquités aux 18e et 19e siècles,* ed. A.-F. Laurens and K. Pomian (Paris, 1992); *Ancient History and the Antiquarian: Essays in Memory of Arnaldo Momigliano,* ed. M. H. Crawford and C. R. Ligota (London, 1995).

like, since very little of this learned literature has survived except in the form of quotations or epitomes. But it seems almost certain that it included not only coherent texts, but also considerable amounts of primary source material. A direct interest in documentary sources did not establish itself at once. Herodotus saw oral testimony rather than written documents as the core of the traditions he reported—an attitude which helps to explain the numerous errors and inconsistencies in his accounts of the inscriptions and objects he supposedly saw in Greece and Egypt.[53] Thucydides also saw no reason to report the exact wording of the treaties and other documents he cited. He may well have regarded his quotations of them as summaries, not meant to be more literally accurate than the speeches he retrospectively composed for his protagonists.[54] By the fourth century B.C.E. at the latest, however, scholars began to work systematically on written records. One example is provided by the work, now largely lost, of Krateros of Macedon, a student of Athenian history who probably had connections with Aristotle. The great philosopher was also, as is well known, a great scholar. He collected historical and legal texts from the whole Greek world in order to carry out his comparative studies of societies and constitutions. Krateros, seemingly, applied a similar empirical method to the study of Athenian history. In order to establish the truth about debated points of history and chronology, he went to the Athenian archives in the Metroon and

53. S. West, "Herodotus' Epigraphical Interests," *Classical Quarterly*, n.s. 35 (1985), 278–305: "His epigraphical studies apppear to have been more for ornament than for use" (303).

54. See O. Luschnat in Pauly-Wissowa-Kroll, *RE*, Supplementband 12 (Stuttgart, 1970), 1124–32.

copied out the inscriptions recording the public decisions of
the Athenian people and other texts.[55] Plutarch, who wrote his
lives of the great Athenian leaders some centuries after Krateros, cited him twice. Once he drew a document "from among
the decrees that Krateros collected" to refute another historian,
Kallisthenes; once he attacked an assertion of Krateros himself,
remarking that the earlier historian had cited no "written . . .
evidence, though he usually records such things with the
proper fullness and cites those who support his account."[56] The
two citations differ in tone but coincide in suggesting that
Krateros wrote something like a document-based, meticulously
detailed work of history, unlike any of the surviving texts—
though precise conclusions can hardly be drawn, given the frag-
mentary nature of the texts and the fact that Plutarch may not
have used Krateros directly. For the same reason, debate con-
tinues to swirl about the local historians of Athens, or Atthi-
dographers, who may have carried out research on similar lines.

The antiquarian genre sprouted new buds in the fourteenth
and fifteenth centuries and bloomed outrageously in the sixteenth and seventeenth. Scholars scoured the cities and coun-
tryside of Europe for Greek and Roman inscriptions, which
they assembled in notebooks and, from the early sixteenth century on, published in more or less faithfully printed collections.
Carlo Sigonio, Onofrio Panvinio, and others restructured the
whole chronological spine of Roman history on the basis of the

55. The texts are collected and discussed by F. Jacoby in *FrGrHist* 342; cf.
M. Chambers in *Classical Philology,* 52 (1957), 130–132.
56. The passages are respectively *Kimon* 13.5 (*FrGrHist* 342 F 13) and *Ar-
istides* 26.4 (*FrGrHist* 342 F 12). Jacoby understands Plutarch as saying that
Krateros normally cited previous authors—not the stone monuments themselves.

fasti, or inscriptions, found in the 1540s in the Roman Forum. These were reassembled, by no less an artist than Michelangelo, in the Palazzo dei Conservatori.[57] The Roman constitution and the Athenian calendar, Roman wedding ceremonies and Byzantine military customs, became the subject of detailed, systematic analysis. The calipers and the engraver's burin joined the pen in the scholar's toolbox. Antiquaries not only read texts but weighed and measured ancient coins, excavated and illustrated ancient buildings and statues, and tried to recover the look of ancient objects, from arms and armor to the cross on which Jesus had died. The most adventurous of them followed the example set by Cristoforo Buondelmonti and Cyriac of Ancona, braving the pirates of the Mediterranean and the difficulties of living in Muslim regions to explore Greek ruins in Athens and elsewhere.[58] Others reconstructed the history of medieval Europe, editing and assessing chronicles and beginning to sound the depths of national and local archives.[59] Cab-

57. See R. Weiss, *The Renaissance Discovery of Classical Antiquity* (Oxford, 1988); E. Mandowsky and C. Mitchell, *Pirro Ligorio's Roman Antiquities* (London, 1963); *Pirro Ligorio,* ed. R. W. Gaston (Florence, 1988); W. McCuaig, *Carlo Sigonio* (Princeton, 1989); McCuaig, "The *Fasti Capitolini* and the Study of Roman Chronology in the Sixteenth Century," *Athenaeum,* 79 (1991), 141–159; *Antonio Agustín between Renaissance and Counter-Reform,* ed. M. H. Crawford (London, 1993); J.-L. Ferrary, *Onofrio Panvinio et les antiquités romaines* (Rome, 1996).

58. See C. Bodnar, *Cyriacus of Ancona and Athens* (Brussels/Berchem, 1960); P. W. Lehmann and K. Lehmann, *Samothracian Reflections* (Princeton, 1973); P. W. Lehmann, *Cyriacus of Ancona's Egyptian Visit and Its Reflections in Gentile Bellini and Hieronymus Bosch* (Locust Valley, N.Y., 1977).

59. For a particularly elaborate example of critical use of sources see A. de Valois, *Rerum Francicarum usque ad Clotharii Senioris mortem libri viii* (Paris, 1646–1658); de Valois emphasizes that he has preferred older sources to new, and multiple witnesses to isolated ones (I, sig. e ii verso); also that he has tried to read all relevant sources and cite by name all those on which he has drawn ([e iv verso]). In volume II, he explained why his work had taken so long—and in

inets of antiquities and *Kunst- und Wunderkammern* offered their learned visitors neat assortments of coins and long rows of ancient statues and inscriptions. Their habitués often developed visual sensibilities as acute as their formidable verbal learning. The Mediterranean academies and palaces where French and Italian antiquaries compiled and debated became the setting for an intellectual adventure. The interdisciplinary and collaborative methods of antiquarianism enlivened the curricula of many universities, especially in the Holy Roman Empire and Scandinavia.[60]

---

doing so offered what might serve as the antiquaries' credo: "Caussa morae diligentia fuit. Statueram enim auctoribus quam emendatissimis uti. Quare undique exemplaria scripta et antiquos codices membranasque conquisivi: qua ratione plurima me observaturum incognita maioribus nostris, plurimos errores vitaturum videbam" ("Diligence was the cause of my delay. For I had decided to use the authors in as correct as possible a state. Therefore I searched everywhere for manuscripts and ancient codices and parchments. By doing so I saw that I would both notice many points unknown to our predecessors and avoid many errors") (II, a iii verso). For the rise of archival scholarship in England, see esp. *English Historical Scholarship in the Sixteenth and Seventeenth Centuries,* ed. L. Fox (London and New York, 1956).

60. On antiquarian practice see further M. Wegner, *Altertumskunde* (Freiburg and Munich, 1951); A. Ellenius, *De arte pingendi* (Uppsala and Stockholm, 1960); P. Fuchs, *Palatinatus illustratus* (Mannheim, 1963); Barret-Kriegel, III, pt. 2; *Medals and Coins from Budé to Mommsen,* ed. M. H. Crawford, C. R. Ligota, and J. B. Trapp (London, 1990); *Documentary Culture,* ed. Cropper et al. On the teaching of antiquities see the case studies of H. Kappner, *Die Geschichtswissenschaft an der Universität Jena vom Humanismus bis zur Aufklärung, Zeitschrift des Vereins für Thuringische Geschichte und Altertumskunde, Neue Folge,* Supplement 14: *Beiträge zur Geschichte der Universität Jena,* 3 (Jena, 1931); L. Hiller, *Die Geschichtswissenschaft an der Universität Jena in der Zeit der Polyhistorie (1674–1763), Zeitschrift des Vereins für Thuringische Geschichte und Altertumskunde, Neue Folge,* Supplement 14: *Beiträge zur Geschichte der Universität Jena,* 6 (Jena, 1937); G. Wirth, *Die Entwicklung der Alten Geschichte an der Philipps-Universität Marburg, Academia Marburgensis,* vol. II (Marburg, 1977); O. Klindt-Jensen, *A History of Scandinavian Archaeology* (London, 1975), chaps. 2–3; G. Parry, *The Trophies of Time* (Oxford, 1995).

Most of the crucial works in this tradition—like Justus Lipsius' brilliant manual *De militia Romana,* which played a central role not only in the study of Roman history but also in the creation of the first modern armies—were more systematic than chronological in organization. All of them cited their authorities lavishly. Lipsius, for example, built his account of the Roman army around the relevant sections of the Greek text of book VI of Polybius' history of Rome, which he translated and analyzed in an extensive commentary.[61] He thus taught a formidable lesson in the importance of using primary sources. So, even more directly, did the seventeenth- and eighteenth-century antiquaries who collected medieval historical and legal texts in vast folios that remain essential parts of any working historical library—even though most of these editors found the texts themselves, considered as literature, impoverished. Most excused, rather than praised, themselves for printing such unpleasant but indispensable sources.

Many antiquaries insisted on the importance of full bibliographies, precise citations, and exact transcripts (often their practices did not quite live up to their precepts).[62] The basic tools of their trade, moreover, made them highly conscious of the importance of seeing their evidence at first hand. Collectors of Greek and Roman inscriptions took care to tell their readers who had seen a particular object, and in what conditions. This

---

61. J. Lipsius, *De militia Romana libri sex* (Leiden, 1596). See A. Momigliano, "Polybius between the English and the Turks," *Sesto Contributo alla storia degli studi classici e del mondo antico* (Rome, 1980), I, 125–141.

62. See e.g. C. R. Cheney, "Introduction: The Dugdale Tercentenary," *English Historical Scholarship,* ed. Fox, 1–9 at 8; H. A. Cronne, "The Study and Use of Charters by English Scholars in the Seventeenth Century: Sir Henry Spelman and Sir William Dugdale," ibid., 73–91 at 89–90. For similar statements in a German context, see W. Ernst, "Antiquarianismus und Modernität: eine historische Verlustbilanz," *Geschichtsdiskurs,* ed. Küttler et al., II, 136–147 at 140.

practice became normal in the fifteenth century, when humanist collectors of inscriptions gave precise indications of where
they had found each stone. These romantic archaeologists included Mt. Olympus among the sites they had supposedly visited, and some of them freely supplemented the headless statues
and incomplete inscriptions that they encountered.[63] Over
time, however, epigraphy lost most of its imaginative element.
Registration of sites and conditions became increasingly precise—even to the point where archaeologists recorded uncer-
tainties when necessary. Janus Gruter, the German antiquary
who produced the seventeenth century's standard epigraphic
corpus, reported that his predecessor Henricus Smetius had examined a set of ancient weights in the collection of Achille
Maffei at Rome in 1562. In many other cases, Gruter could
state only that Smetius had "seen" a given object himself, no
one knew where. Where possible, documents were simply reproduced. To clarify the nature and use of a bronze abacus from
Markus Welser's collection, Gruter wrote, "nothing prevents
us from hearing his own clear words"—which he promptly
quoted.[64] Like natural historians, antiquaries eagerly assembled
specimens: many prominent intellectuals, like Ulisse Aldro-
vandi of Bologna and Kircher, practised both disciplines, collecting ancient weapons and inscriptions as well as narwhal
horns and curious flowers in their museums. Like the natural
historians, the antiquaries assembled albums of drawings and
arranged for the creation of elaborate series of prints to preserve
uncollectable details like the arrangement of outdoor sites.[65] A

63. See C. Mitchell, "Archaeology and Romance in Renaissance Italy," *Italian Renaissance Studies*, ed. E. F. Jacob (London, 1960), 455–483.

64. *Inscriptionum Romanarum corpus absolutissimum*, ed. J. Gruter (Heidelberg, 1616), ccxxi, ccxxiv.

65. G. Olmi, *L'inventario del mondo* (Bologna, 1992); I. Herklotz, "Das *Museo*

profusion of evidence and a clear set of standards for using it gave antiquaries across Europe a basis for precise discussion of a vast range of problems in ancient history.

Antiquarian controversy was not eliminated by these methodological refinements. Instead it came to revolve around an interestingly sophisticated version of the old question "Button, button, who's got the button?"—"Evidence, evidence, who can cite the first-hand evidence?" When Ralph Brooke, York Herald and antiquary, set out to discredit his new colleague William Camden, formerly the headmaster of Winchester School, he quoted both documents and monuments in order to show that Camden should have remained in his "inferior province of boy-beating." Camden, who used the material evidence of Queen Philippa's tomb in his defense of his *Britannia,* retorted that this primary source provided ocular proof of his theory: "Let him goe to the tombe," he urged his adversary, "lett him looke upon it." "I have been to see," Brooke replied, and noted that Camden had "untruly reported" the arms he claimed to have found.[66] For all his learning, Camden was not above citing the occasional dubious text—like the passage, supposedly from Asser, describing the early history of Oxford, which he printed in 1603 even though he knew that the antiquary Henry ("Long Harry") Savile of Banke had very likely forged it.[67] Similar

cartaceo des Cassiano dal Pozzo und seine Stellung in der antiquarischen Wissenschaft des 17. Jahrhunderts," *Documentary Culture: Florence and Rome from Grand-Duke Ferdinand I to Pope Alexander VII,* ed. E. Cropper et al. (Bologna, 1992), 81–125; and Findlen.

66. T. D. Kendrick, *British Antiquity* (London, 1950), 152–155.

67. See J. Parker, *The Early History of Oxford,* 727–1100 (Oxford, 1885), 40–47; S. Gibson, "Brian Twyne," *Oxoniensia,* 5 (1940), 94–114 at 98–99. Cf. the case of John Selden, whose erudite and polemical antiquarian works swarmed with quotations from documents, and who reacted with special fury to the suggestion that he had misquoted or misrepresented documents (as he some-

controversies and arguments filled the Latinate pages of continental antiquarian literature.[68] No one negotiated the bibliographical and moral minefields of this brand of scholarship
more expertly than the great philosopher Leibniz—who not
only proved by metaphysical argument that he was living in
the best of all possible worlds, but also proved by extensive
archival research and the publication of any number of texts
that his patrons, the house of Braunschweig-Lüneburg, could
boast of the best of all possible genealogies.[69]

Gibbon and his colleagues could thus draw, for models of
source-criticism and source-citation, on a tradition of secular
scholarship that ran back to the Renaissance and before.[70] True,
Gibbon did not accord all antiquarians equal respect. The fantastic speculations of carnivalesque chronologists like Kircher,
who rewrote the entire history of the ancient world to suit their
neo-Platonic or patriotic tastes, left him as cold as the fanati-
cism and credulity of hagiographers. He withered the bright
buds of their imaginative recreations of the past with one Arctic
blast of neoclassical contempt:

> The last century abounded with antiquarians of profound learn-
> ing and easy faith, who, by the dim light of legends and
> traditions, of conjectures and etymologies, conducted the great
> grandchildren of Noah from the Tower of Babel to the extrem-

---

times had). He too sometimes relied on forgeries, or took late sources as authoritative for periods long before their own dates. See D. Woolf, *The Idea of
History in Early Stuart England* (Toronto, Buffalo, and London, 1990), chap. 7.

68. For a particularly rich case study see J. Levine, *Dr. Woodward's Shield*
(Berkeley, Los Angeles, and London, 1977).

69. H. Eckert, *Gottfried Wilhelm Leibniz' Scriptores Rerum Brunsvicensium. Entstehung und historiographische Bedeutung* (Frankfurt a. M., 1971).

70. Momigliano, *Classical Foundations of Modern Historiography*, chap. 3. See
also Fuchs, *Palatinatus illustratus*.

ities of the globe. Of these judicious critics, one of the most
entertaining was Olaus Rudbeck, professor in the university of
Upsal. Whatever is celebrated either in history or fable, this
zealous patriot ascribes to his country. From Sweden (which
formed so considerable a part of ancient Germany) the Greeks
themselves derived their alphabetical characters, their astronomy, and their religion. Of that delightful region (for such it
appeared to the eye of a native) the Atlantis of Plato, the country of the Hyperboreans, the gardens of the Hesperides, the
Fortunate Islands, and even the Elysian Fields, were all but
faint and imperfect transcripts. A clime so profusely favoured
by Nature, could not long remain desert after the flood. The
learned Rudbeck allows the family of Noah a few years to mul-
tiply from eight to about twenty thousand persons. He then
disperses them into small colonies to replenish the earth, and
to propagate the human species. The German or Swedish de-
tachment (which marched, if I am not mistaken, under the
command of Askenaz the son of Gomer, the son of Japhet)
distinguished itself by a more than common diligence in the
prosecution of this great work. The northern hive cast its
swarms over the greatest part of Europe, Africa, and Asia; and
(to use the author's metaphor) the blood circulated from the
extremities to the heart.[71]

Contempt oozes from every sentence of this paraphrase: no
reader will be brought up short by Gibbon's caustic comment
that "all this well-laboured system of German antiquities is
annihilated by a single fact." Gibbon felt amused, not stimulated, when contemplating the wild efforts of the too learned

71. Gibbon, *History,* chap. 9; ed. Womersley, I, 234. For modern treatments
of Rudbeck's theory see P. Vidal-Naquet, "L'Atlantide et les nations," *La dé-
mocratie grecque vue d'ailleurs* (Paris, 1990), 139–161, esp. 152–154, and G. Er-
iksson, *The Atlantic Vision: Olaus Rudbeck and Baroque Science* (Canton, Mass.,
1994).

Jesuit Jean Hardouin to prove, on the basis of the incontestable evidence of coins, that virtually the entire corpus of classical literature consisted of forgeries. In his discussion of whether St. Peter actually visited Rome, Gibbon listed opinions *pro* and *contra* in a footnote. He made his own view clear by the simple expedient of summarizing Hardouin's theory: "According to father Hardouin, the monks of the thirteenth century, who composed the Aeneid, represented St. Peter under the allegorical character of the Trojan hero."[72]

In general, moreover, Gibbon showed little tolerance for many of the most characteristic features of antiquarian literature. He ridiculed efforts to tie the histories of divergent nations together by identifying common cultural and religious traits. Comparative ethnology could explain such evidence far more plausibly than speculative philology: "Much learned trifling might be spared, if our antiquarians would condescend to reflect, that similar manners will naturally be produced by similar situations."[73] Pedantry always repelled Gibbon—especially when exhibited in support of what he saw as wild hypotheses. He deplored the tendency of even the most learned antiquarians to enter into far more detail than their readers could desire or their sources could supply. Scholarly efforts to reconstruct "the religious system of the Germans (if the wild opinions of savages can deserve that name)" he dismissed with a characteristically cutting parallel sentence: "Tacitus has employed a few lines, and Cluverius one hundred and twenty-four pages, on this obscure subject."[74] These and other critical re-

72. Gibbon, *History,* chap. 15, n. 122; ed. Womersley, I, 489.
73. Ibid., chap. 9, n. 71; I, 247.
74. Ibid., chap. 9, n. 62, I, 245.

marks make clear that Gibbon regarded the older, Latin literature of antiquarianism with considerable ambivalence.

Still, the antiquaries taught Gibbon much. Their minute care in citation gave him a model of careful scholarship and close attention to the location and quality of sources. A habitué not only of libraries but of the antiquarian collections of the Continent, he knew their precision and erudition at first hand. In May 1764, the learned savant Giuseppe Bartoli, a model of orderliness and "politesse," showed Gibbon through the royal Cabinet of Antiquities at Turin. Though "un peu Charlatan," he proved able to use monuments and texts in conjunction with a deftness which impressed his visitor. Gibbon took a special interest in the thirty-volume collection of antiquities on paper assembled by the sixteenth-century Roman antiquary Pirro Ligorio. He knew that many scholars had criticized Ligorio, an artist and architect rather than a humanist, "for a lack of faithfulness, and for inventing monuments that he did not know." But as Gibbon read, he found in the manuscripts

> evidences of candor, which predispose me to view him with some favor. I see a man who often doubts if he has read correctly, who leaves gross errors in the monuments, only using a *sic* to show that he had noticed them, and who leaves blank spaces which he could easily have filled in. I may also add that he was only a compiler and had no system, the interests of which he had to serve. He often cites the city, the house and the cabinet from which he took a given piece.[75]

75. *Gibbon's Journey from Geneva to Rome. His Journal from 20 April to 2 October 1764,* ed. G. A. Bonnard (Edinburgh, 1961), 21–31 at 29: "Le reproche qu'on a toujours fait à Ligorio c'est le defaut de fidelitè, et d'avoir supposè des monumens qu'il ne connoissoit point. Cependant j'y ai vû des traits de candeur qui me previennent en sa faveur. Je vois un homme qui doute souvent s'il a bien

More erudite antiquaries showed Gibbon how to cut up classical texts, turning them into collections of facts about social and cultural history. He acted as their faithful disciple, not their scathing critic, when he remarked that "Ovid employs two hundred lines in the research of places the most favourable to love. Above all, he considers the theatre as the best adapted to collect the beauties of Rome, and to melt them into tenderness and sensuality."[76] And in the antiquarian collections of the eighteenth century, mostly written in French and usually characterized by an elegant economy of intellectual and scholarly means not visible in the older treatises he ridiculed, Gibbon discovered a model for his own ability to muster humanist erudition and philosophical irony together. In the essays published by the members of the Académie des Inscriptions et Belles-Lettres, whose twenty volumes of *mémoires* formed the foundation of Gibbon's professional library, he found what he had looked for in vain in Rudbeck and Cluverius: sensible treatments of such obscure topics as the origins and migrations of peoples. "It is seldom," he observed of one such essay, "that the antiquarian and the philosopher are so happily blended."[77]

In this updated form, Gibbon gained access to and appreciation for the results of the antiquarian enterprise of the last two centuries. The members of the Académie, as he knew, subjected ancient and modern reports on the foundation of Rome

---

lû, qui laisse des fautes grossieres dans les monumens, en avertissant seulement par un *sic* qu'il les avoit remarquèès, et qui laisse des endroits en blanc qu'il lui etoit très facile de remplir. J'ajoute encore qu'il n'etoit que Compilateur et qu'il n'avoit aucun systeme dont il falloit servir les interets. Il cite souvent la ville, la maison et le cabinet dont il a tirè telle ou telle piece." On the vexed question of Ligorio's accuracy as a scholar see above all the essays edited by R. Gaston.

76. Gibbon, *History,* chap. 9, n. 57; ed. Womersley, I, 244.

77. Ibid., chap. 9, n. 86; I, 251.

to a corrosive bath of historical skepticism. In doing so, they sometimes went over ground already cleared in earlier treatments by Renaissance scholars—Johannes Temporarius, Philip Cluverius, Joseph Scaliger—who had not only sorted out the real sources from the fakes of Annius of Viterbo, but had also shown that Roman accounts of the dates and details of the city's early history rested only on late reports. Since the Gauls had burned the city and its records, moreover, these must have been transmitted orally for some time—perhaps in the form of banquet songs—and no doubt changed in the course of transmission. H. J. Erasmus showed decades ago that De Beaufort and Niebuhr had little to teach the humanists of the Renaissance and their baroque successors about historical criticism.[78] By steeping himself in the precocious and elegant essays of the French scholars, Gibbon learned to appreciate the antiquarian tradition, even if he showed little sympathy for individual antiquaries.[79]

The ecclesiastical historians and secular antiquaries often collaborated, and individual scholars, like Kircher, often practiced both forms of history. Their compilations of sources provided the raw materials that Enlightenment historians sawed, turned, and polished; their methodical criticism provided the model for the analytical, though not the narrative, procedures that Robertson and Möser used. Yet the antiquaries did not provide anything like a full literary model for their secular successors. When they wrote about historical problems, for the most part, they produced not annotated narratives but unannotated ar-

78. H. J. Erasmus, *The Origins of Rome in Historiography from Petrarch to Perizonius* (Assen, 1962); cf. C. Grell, *L'histoire entre érudition et philosophie* (Paris, 1993), 81ff.

79. On Wolf and earlier scholarship see Grafton, *Defenders of the Text,* chap. 9.

guments. The sources to be discussed and the alternate theses to be refuted were quoted and analyzed in the text proper. And even the occasional presence of footnotes or glosses—as in Kircher's works, with their marginal apparatus of references in small print—did not stem from a clear separation between text and apparatus. One can read through most of the classics of seventeenth- and early eighteenth-century erudition, from Mabillon's *De re diplomatica* to Muratori's *Annali d'Italia* to Jean LeClerc's *Ars Critica,* without encountering a double narrative in the Gibbonian style.

Gibbon, who regularly confessed his debt to these traditions, made clear that he found in such works not a model but a foundation for his narrative. Of Muratori, for example, he wrote:

> His Antiquities, both in the vulgar and the Latin tongue, exhibit a curious picture of the laws and manners of the middle age; and a correct text is justified by a copious Appendix of authentic documents. His Annals are a faithful abstract of the twenty-eight folio volumes of original historians; and whatsoever faults may be noticed in this great collection, our censure is disarmed by the remark, that it was undertaken and finished by a single man. Muratori will not aspire to the fame of historical genius: his modesty may be content with the solid, though humble praise of an impartial critic and indefatigable compiler.[80]

The verdict was not idiosyncratic. In 1747 the German translator of the *Annali* praised Muratori's systematic use of original sources, which gave his crowded work "das eigentliche Le-

80. E. Gibbon, *Miscellaneous Works,* ed. John, Lord Sheffield (London, 1814), III, 367.

ben"—"its genuine life." But he hoped that his version might gain preference over the original, precisely because he had tested Muratori's sources and added "Anmerckungen." These footnotes identified the Catholic opponents Muratori had not wished to attack explicitly and modified, qualified, or enhanced his theses with new evidence from the sources. The translator had, in short, turned a deeply worthy but deeply traditional compilation into an up-to-date, critical piece of history—at the price of radical alterations in its form.[81]

Ecclesiastical history and antiquarianism—like the critical history of de Thou and his contemporaries—form necessary parts of the story of the footnote.[82] But they are insufficient, either together or separately, to explain its creation. To understand how the historical tradition mutated, we must examine one more of the strands that formed its intellectual gene pool.

81. L. von Muratori, *Geschichte von Italien*, pt. V (Leipzig, 1747), Vorrede.

82. Here I disagree, mildly, with Woolf, who convincingly argues that systematic use of documentation in historical texts was normally the result of "virulent historical controversy," but oddly concludes that Selden and his other protagonists did not adumbrate "the enterprises of Enlightenment and nineteenth-century historiography" (221). These enterprises too, after all, had their origins as much in polemic as in the disinterested, unemotional search for the truth.

CHAPTER SEVEN

Clarity and Distinctness in the Abysses of Erudition: The Cartesian Origins of the Modern Footnote

✳ One prominent but neglected piece of evidence makes it possible to narrow the chronological focus of this inquiry further. In writing to Walpole to apologize for "my negligence in not quoting my authorities," Hume took care to point out that he had done his research systematically and could perfectly well have annotated his text: "I own that I was so much the less excusable for not taking this precaution, that such an exactness would have cost no trouble; and it wou'd have been easy for me, after I had noted and markd all the passages, on which I founded my narration, to write the references on the margin." The problem was one of style, not of research. Hume confessed that "I was seduc'd by the example of all the best of the historians even among the moderns, such as Matchiavel, Fra paolo, Davila, Bentivoglio"—or, in other words, that he had followed the high political historians of the Renaissance, writing, as they did, in the classical tradition. He now thought, however, that he had quite simply missed the central point in making them his models and avoiding the use of footnotes: "that practice was more modern than their time, and having been once introduc'd, ought to be follow'd by every writer."[1] This clue, the most precise we have yet turned up, indicates that we should look for the origins of the historical footnote a generation or two before Hume—sometime around 1700, or just before. And in fact, as Lionel Gossman and Lawrence Lipking have pointed out, one of the grandest and most influential works of late seventeenth-century historiography not only has footnotes, but largely consists of footnotes, and even footnotes to footnotes. The vast pages of that unlikely best-seller, Pierre Bayle's *Historical and Critical Dictionary,* offer the reader only a thin and fragile crust of text on which to cross the deep, dark swamp of commentary.[2]

Bayle was a characteristic as well as a dominant figure of the French Calvinist emigration of the late seventeenth century— the wave of Huguenots, which included thousands of artisans as well as dozens of leading intellectuals, who were driven from France by religious persecution under Louis XIV.[3] A student of the new philosophy of Descartes and an amateur, but expert, connoisseur of Protestant theology and exegesis, Bayle taught at the Protestant Academy of Sedan and, after it was closed, at the Gymnasium Illustre in Rotterdam. But above all he made his way as an editor and writer. His monthly journal of extended reviews, the *Nouvelles de la République des Lettres,* reached

1. D. Hume, *Letters,* ed. J. Y. T. Greig (Oxford, 1932), I, 284.
2. See the concise treatments in L. Gossman, *Between History and Literature* (Cambridge, Mass., and London, 1990), 290–291, and L. Lipking, "The Marginal Gloss," *Critical Inquiry,* 3 (1976–77), 609–655 at 625–626; cf. also Lipking, *The Ordering of the Arts in Eighteenth-Century England* (Princeton, 1970).
3. See in general E. Haase, *Einführung in die Literatur des Réfuge* (Berlin, 1959), and A. Goldgar, *Impolite Learning* (New Haven and London, 1995).

a wide public soon after it started publication in 1684. Bayle soon found himself in possession of a well-known name and a European network of correspondents. At the same time, however, he found himself more and more in difficulties. The French authorities, who detested the ironic brilliance of this Protestant critic whom they could not reach, arrested his brother, who refused to convert. The severity of his imprisonment proved fatal. Meanwhile Bayle's political tolerance and certain personal loyalties brought him into sharp conflict with his former friend, the Calvinist theologian Pierre Jurieu. Bayle lost his teaching post and came under sharp literary assault.[4]

Despite these pressures, Bayle maintained his personal and intellectual independence and went on fighting smug orthodoxies on all sides (he described himself, wonderfully, as a real protestant—the sort who on principle protests against everything).[5] But he saw that he would have to make his way by writing. Amazingly enough, a vast, unruly reference work that took him years to complete also earned him a living. Bayle set out, early in the 1690s, to provide a dictionary of all the mistakes in other works of reference, above all those in the vastly popular *Grand dictionnaire historique* of Louis Moréri (Paris, 1674), which would reach its twentieth(!) edition, despite Bayle's criticisms, in 1759.[6] In a sketch that Bayle circulated

4. For a fully documented and excellent recent account of Bayle's life and works, see E. Labrousse, "Pierre Bayle," in *Grundriss der Geschichte der Philosophie, Die Philosophie des 17. Jahrhunderts,* II: *Frankreich und Niederlande,* ed. J.-P. Schobinger (Basel, 1993), 1025–1043. Her now generation-old biography and analysis of his thought, *Pierre Bayle* (The Hague, 1963–64), remains standard.

5. E. Gibbon, *Memoirs of My Life,* ed. G. A. Bonnard (New York, 1969), 65: " 'I am most truly (said Bayle) a protestant; for I protest indifferently against all Systems, and all Sects.' "

6. A manuscript in the Royal Library, Copenhagen, preserves part of Bayle's

to test market and reader response he described the task with characteristic modesty: "It's worse than setting out to fight monsters. It's trying to wipe out the Hydra's heads: at the least it's trying to clean the Augean Stables."[7] His basic idea was as simple as it was ambitious. In collecting material about the Roman philosopher Seneca, for example, Bayle would list all the omissions and errors in existing reference books. Anything the reader learned elsewhere and did not find contradicted in Bayle would be true.[8] Bayle was anything but naive. He knew that controversies raged about many facts, that the reader could not always determine where truth lay. Even the harshest and apparently most credible critics committed dozens of errors. The greatest scholars of the previous two centuries—even Joseph Scaliger and Claude Saumaise—had not only discovered others' mistakes but made their own. In the course of the bitter controversies that continually broke out between historians and philologists, the truth bounced and flew as hard, and at times as wildly, as a tennis ball at Wimbledon.[9] Only a dictionary of errors, Bayle held, could give readers an Ariadne's thread to

---

preparatory work from as early as 1689: see L. Nedergaard-Hansen, "La genèse du 'Dictionaire historique et critique' de Pierre Bayle," *Orbis litterarum,* 13 (1958), 210–227 (my thanks to E. Petersen for examining the manuscript in question at my request). See also S. Neumeister's fine essay "Pierre Bayle oder die Lust der Aufklärung," in *Welt der Information,* ed. H.-A. Koch and A. Krup-Ebert (Stuttgart, 1990), 62–78, to which I am much indebted.

7. P. Bayle, "Projet d'un Dictionaire critique," in *Projet et fragmens d'un Dictionaire critique* (Rotterdam, 1692; repr. Geneva, 1970), sig. *2 verso: "c'est pis qu'aller combattre les monstres; c'est vouloir extirper les têtes de l'Hydre; c'est du moins vouloir nettoyer les étables d'Augias."

8. Ibid., sig. [*8] recto-verso: "Car si c'étoit une fausseté, elle seroit marquée dans le recueil, et dès qu'on ne verroit pas dans ce recueil un fait sur le pied de fausseté, on le pourroit tenir pour veritable."

9. Ibid., sigs. *4 verso–[*6] recto.

lead them through the labyrinthine scholarly polemics of the last two hundred years. Hurling all his metaphors, traditional and modern, into one basket, he suggested that one might call his projected book "the touchstone for all other books" and "the insurance exchange of the Republic of Letters."[10]

The public response to Bayle's proposal took two forms: criticism from readers he respected, like Leibniz, and a vast, collective yawn from the rest. Even the immensely erudite Gilles Ménage, for example, found the proposal for a dictionary of errors unappealing, much though he respected Bayle's talent and hoped he could succeed.[11] Accordingly, Bayle set out to produce something even grander: a historical dictionary of persons (and a few places) ancient, medieval, and modern, all of it supported by a vast apparatus of references and citations. The *Dictionary* appeared in December 1696; was enlarged in 1702; and formed the favorite reading matter of just about every literate European for much of the next century. Students queued up to use it in the Bibliothèque Mazarine; all serious collectors bought it. Voltaire devoted an immense amount of time to reading, annotating, and reacting to Bayle's articles, to which he owed endless stimulation and productive irritation.[12] Those who tried to combine erudition and philosophy found the book especially fascinating. The pioneering historian of art J. J. Winckelmann, another of the eighteenth-century writers who

10. Ibid., sig. [*8] recto.
11. *Menagiana,* 2nd. ed. (Paris, 1694), I, 118: "Il paroît que M. Bayle a dessein de faire un ouvrage touchant les fautes que les Biographes ont fait en parlant de la mort et de la naissance des Savans; mais c'est une matiere que est bien seche, cependant comme il a de l'esprit elle peut devenir riche entre ses mains. Je meurs d'envie de voir l'essay de son Dictionaire critique qu'il nous a promis."
12. H. T. Mason, *Pierre Bayle and Voltaire* (Oxford, 1963).

transformed the tradition of antiquarian scholarship into something rich and strange, read the *Dictionary* twice and copied from it what he called a "iustum . . . volumen," 1300 pages' worth of articles, written out in a minute hand.[13]

It may seem odd to identify Bayle, a thinker usually regarded as the one who taught the intellectuals of the Enlightenment to doubt everything, as a founder of historical learning. Many readers have found the *Dictionary* a vast subversive engine, designed to undermine the Bible, Protestant orthodoxy, the very notion of exact knowledge.[14] And certainly the man who saw history as "nothing but the crimes and misfortunes of the human race" did not share de Thou's—or Gibbon's—optimism. Bayle repeatedly exposed errors and contradictions: between the despised Moréri, his predecessor in the dictionary-making game, and the sources; between the sources themselves; between the sources and common sense. He insisted that massive falsification had interfered with the historical record. All writers, pagans and Christians alike, distorted in order to condemn: "This method has been used in all times and places. Men have always tried, and still try, to ridicule the doctrine and the person of their adversaries: to achieve this they invent thousands of stories."[15] In the dour footnote D to his account of Giacomo

13. A. Tibal, *Inventaire des manuscrits de Winckelmann déposés à la Bibliothèque Nationale* (Paris, 1911), 12: "Baylii Dictionarium bis perlegi et iustum inde volumen miscellaneorum conscripsi."

14. See Gibbon, *Memoirs of My Life,* 64–65: "His critical Dictionary is a vast repository of facts and opinions; and he balances the *false* Religions in his sceptical scales, till the opposite quantities, (if I may use the language of Algebra) annihilate each other . . . in a conversation with the ingenious Abbé, (afterwards Cardinal) de Polignac, he freely disclosed his universal Pyrrhonism."

15. Bayle, *Dictionaire historique et critique* (Rotterdam, 1697, 3rd ed., Rotterdam, 1720, 4th ed., Amsterdam, 1730), Lacyde, footnote F (1720, II, 1638,

Bonfadius—a historian whose enemies arranged his condemnation and execution for sodomy—Bayle ridiculed the Ciceronian notion that historians should and could tell the whole
truth:

> Nothing is finer in theory than the ideas of the lawgiver of
> historians. He commands them not to dare to say anything that
> is false, and to dare to say everything that is true. But these
> are impractical laws, like those of the Decalogue, given the
> condition in which the human race finds itself . . . In addition,
> let us observe a great difference between such similar laws.
> Only a perfect wisdom can live according to the Decalogue;
> and it would be a complete folly to carry out the laws of history.
> Eternal life is the fruit of obedience to the Decalogue; but
> temporal death is the almost inevitable consequence of obedi-
> ence to the lawgiver of historians.[16]

Many readers, accordingly, have seen Bayle as the sworn enemy
of the notion that history could ever recover solid facts—and
have interpreted the swarming irreverences of his footnotes as
a massive effort to subvert all certainties.

1730, III, 31): "Cette méthode est de tous les tems, et de tous les lieux: on a
toûjours cherché, et l'on cherche encore à tourner en ridicule la doctrine, et la
personne de ses Adversaires; et afin d'en venir à bout on supose mille fables."
Here and elsewhere, I use where possible the modern partial rendering by R.
Popkin, with C. Brush (Indianapolis, 1965). My interpretation of Bayle owes
much to Popkin's introduction; cf. also Mason, 128–133.

16. Bayle, *Dictionaire*, Bonfadius, footnote D (not in 1697, 1720, I, 596,
1730, I, 602): "Rien n'est plus beau dans la théorie, que les idées du Législateur
des Historiens: il leur commande de n'ôser dire rien qui soit faux, et d'ôser dire
tout ce qui est vrai; mais ce sont des loix impraticables, tout comme celles du
Décalogue dans l'état où le genre humain se trouve . . . Remarquons d'ailleurs
une grande différence entre des loix si semblables. Il n'y a qu'une parfaite sa-
gesse, qui puisse accomplir le Décalogue; et il faudroit être d'une folie achevée,
pour accomplir les loix de l'Histoire. La vie éternelle est le fruit de l'obéissance
au Décalogue, mais la mort temporelle est la suite presque inévitable de
l'obéissance au Législateur des Historiens."

Yet Bayle's readers could—and can—learn many lessons from him, some of which apparently contradict others. Bayle emphasized the rules of good scholarship as well as the defects of bad. And in doing so he stated, formally, rules of scholarly procedure—the very rules that Gibbon and Davis, a century later, took for granted. In his article on David, for example, Bayle writes that

> The life of this great prince, published by the Abbé de Choisi, is a very good book, and would have been much better if someone had taken the trouble to set down in the margin the years of each action and the passages from the Bible or Josephus that furnished him his data. A reader is not pleased to be left ignorant about whether what he reads comes from a sacred source or a profane one.[17]

Citation, evidently, must be full and precise. So must the collection of testimonies. Bayle's footnotes buzz with the salacious twaddle of the Republic of Letters, with every pornographic interpretation of a biblical passage and every sexual anecdote about a philosopher or a scholar. We owe to him the preservation of Caspar Scioppius' description of the sparrow he watched, from his student lodgings at Ingolstadt, having intercourse twenty times and then dying—as well as Scioppius' reflection, "O unfair lot. Is this to be granted to sparrows and denied to men?"[18] Readers have often wondered if Bayle hoped to hide the most scandalous and irreverent bits of his work

17. Ibid., David (1730, II, 254; different in wording, but not in substance, in 1697, I, pt. 2, 930, and 1720, II, 967*): "La Vie de ce grand Prince publiée par Mr. l'Abbé de Choisi est un bon Livre, et seroit beaucoup meilleur, si l'on avoit pris la peine de marquer en marge les années de chaque fait, et les endroits de la Bible ou de Josephe qui ont fourni ce que l'on avance. Un Lecteur n'est pas bien aise d'ignorer si ce qu'il lit vient d'une source sacrée, ou d'une source profane."

18. Ibid., Scioppius (1720, III, 2551, 1730, IV, 173).

from censorship by placing them in his apparatus rather than in the text. But it seems certain, as Walter Rex argued a generation ago, that Bayle did not try to evade detection. His most hostile readers, after all, were also habitués of works of erudition, expert explorers of scholarly apparatus. No nook or cranny in a suspect commentary could escape their attention.[19]

When wicked passages in Bayle's notes attracted flak from orthodox batteries, Catholic and Calvinist, he not only refused to take evasive action but also deployed a powerful defense:

> This is a historical dictionary, with commentary. "Laïs" ought to have its place in it as well as "Lucretia" . . . It is necessary to give in it not only a recital of the best known events, but also an exact account of the least known ones, and a collection of what has been dispersed in various places. It is necessary to bring to bear proofs, to examine them, confirm them, and clarify them. In a word, this is a work of compilation.[20]

The claim to be a compiler, however, amounted to more than a defense of the naughty bits of the footnotes. Bayle made compilation into a term of pride. More elegant writers, who refused

19. W. Rex, *Essays on Pierre Bayle and Religious Controversy* (The Hague, 1965). Rex also offers a provocative analysis of the sources and structure of Bayle's article "David."

20. Bayle, *Dictionaire*, Eclaircissements (1720, IV, 3021, 1730, IV, 651): "C'est un Dictionaire Historique commenté. LAIS y doit avoir sa place aussi bien que LUCRECE . . . Il faut y donner non seulement un Récit des actions les plus conues, mais aussi un détail exact des actions les moins conues; et un Recueil de ce qui est dispersé en divers endroits. Il faut aporter des preuves, les examiner, les confirmer, les éclaircir. C'est en un mot un Ouvrage de Compilation." Cf. *Gibbon's Journal to January 28th, 1763,* ed. D. M. Low (New York, n.d.), 110: "If Bayle wrote his Dictionary to empty the various collections he had made, without any particular design, he could not have chose a better plan. It permitted him everything, and obliged him to nothing. By the double freedom of a Dictionary and of notes, he could pitch on what articles he pleased, and say what he pleased on those articles."

to provide the evidence in full, had brought scholarship into discredit. Bayle's vast accumulation of passages from other texts, of exegesis, summary, and rebuttal, was a profound exercise in truth-seeking—the only one, indeed, that could allay the fears of readers rightly discouraged by the usual methods of uncritical scholarship. Historians of the normal kind distorted; but the "compiler," who necessarily preserved even what was distasteful, offered the critical reader as much truth as human effort could attain. Bayle described such obsessive researchers, who insisted on checking every fact, with eloquence, even fire: "They try to verify everything, they always go to the source, they examine the author's intent, they do not stop at the passage they need, but examine closely what precedes and what follows it. They try to make suitable applications, and to link their authorities well. They compare them with one another—or, indeed, they show that they conflict. Moreover, they are people who make it their religion, when points of fact are concerned, to make no assertion that has no proof."[21] Bayle, in short, filled his dictionary not only with random, entertaining facts, but also with crisp, explicit, persuasive statements of the previously developed forms of antiquarian practice. At the touch of his philosopher's stone, the lead of practice was transmuted into the gold of precepts.

Bayle clearly thought that the redoubled form of his work

---

21. Bayle, *Dictionaire,* Epicure, footnote D (1697, I, pt. 2, 1046) = footnote E, n. α (1720, II, 1077, 1730, II, 367): "Ils veulent tout vérifier, ils vont toûjours à la source, ils examinent quel a été le but de l'Auteur, ils ne s'arrêtent pas au Passage dont ils ont besoin, ils considérent avec attention ce qui le précéde, ce qui le suit. Ils tâchent de faire de belles aplications, et de bien lier leurs Autoritez: ils les comparent entre elles, ils les concilient, ou bien ils montrent qu'elles se combatent. D'ailleurs ce peuvent être des gens qui se font une religion, dans les matieres de fait, de n'avancer rien sans preuve." This passage is cited and discussed by Neumeister, 71.

made it radically new; he believed that he had departed from the literary rules of the game. He explained that he had had to sustain "in this mass of all sorts of things a dual personality, that of historian and that of commentator." As the historian he recounted in the text his countless odd, ill-chosen stories of the lives and deaths, the views and bizarreries of thousands of individuals. "In his commentary," he told his readers, he had tried to "compare the arguments for and against something, with all the impartiality of a faithful reporter."[22] Bayle devised and defended a double form of narrative: one which both stated final results and explained the journey necessary to reach them. Pressed by a thousand enemies, Catholic and Protestant, enraged at the reign of error in a thousand books, and unsupported by any institution, Bayle had only the authority of his own scholarly workmanship to rely on. The format he chose reinforced his criticisms of error as nothing else could have— and gave him, as it would Gibbon, endless space as well for subversive ironies.[23]

Bayle was not, of course, the only scholar of his day to use footnotes. The Protestant polymaths of the Holy Roman Empire matched him, note for note. J. F. Buddeus used detailed source-notes to support his remarkable *History of the Philosophy of the Hebrews,* published by the Halle Orphanage in 1702; so did Christian Thomasius, in the sharp treatise of 1712 in which

22. Bayle, *Dictionaire,* Eclaircissements (1720, IV, 2986, 1730, IV, 616): "il a falu que dans cet amas de toutes sortes de matieres je soutinsse deux personnages, celui d'Historien et celui de Commentateur . . . discuter les choses, et comparer ensemble les Raisons du pour et du contre avec tout le desintéressement d'un fidelle Raporteur."

23. For this analysis see the classic works of E. Cassirer, *Die Philosophie der Aufklärung,* 2nd ed. (Tübingen, 1932), 269–279; Haase, 418–454.

he demolished the legend of the Witches' Sabbath, and Friedrich Otto Mencke, in his vastly erudite life of the fifteenth-century scholar and poet Angelo Poliziano, which built on the heavily documented article on Poliziano in Bayle's *Dictionary*.[24] Catholic scholars searched at least as passionately as Protestants for documentation. French and Italian Jansenists, in particular, anticipated Bayle's effort to provide a theoretical grounding for documentary research, and matched or exceeded the precision of his practices.[25] Pascal, after all, made the *Provincial Letters,* in which he denounced the Jesuit casuists who excused priestly lust and mercantile usury, into a tissue of quotations from his enemies' manuals. He insisted, over and over again, on his bibliographical probity: "I keep forgetting to tell you," he informed his correspondent at one point, "that there are Escobars of different impression. If you buy any, get those printed at Lyons, which have at the beginning a picture of a lamb standing on a book sealed with seven seals, or the Brussels ones of 1651."[26] He argued that the Jesuits who retaliated,

24. C. Thomasius, *Vom Laster der Zauberei. Über die Hexenprozesse,* ed. R. Lieberwirth (Weimar, 1963; repr. Munich, 1986); F. O. Mencke, *Historia vitae et in literas meritorum Angeli Politiani* (Leipzig, 1736), sigs. [)()(4] verso -)()(recto, esp.)()(recto: "maximi nominis Criticus et Philologus, felicissimusque rerum historicarum indagator, PETRUS BAELIUS, cuius amplissimam rebusque optimis et doctrina multiplici refertam *de Vita et moribus Politiani* Commentationem habemus in *Lexici,* quod stupendo labore emisit vir incomparabilis, *Historici atque Critici* editione altera" ("that famous critic and philologist and very effective historical researcher, Pierre Bayle, whose very informative and erudite treatment of the life and character of Poliziano appears in the second edition of the *Dictionary,* to the publication of which that incomparable man devoted incredible effort"). Mencke cites other sources as well, but with less sumptuous adjectives.

25. A. Momigliano, "La formazione della storiografia moderna sull'impero romano," *Contributo alla storia degli studi classici* (Rome, 1955), 110–116.

26. B. Pascal, *The Provincial Letters,* tr. A. J. Krailsheimer (Harmondsworth,

dismissing him as a heretical Jansenist or complaining that he had misquoted the casuits, themselves distorted the sources they relied on: "Find some other way then of proving me a heretic, or everyone will recognize how feeble you are. Prove from my writings that I do not accept the Constitution; they are not so very numerous. There are only sixteen *Letters* to look at, and I defy you, or anyone else, to produce from them the slightest sign of such a thing."[27] In the preface to his *Treatise on the Vacuum* he argued, more generally, for the validity and autonomy of historical research based on precise use of sources, so long as it concerned itself only with questions of what particular authors had written.[28] Dogged, black-wearing, straightforward Jansenists like le Nain de Tillemont followed Pascal's precept and example, producing some of the most exhaustive and influential learned compendia of the Enlightenment.

As savage pruning makes hedges bloom and flourish, so savage polemics produced the richest growths of source-notes. The Catholic biblical scholar Richard Simon enraged both Catholic authorities and Protestant divines with his *Critical History of*

1967), 131 = Pascal, *Oeuvres complètes,* ed. L. Lafuma (Paris, 1963), 407: "J'ai toujours oublié à vous dire qu'il y a des Escobars de différentes impressions. Si vous en achetez, prenez de ceux de Lyon, ou à l'entrée il y a une image d'un agneau qui est sur un livre scellé de sept sceaux, ou de ceux de Bruxelles de 1651."

27. Pascal, *Letters,* 260 = *Oeuvres,* 454: "Prouvez donc d'une autre manière que je suis hérétique, ou tout le monde reconnaîtra votre impuissance. Prouvez que je ne reçois pas la Constitution par mes écrits. Ils ne sont pas en si grand nombre. Il n'y a que 16 Lettres à examiner, où je vous défie, et vous et toute la terre, d'en produire la moindre marque." Pascal's citation practices, were, as usual, not so precise and scrupulous as he claimed. See Krailsheimer's introduction, 22.

28. Pascal, "Préface sur le Traité du Vide," *Oeuvres,* ed. Lafuma, 230–233 at 230.

the Old Testament. Here he argued that the Pentateuch represented not the literally inspired words of Moses but a selection made by public scribes from what had originally been a much larger set of documents. Simon not only repeated the dangerous suggestion, already ventured by many others, that Moses could not have written the whole Bible, but offered an alternate theory of the text's development. This he supported with rich documentation, quoted liberally in his text.[29] Scandalized critics on both sides of the religious divide claimed that Simon had cited his sources incorrectly or imprecisely. The accusation infuriated him, especially since the critics themselves copied one another's false accusations and failed to check the original sources that Simon supposedly misused.[30]

29. R. Simon, *Histoire critique du Vieux Testament* (Suivant la Copie, imprimée à Paris, 1680): brief marginal glosses name the authors and sometimes give the titles of Simon's later sources and identify biblical verses cited. On Simon's Old Testament scholarship see H. Graf Reventlow, "Richard Simon und seine Bedeutung für die kritische Erforschung der Bibel," *Historische Kritik in der Theologie. Beiträge zu ihrer Geschichte,* ed. G. Schwaiger (Göttingen, 1980), 11–36; W. McKane, *Selected Christian Hebraists* (Cambridge, 1989), chap. 4.

30. [R. Simon], *Apologie pour l'Auteur de l'Histoire Critique du Vieux Testament* (Rotterdam, 1689; repr. Frankfurt, 1973), 94–95: "L'erudition de nôtre copiste [Pere le Vassor] paroit encore mieux lorsqu'il copie au méme endroit jusquaux fautes *des Theologiens de Hollande.* Ces Messieurs dont il admire la capacité, parce qu'il n'en a aucune, avoient objecté à M. Simon, que lorsqu'il a cité Josephe il n'a pas été exact à marquer le Livre et le Chapitre. Mais comme il s'agissoit de l'Apologie de cet Historien contre Apion, laquelle ne contient que deux Livres forts petits sans aucune distinction de Chapitres, on leur avoit repondu, que c'étoit assez d'avoir cité le livre. Le P. le Vassor qui est bien autrement exact repetant la méme objection marque la page. Le malheur est que ce qu'il cite de l'edition Greque Latine de Josephe ne s'y trouvve point, bien qu'il ait marqué la page avec grande soin; mais seulement dans le Livre François *des Theologiens de Hollande* qui ont mal traduit cet endroit de Josephe, comme M. Simon leur a fait voir dans sa réponse" ("Our copyist's learning appears still better when he copies even the errors of the 'Theologians of Holland' in the same passage. He

To defend both his honor and his arguments, Simon devised what he described as a new form of documentation for his *Critical History of the Text of the New Testament,* which appeared in 1689. In the text, he explained in his preface, he normally cited his sources "in abridged form, and following only the sense." But to satisfy readers who wanted to know the exact wording of his sources, he placed full texts "at the bottom of each page, where everyone will be able to read them at full length and in the language of the authors."[31] In fact, Simon was better than his word. He normally indicated the precise source of every quotation or paraphrase in his text with a marginal gloss, and then provided the whole text in question, and a second indication of its origin, in a footnote. Critics, if not disarmed, were certainly wrong-footed by this preemptive strike.

All authors who addressed controversial questions in the

---

admires these gentlemen's capacities, having none himself. They had objected to M. Simon that he did not note the book and chapter when he cited Josephus. But the text in question was the historian's apology *Against Apion,* which contains only two short books not divided into chapters, and in reply to them it was explained that it sufficed to cite the book. Father le Vassor, whose accuracy is of quite a different kind, repeats the same criticism and notes the page. Sadly, the passage he quotes from the edition of Josephus in Greek and Latin is not in fact there, though he cites the page with great care. It is only in the French book of the 'Theologians of Holland,' who mistranslated this passage in Josephus, as M. Simon has shown them in his reply").

31. R. Simon, *Histoire critique du texte du Nouveau Testament* (Rotterdam, 1689), sig. **2 recto: "on a tâché de les satisfaire là-dessus, sans neanmoins changer rien de nôtre premiere methode. On les a mis au bas des pages, où chacun pourra les lire dans toute leur étenduë et dans la langue des Auteurs." The great paleographer Jean Mabillon, whose criticism of traditions about medieval saints won him much enmity, also showed a sharp sensitivity to the importance of sources and citation procedures, which he saw as crucial to the interpretation and evaluation of historical sources. See his *Brèves réflexions sur quelques Règles de l'histoire,* ed. B. Barret-Kriegel (Paris, 1990).

years around 1700 knew that they were entering minefields: footnotes naturally appealed to many of those who discussed historical and philological topics as the best way to protect themselves against hidden and overt attack. But other social and cultural conditions also helped to make intellectuals self-conscious about the problem of authority in writing about the past—and, in Bayle's case, sharply articulate about the way to avoid disaster. The seventeenth century, after all, saw the scientific authority of the ancients deconstructed by Bacon, Descartes, Boyle, and Pascal; the political authority of kings deconstructed by French Frondeurs and English Puritans; and the historical authority of the Bible deconstructed by La Peyrère and Spinoza. Questions of authority and evidence posed themselves on every side. Whose descriptions of the behavior of a barometer or a comet, a new substance or a new island, deserved belief? What made one account authoritative and another implausible? Any intellectual of the late seventeenth century necessarily confronted these and other questions of intellectual authority—and had to devise protocols for providing assurances that could quell the doubts of skeptical readers.[32]

Students of the past, however, faced special problems. Bayle, as Carlo Borghero has shown, was one of dozens of European scholars who were forced in the course of the later seventeenth century to resist not only the normal forms of clerical intolerance, but also a far more fundamental attack on their whole

---

32. See B. J. Shapiro, *Probability and Certainty in Seventeenth-Century England* (Princeton, 1983); P. Dear, "*Totius in verba:* Rhetoric and Authority in the Early Royal Society," *Isis,* 76 (1985), 145–161; S. Shapin, *A Social History of Truth* (Chicago and London, 1994); P. Dear, *Discipline and Experience* (Chicago and London, 1995); Q. Skinner, *Reason and Rhetoric in the Philosophy of Hobbes* (Cambridge, 1996).

discipline. Descartes's vastly influential *Discourse on the Method* included a withering critique of historical knowledge as well as a program for a new philosophy. Descartes dismissed history and the humanities as a pastime no more informative or rigorous than travel (both showed only that human opinions and customs diverged endlessly). But he also supplied his opponents with weapons that could be used against him. In both his mathematical and his philosophical works, Descartes made clear that the formal qualities of mathematical arguments lent them the rigor and generality that humanistic ones lacked. Some defenders of historical knowledge, like Pierre-Daniel Huet and John Craig, applied this argument directly to their work. They tried to make their historical criticism proof against skeptical attack by casting it in the Cartesian or Newtonian form of quasi-geometrical chains of deductions. Craig, for example, went so far as to devise formulas for measuring the decrease of authority over time that the testimony of any witness must undergo. He even computed the date at which the witnesses to the life of Christ himself would lose their credibility.[33]

Bayle and his fellow footnoters responded to Descartes in a more constructive way. They not only applied but stated the rules that verified or falsified historical propositions. And they created the double form of the double narrative, as one that would make explicit, just as the Cartesian *Regulae* did, that each argument followed from all the relevant evidence.[34] Scholars who lacked their inspiration—like Jacob Thomasius—

33. C. Borghero, *La certezza e la storia* (Milan, 1983).

34. See also J. Solé, "Religion et méthode critique dans le 'Dictionaire' de Bayle," *Religion, érudition et critique à la fin du xviie siècle et au début du xviiie* (Paris, 1968), 70–117 at 104–106.

might emphasize the ethical importance of honest source-citation. But Thomasius did not anticipate the characteristic formalism of Bayle and his contemporaries, their insistence on frequent, precise references cast in a particular form.[35] To become modern, philology needed the unkind assistance of philosophy. Bayle needed Descartes.

The early history of Bayle's project for his dictionary supports this analysis. In his "Projet" Bayle insisted that his work would find many readers, precisely because the sciences of historical and philological criticism were flourishing as never before:

> I do not wish to be told that our century, which has been restored and cured from the critical spirit that reigned in the preceding one, regards as mere pedantry the writings of those who correct errors of fact, with regard either to the individual lives of great men or the names of cities or similar points. For it is certain, on the whole, that this sort of enlightenment has never found more support than it does at present. For every investigator of physical experiments and every mathematician you will find a hundred profound students of history and all its subdisciplines. The science of antiquities, by which I mean

35. See J. Thomasius, *praeses, Dissertatio philosophica de plagio literario,* resp. Joh. Michael Reinelius (Leipzig, 1692), §249, 106: "Quod si e variis autoribus librum colligas, non multum referet, sive sub exordium operis universi, quod Plinius fecit historiae naturalis scriptor, sive principio singulorum librorum, quod Thuanus in Historia sui temporis, Catalogum eorum ponas, quorum opera es usus; qui nec male finem, quod solent alias indices, occupabit. Verum nec in titulo dedecebit aut praefatione apem profiteri, quae non ex unius horto flores delibaverit" ("If you compile a book from several authors, it will not matter much whether you put a list of them at the start of the whole work, as Pliny, the author of the Natural History, did, or at the start of each book, as de Thou did in his history of his own time. This can also perfectly well come at the end, where in other cases the indices normally stand. But it will also be quite suitable to profess in your title or preface that you are a bee that took flowers from more than one person's garden").

the study of medals, inscriptions, bas-reliefs, and so on, has never been cultivated as it is now.[36]

Bayle's voice sounds proud and positive here. But he introduced this passage, revealingly, as a response to a hypothetical objection. He knew perfectly well that popular opinion was against him. Many dedicated scholars had already despaired of regaining a central place in the curriculum, given the vogue for Cartesian philosophy and experimental science. That, in turn, explains why Bayle felt it necessary to argue, at length, against the fashionable view that mathematics had an advantage over historical knowledge, in that it "leads us to truths not susceptible of doubt." On the contrary, Bayle insisted, the "certitudes" of history, though different from those of mathematics, were far more concrete, more applicable to human life, and even "more certain, in a metaphysical sense," than "the profound abstractions of mathematics."[37]

In this same sketch, but in another context, Bayle acknowledged that problems of citation played an important role in making history seem less certain than it was:

> If an author asserts things without citing his source, the reader has occasion to believe that he speaks only on the basis of hear-

36. Bayle, "Projet," *Projet*, sig. [∗∗6] verso: "Et qu'on ne me dise pas que nôtre siécle, revenu et gueri de l'esprit Critique qui regnoit dans le precedent, ne regarde que comme des pedanteries, les Ecrits de ceux qui corrigent les faussetez de fait, concernant ou l'Histoire particuliere des grands hommes, ou le nom des villes, ou telles autres choses; car il est certain à tout prendre, qu'on n'a jamais eu plus d'attachement qu'au'jourdhuy à ces sortes d'éclaircissemens. Pour un chercheur d'experiences Physiques, pour un Mathematicien, vous trouvez cent personnes qui étudient à fond l'Histoire avec toutes ses dependances; et jamais la science de l'Antiquariat, je veux dire l'étude des medailles, des inscriptions, des bas-reliefs etc. n'avoit été cultivée comme elle l'est presentement."

37. Ibid., sigs. ∗∗∗ recto–∗∗∗3 recto.

say. If he does cite, the reader fears that he quotes the passage wrongly or misunderstands it . . . What, then, is to be done in order to remove these reasons for mistrust? There are a great many books that have never been refuted, and a great many readers who do not possess the books that contain the full series of literary disputations.[38]

The last of the draft dictionary entries that Bayle printed with his *Projet* was the hilarious "Zeuxis," with its brilliantly ironic account of the difficulties that had confronted the great Greek artist when he asked to see his models naked. In footnote A, Bayle insisted on the positive importance of proper citation. As usual, Moréri had gone about the matter in exactly the wrong way: "He piles up all his citations at the end of each article, without informing us that a particular author said one thing, and a second author another. He thus gives his reader a great deal of trouble: one must sometimes knock at five or six doors before finding someone with whom one may speak." The same point, Bayle noted with pleasure, had already been made by the ecclesiastical historian le Nain de Tillemont, a favorite source of Gibbon's, whose own works, as we have seen, consisted for the most part of extracts from the sources. Bayle praised Tillemont's "method of citation" as "of the utmost exactness."[39]

38. Ibid., sig. [*8] recto: "Si un Auteur avance des choses sans citer d'où il les prend, on a lieu à croire qu'il n'en parle que par oui-dire; s'il cite, on craint qu'il ne raporte mal le passage, ou qu'il ne l'entende mal . . . Que faire donc, Monsieur, pour ôter tous ces sujets de defiance, y ayant un si grand nombre de livres qui n'ont jamais été refutez, et un si grand nombre de lecteurs, qui n'ont pas les livres où est contenue la suitte des disputes literaires?"
39. Ibid., 387: "Il entasse toutes ses citations à la fin de chaque article, sans faire savoir qu'une telle chose a été dite par celuy-cy, et une telle autre par celuy-là: il laisse donc à son lecteur une grande peine, puis qu'il faut quelquefois heurter à plus de cinq ou six portes, avant que de trouver à qui parler."

Evidently, Bayle saw his dictionary as connected with the defense of the historical sciences, and the proper mode of citation as vital to that enterprise. But the full connection apparently did not become clear even to him until the most erudite and brilliant of his critics tied these threads of argument and practice together. Leibniz, in his response to Bayle's "Projet," discouraged his erudite correspondent from compiling a list of errors or a doxography of scholarly debates. But he agreed with Bayle "that those pure mathematicians and physicists, who are ignorant of and despise all other forms of knowledge, are wrong."[40] And he insisted that a trimmed-down and reoriented version of the project, one that addressed itself to truths rather than errors, would be very useful. Vital to this reference work would be a form of citation designed not to confuse the reader further but to demonstrate, conclusively, where the truth lay. Leibniz was an experienced editor (and entrepreneur for editions that lesser men carried out). He gave Bayle crisp, specific advice:

> I suppose that the best way to attain this end would be to speak about the subject in question, and generally to quote the passages from texts, on which one relies, often giving the authors' exact words, in imitation of M. Ducange's excellent work. It will be possible to put these words in the margin, since generally there seems to be some reluctance about putting Greek or Latin directly into the French text. If you had set out to produce a work in Latin, you would have more freedom in this respect, for in points of fact there is nothing like seeing the authors' own words.[41]

40. G. W. Leibniz, *Die philosophischen Schriften*, ed. C. J. Gerhardt, VI (Berlin, 1885; repr. Hildesheim and New York, 1978), 19: "que des mathematiciens ou physiciens purs qui ignorent et meprisent toutes les autres connoissances, ont tort." On the importance of this text see Neumeister.

41. Leibniz, *Philosophische Schriften*, ed. Gerhardt, VI, 16–17: "Pour cet effect

The close connections between philosophy and philology emerge clearly here, as Leibniz and Bayle cast about for models of accurate citation in the philological literature of their time. So does the high quality of Catholic learning, as evidenced both by Bayle's reference to the Jansenist church historian Tillemont and Leibniz's to the huge dictionaries of Byzantine Greek and medieval Latin by Charles Ducange.

Most important, Bayle arrived at his new method of citation after engaging in sustained reflection and debate. Footnotes mattered to him—mattered enough not only to be compiled with endless energy and laced with sardonic humor, but also to be the object of serious epistemological effort. Whatever his ultimate intentions, then, Bayle shored up the very historical discipline that many have seen him as challenging. True, his practice did not live up to his principles. Bayle, like his enemies, silently abridged and consciously or unconsciously misread the texts he instructed his printers to excerpt (Bayle tried to avoid copying out long extracts, which he saw as a waste of time, even though he thus apparently violated his own strict principles for the critical use of sources). Though he insisted that scholars should give the exact titles and editions of the works they cited, he often gave incomplete bibliographical details in his own references. He regularly found himself forced to cite books no longer in his hands from memory or from notes that he could not verify. Worse still, he cited sources that

---

je m'imagine que le meilleur seroit de parler de la matiere en elle même, de rapporter le plus souvent les passages des auteurs, sur lesquels on s'appuye, et de donner souvent leur propres paroles à l'imitation de l'excellent ouvrage de Mons. du Cange. On pourra mettre ces paroles à la marge, parcequ'on fera scrupule apparement d'inserer souvent le grec ou le latin dans le corps du texte françois. Si l'ouvrage avoit esté entrepris en Latin, on auroit eu plus de liberté là dessus, car en matiere de faits il n'y a rien de tel que de voir les propres paroles des auteurs."

he had not read at all, drawing his information from summaries and reviews.[42] But the novelty and utility of the model he offered are now clear.

So is the stimulus that Bayle offered to younger intellectuals who wished to preserve the possibility of attaining historical knowledge while developing a critical and modern epistemology and practice as well. Writers on the credibility of historical testimony *(de fide historica)* like the German F. W. Bierling followed Bayle's hints as they explicitly addressed the wider problem of establishing rules for the criticism of sources. Long before Ranke made archive-diving fashionable, Bierling had pointed out in a book festooned with footnotes that archives can mislead. He admitted that many of his contemporaries thought this impossible, but a careful analysis of their content proved his point. Archives consisted, he argued, chiefly of documents created by ambassadors and other public officials. But such men normally had to report on deliberations to which they did not have direct access and the intentions of monarchs who did not speak frankly. Their reports, in short, contained "what the ambassador guesses to be true or considers to be memorable, not always what is true." A neat footnote drove the point home: Hugo Grotius, while serving as ambassador in the Swedish service, spent the whole day and much of the night writing theology, and satisfied his employer, the statesman Axel Oxenstierna, with the gossip he picked up in the streets ("des

---

42. For a close analysis of some of Bayle's errors see R. Whelan, *The Anatomy of Superstition,* Studies on Voltaire and the Eighteenth Century, 259 (Oxford, 1989). Still more enlightening, however, is H. H. M. van Lieshout, "Van boek tot bibliotheek" (Diss., Nijmegen, 1992), which describes Bayle's methods of citation, sets them into their historical context, and builds from them a detailed analysis of his library and his practices as reader, scholar, and writer.

nouvelles du Pont-neuf en beau latin"). An archive constituted of such reports—and a narrative derived from them—might yield the right names and dates but would hardly provide the inner history of events. Hence archives and narratives kept and compiled in good faith contradicted each other.[43] Bierling did not take this as reason to despair; but he, like the contemporary Dutch scholar Jacob Perizonius, argued coherently for a mitigated, rather than excessive, faith in historical research.[44] They, in turn, were only two of the best known among the many writers who took part in the sophisticated debates of the late seventeenth and eighteenth centuries on the reasons for historical Pyrrhonism and the conditions of historical credibility.[45] These writers, as Markus Völkel has shown, did not always arrive at new results or rigorous formulations. But they highlighted both the problems connected with establishing historical facts and the accomplishments of scholars who had attacked particular problems, like the dating of manuscripts.

Bayle's expository model, however, still lacked one vital feature, as Gibbon pointed out long ago, and Lipking more recently agreed: economy. Bayle wrote his articles rapidly, and in later versions of them added new information not to the text

43. F. W. Bierling, *Commentatio de Pyrrhonismo historico* (Leipzig, 1724), chap. IV ("De fide monumentorum"), 225–249; see L. Gossman, *Medievalism and the Ideologies of the Enlightenment* (Baltimore, 1968), and Borghero. A segment of Bierling's work is now available, with facing German translation and notes, in *Theoretiker der deutschen Aufklärungshistorie,* ed. H. W. Blanke and D. Fleischer (Stuttgart and Bad Cannstatt, 1990), I, 154–169.

44. On Perizonius see Erasmus, *The Origins of Rome in Historiography from Petrarch to Perizonius* (Assen, 1962), and Th. J. Meijer, *Kritiek als Herwaardering* (Leiden, 1971).

45. M. Völkel, *"Pyrrhonismus historicus" und "fides historica"* (Frankfurt a. M., 1987).

but to the commentary. This became so complex—and sometimes so self-contradictory—that readers found themselves trapped in a sort of morass of erudition. Often the text confined itself to providing a few anecddotes, rather than offering readers clear guidance or a discernible story. In particular, as Markus Völkel and Helmut Zedelmaier have pointed out, Bayle did not firmly distinguish between a text which offered a clear narrative and the footnotes which supported it.[46] The mechanism was simply too haphazard and complex: with its slender, lightweight text hovering over a staggeringly learned and profound commentary, rather like a mayfly hovering over a swamp, it offered a wonderful model of critical reflection but a poor one of historical narrative. Even Bayle's pointed theoretical discussions, for the most part scattered and inaccessible, could easily escape the notice of his readers.

Fortunately, many scholars were at work on the same expository problems that Bayle attacked: their eventual solution, which took many years, engaged the efforts of scholars from any number of intellectual camps. For example, one of Bayle's enemies, his fellow Huguenot and refugee intellectual Jean Le Clerc, devised a theory of the footnote that took more account of the reader than Bayle had managed to.[47] Born in Geneva, Le

46. For Bayle's method of composition see van Lieshout, chap. 2. For an elegant analysis and defense of his method of presenting "a choir of voices" on each page, see M. Völkel, "Zur Text-logik im *Dictionnaire* von Pierre Bayle. Eine historisch-kritische Untersuchung des Artikels *Lipsius (Lipse, Juste),*" *Lias,* 20 (1993), 193–226. Cf. also H. Zedelmaier, "Fussnotengeschichte(n) und andere Marginalien: Anthony Grafton über die Ursprünge der modernen Historiographie aus dem Geist der Fussnote," *Storia della storiografia,* 30 (1996), 151–159 at 155–156.

47. Cf. *Gibbon's Journal,* ed. Low, 105: "I read the articles of Jupiter and Juno, in Bayle's dictionary. That of Jupiter is very superficial. Juno takes up

Clerc came to the Low Countries after studying there and traveling to Grenoble and Saumur. Like Bayle, he taught at Rotterdam, not at the Gymnasium Illustre but in the theological seminary of the Remonstrants (relatively liberal Calvinists who had broken with the main Dutch Calvinist church). Like Bayle, he became a brilliant journalist, filling the mailboxes of the citizens of the Republic of Letters with a whole series of periodicals in which he reviewed the newest novelties in scholarship and science. Like Bayle, he knew the modern philosophy of the time—above all that of Locke, which he encountered during a stay in England—and spun a web of correspondence that spread across Europe.[48]

Le Clerc had a gift for lucid, rapid synthetic formulations of complex problems and procedures. His *Ars critica,* for example, summed up two centuries of work on textual and historical criticism with authority and elegance.[49] Le Clerc published his *Parrhasiana,* or mock table talk, himself (the usual practice was to die and leave the agreeably scandalous task to a disciple), and in it he analyzed both the scholarly function and the lit-

---

seventeen pages; but great part of it, as usual, very foreign to the purpose. A long inquiry when horns began to be an emblem of cuckoldom; numberless reflexions, some original, and some very trivial; and a learning chiefly confined to the Latin Writers . . . Upon the whole, I believe that Bayle had more of a certain multifarious reading, than a real erudition. Le Clerc, his great antagonist, was as superior to him in that respect, as inferior in every other."

48. See J. Le Brun, "Jean Le Clerc," in the new Gudemann's *Grundriss, Die Philosophie des 17. Jahrhunderts,* II, 1018–1024; Goldgar.

49. See M. Sina, *Vico e Leclerc* (Naples, 1978); S. Timpanaro, *La genesi del metodo del Lachmann* (Padua, 1985), 20–22; M. C. Pitassi, *Entre croire et savoir* (Leiden, 1987); P. Lombardi, "Die *intentio auctoris* und die Streit über das Buch der Psalmen. Einige Themen der Aufklärungshermeneutik in Frankreich und Italien," *Unzeitgemässe Hermeneutik,* ed. A. Bühler (Frankfurt, 1994), 43–68 at 52–60; H. Jaumann, *Critica* (Leiden, 1995), 176–180.

erary form of the footnote. Many critics, he admitted, held that
one should follow the example of the ancients, "who only rarely
cited the authors they used: for example, when they showed
some disagreement."[50] But Le Clerc insisted that mere age did
not lend authority to a bad practice. In history as in science,
moderns had the right to improve on classical forms and ideas.
The historian's willingness to use footnotes became, for Le
Clerc, a sign of critical rationality:

> In fact, if a thing is bad in itself, the example of the ancients
> does not make it better. Nothing should stop us from improv-
> ing on them. The Republic of Letters has finally become a land
> of reason and light, and not of authority and blind faith, as it
> was for all too long a time. Nowadays numbers prove nothing,
> and there are no more cabals. No divine or human law forbids
> us to perfect the art of writing history, as others have tried to
> perfect the other arts and sciences.[51]

Le Clerc did not condemn all historians who wrote without
notes. Typically, he had more than one good word to say for de
Thou.[52] But he made clear that, in his time, only a historian
who wished his assertions to go unchecked could refuse to cite

50. J. Le Clerc, *Parrhasiana* (Amsterdam, 1699–1701), I, 144: "qui ne citent
que très-rarement les Auteurs, dont ils se sont servis; comme lors qu'il y a entre
eux quelque diversité de sentimens."

51. Ibid., 145: "En effet, si la chose est mauvaise en soi, l'exemple des
Anciens ne la rend pas meilleure, et rien ne nous doit empêcher de faire mieux
qu'eux. La République des Lettres est enfin devenue un païs de raison et de
lumière, et non d'autorité et de foi aveugle, comme elle ne l'a été que trop longtemps. La multitude n'y prouve plus rien, et les cabales n'y ont plus de lieu. Il
n'y a aucune Loi divine, ni humaine, qui nous défende de perfectionner l'Art
d'écrire l'Histoire; comme on a tâché de perfectionner les autres Arts et les autres
Sciences."

52. Ibid., 148–149; cf. 193–194.

his sources.[53] The intellectual modernity of the footnote—the novelty and rationality of the device, which Hume both appreciated and deprecated—was dramatically emphasized by Le Clerc.

So, too, was a modern practical requirement to which Bayle had been at best inattentive. Bayle's literary practice, as more than one modern scholar has noted, is typical of the scholars of the late sixteenth and seventeenth centuries. Many of them preferred synthesis to analysis and the making of massive compilations to the drawing of minute distinctions. Among their typical products were the huge variorum editions that Pope and his friends found so laughable—anthologies of learned exegesis in which notes, or whole commentaries, by a troupe of scholars clustered around a single classical text. Such an apparatus preserved a wonderful cacophony of scholarly voices, but also threatened to obscure both the text to be explained and the methods and interests of each individual commentator.

Le Clerc, an experienced and attentive reviewer of learned works of every sort, explained not only what services notes should provide but also what form they should take. He argued that one should divide variorum commentaries into their components, reorganizing these for the reader's benefit. Under the text, the editor should provide something quite specific, which combined Bayle's care for authenticity of sources with an eye to the reader's convenience:

> Notes expressed in good terms, in few words, and where one asserts nothing without proving it, or without at least citing

---

53. Ibid., 146: "On soûtient donc que l'on n'évite de citer, qu'afin que personne ne puisse examiner l'Histoire, que l'on raconte, en comparant la narration avec celles des Historiens, qui ont écrit auparavant."

some good author where one can see the assertion verified, indicating the passage in question so well that the reader can easily find it, if necessary: most readers, I say, will find notes like this of the greatest value.[54]

At the end of the book should go full commentaries by individuals and excursuses on points of detail. Readers were, Le Clerc admitted, delighted to have at their disposal all the material that the variorums provided.[55] But the full commentary that experts might look for at the end of an edition should be firmly distinguished from the brief, but well-documented, guidance that the notes beneath the text should provide. Even the more extensive notes should also be set out line by line, not commentary by commentary, as some editors had done. Otherwise the flood of information would become too overwhelming to be useful. Gottfried Jungermann's edition of the works of Caesar, for example, confronted the reader with a series of discrete commentaries, written by more than twenty authors and totalling more than 1100 double-columned pages, rather than a single coherent exposition of the text.[56] Le Clerc con-

54. Ibid., 229: "Des Notes conçues en bons termes, en peu de mots, et où l'on n'avance rien sans le prouver, ou sans indiquer au moins quelque bon Auteur, où l'on puisse voir la verification de ce qu'on dit; en marquant si bien l'endroit, qu'il soit facile au Lecteur de le trouver, si il a besoin de le chercher; des Notes, dis-je, de cette sorte, sont un thrésor pour la plupart des Lecteurs."
55. Ibid., 230.
56. *C. Julii Caesaris Quae exstant* (Frankfurt, 1669). Jungermann explained that the chief merit of his variorum commentary was that it enabled readers to work out "what each of them [the commentators] derived from the others, and what he contributed of his own: this will be of no little help in understanding and explicating Caesar" ("quid alter ab altero derivasset, quid de suo contulisset: quod Caesari intelligendo et illustrando non parum futurum fore") (II, sig. a2 recto). The editor, typically, had more precise ideas about how he should present

demned it. In no circumstances, he explained, must a reader of a well-made edition be forced "to leaf through a whole volume to find out what each critic said. That is too long and boring."[57]

Le Clerc, in other words, not only underlined the need for the intellectual support footnotes could provide but outlined a program for their composition—one on which, as he well knew, scholars and printers would have to collaborate. Naturally it took time for anything resembling a uniform citation practice to establish itself in the varied ecologies where Europe's scholars fought with note and claw for intellectual space. Even within a single province of the Republic of Letters, moreover, one writer's citation practices often provided ammunition for another's polemical broadsides. When the erudite curé Jean-Baptiste Thiers set out to excoriate Jacques Boileau's critical history of the place of flagellation within the Christian tradition, he flailed his opponent, who had denied the antiquity of the practice, for swelling his book by including irrelevant details about his sources: "Often he cites the year and place of publication of books, the names of the printers or publishers, the pages and leaves in the books, and sometimes even the capital letters found at the margins and the lines on the pages."[58] Boileau,

---

the history of scholarship on Caesar than he did on how this would help readers to master the texts themselves.

57. Le Clerc, *Parrhasiana,* 231: "feuilleter tout un Volume, pour trouver ce que chacun a dit, ce qui est long et ennuieux."

58. J.-B. Thiers, *Critique de l'Histoire des Flagellans* (Paris, 1703), 29: "Souvent il cite l'année et le lieu de l'Edition des Livres, le nom des Imprimeurs ou Libraires, les pages et les feüillets des Livres, et quelquefois même les létres majuscules qui sont aux marges et les lignes des pages. En voici la preuve . . . [which takes up two pages, 29–31]." (Early printed books in large formats often used capital letters in the margins to divide the text into sections for easy and

Thiers complained, filled his work with such unnecessary bibliographical facts, such "bookseller's learning," even when only one edition of the work in question existed. Sometimes Boileau reached a level of pedantry not seen in the whole period since the invention of printing. Yet in other cases he had omitted all details. "What purpose," Thiers demanded, "do all these meticulous and affected citations serve, except to enlarge his history?"[59] Even in the erudite precincts of the French clergy, evidently, too much learning could prove a passport to dismissal as the social inferior of those who wore their documentation more lightly.

In the course of the later seventeenth and eighteenth centuries, however, a long series of debates and discussions among writers, translators, and printers gradually yielded something like the modern system of documentation—even if the process did not then reach, and still has not reached, completion. Across Europe, writers and publishers collaborated more intensively than ever before, trying to make every aspect of the physical presentation of text mirror and guide the reader through its content.[60] A revolution in book design took place, as those concerned with authorship and publication carried out exper-

---

precise citation.) Boileau had indeed incorporated some quite detailed indications of his sources, as well as long quotations from them, in his *Historia flagellantium* (Paris, 1700). On this controversy and its protagonists see B. Neveu, *Erudition et religion aux xviie et xviiie siècles* (Paris, 1994), esp. 201–202.

59. Thiers, *Critique,* 33: "A quoi bon toutes ces citations si scrupuleuses et si afectées, sinon pour grossir son Histoire qui n'eût pas laissé d'être trop grosse sans toutes ces minuties?"

60. N. Barker, "Typography and the Meaning of Words: The Revolution in the Layout of Books in the Eighteenth Century," *Buch und Buchhandel in Europa im achtzehnten Jahrhundert,* ed. G. Barber and B. Fabian, Wolfenbütteler Schriften zur Geschichte des Buchwesens 4 (Hamburg, 1981), 127–165.

iments in layout and design, trying to make books physically as well as intellectually accessible. In this period, for example, classical scholars and printers first collaborated to establish the custom that the lines of each book or section of a classical text should be numbered sequentially throughout. Thus critics all over Europe could discuss a common problem without assuming that all participants knew the texts by heart or having to refer to pages and lines in a single edition—the practices that had remained standard since the invention of printing.[61] The combination of practical and aesthetic considerations that moved the classicists to depart from immemorial procedures also affected historical practice. As footnotes came to be not only intellectually fashionable but also typographically practical, they came to be found in the historian's normal literary toolbox. Through the eighteenth century new standards for precision gradually infected historical exposition, in a process the details of which remain to be established. Historians continued to believe in the moral and literary virtue of a clear, instructive narrative, but also cherished a newer desire for critical discussion of the sources. Publishers needed to reach large markets, but also wanted to work with authors. An interminable struggle resulted, one sometimes fought out to the tune of "two steps forward, one step back." But in the end, thanks as much to wider developments in publishing and education as to the achievements of brilliant individuals, the footnote won its place on the historian's page.[62]

One last time, David Hume offers crucial testimony. He directed the letter in which he insisted that Gibbon make his

61. E. J. Kenney, *The Classical Text* (Berkeley, 1974).
62. See Zedelmaier.

endnotes into footnotes not to Gibbon himself but to their joint publisher, William Strahan. As he said, "I intended to have given him [Gibbon] my Advice with regard to the manner of printing it; but as I am now writing to you, it is the same thing."[63] Hume's new sense of how history should be read went together with a new sense of how it should be written—and that, in turn, with a new sense of what the author could expect of his publisher. For all of this, he—like Gibbon and Möser—owed a considerable debt to those French thinkers of the late seventeenth century who found in Holland a refuge from the religious intolerance of Louis XIV, in learning a refuge from the oppression of theological orthodoxies, and in footnotes a refuge from the intellectual dogmatism of Descartes.

63. Hume, *Letters,* ed. Greig, II, 313.

EPILOGUE

Some Concluding Footnotes

✳ Gibbon and Möser, Robertson and Wolf replicated in full-length narratives the structures that Bayle had erected on a small scale in each article, bearing in mind Le Clerc's directions for users of erudite compilations as well as the practices of generations of historians and antiquaries. So critical history of the modern sort became possible. Ranke had only two ingredients to add—but both proved crucial. Almost against his own will, he gave a new literary life to the process of research and criticism, making the footnote and the critical appendix a source of pleasure rather than an occasion for apology. The scrupulous scholars of seventeenth- and eighteenth-century Europe created many features of modern historical practice. But they rarely anticipated Ranke's glow of enthusiasm, his ability to end a day's immersion in the dust of decaying records with his heart still throbbing with the excitement of discovery and interpretation.

Leibniz, a habitué of archives and an industrial-strength publisher of sources, complained bitterly about the damage deciphering illegible manuscripts had done to his eyes. He showed little interest in the minutiae of the manuscripts whose contents he made accessible to a wide public.[1] Gibbon, for all his mastery of the footnote as a literary form, long felt ambivalent about the relation between scholarship and narrative. He retained a tendency to denigrate what he described as "the dusty parchments and barbarous style of the records of the middle age."[2] In his *Memoirs,* he expressed his regret that he had allowed himself to be persuaded to disfigure his narrative with footnotes. Discussing the two Basel editions of the *Decline,* Gibbon wrote: "Of their fourteen octavo Volumes, the two last include the whole body of the notes. The public importunity had forced *me* to remove them from the end of the Volume to the bottom of the page: but I have often repented of my complyance."[3] It seems characteristically ironic that Gibbon described the advice of David Hume as "the public importunity." Ranke, however, made research and criticism glamorous and attractive.

At the same time, Ranke created, informally at first, a central institution of the new historiography: the nineteenth-century historical seminar, in which young students learned the tools of their trade by attacking technical problems selected by their teacher, under his guidance and with the help of his continual criticism. Most of the early historical seminars resembled Ranke's. Small in scale, not always supported by state grants, they were poorer and less ambitious than eighteenth-century

---

1. H. Eckert, *Gottfried Wilhelm Leibniz' Scriptores Rerum Brunsvicensium. Entstehung und historiographische Bedeutung* (Frankfurt a. M., 1971), brings out the contrast between the sophisticated principles of Leibniz's historical research and the sloppy teamwork by which they were imperfectly applied to the sources.

2. E. Gibbon, *Miscellaneous Works,* ed. John, Lord Sheffield (London, 1814), III, 362.

3. E. Gibbon, *Memoirs of My Life,* ed. G. A. Bonnard (London, 1966), 194, n. 64 to chap. VIII.

Göttingen's stately Historical Institute. Gradually they won modest official funds for scholarships and prizes. A mid-nineteenth-century historian counted himself lucky if he could convince the state minister responsible for education to buy one bookcase full of primary sources and reference works for the students in his seminar. Students who did not come—as many, naturally, did—from professional and academic families had to depend on the kindness of librarians. Otherwise they could not develop the technical and bibliographical competence needed to produce acceptable seminar reports and dissertations.

Nonetheless, the nineteenth-century seminars achieved something new. The forum for technical discussion that they offered and the short, precise dissertations on source-criticism on which their members concentrated eventually created a new disciplinary style and atmosphere. Only a proven ability to wield the tools and techniques of scholarship with dexterity and enthusiasm could open the doors to professional advancement.[4] In the Renaissance, when gentlemen wrote rhetorical history to be read by younger gentlemen, one's scholarship underpinned the utility of one's text. Still, excessive display of learning could only impair, not enhance, the moral and pragmatic impact of a history. Gentlemen must write as they rode—with great skill but no apparent effort. In the seventeenth- and eighteenth-century Republic of Letters, Bayle's and

---

4. For the development of professional history in Germany see W. Hardtwig, *Geschichtskultur und Wissenschaft* (Munich, 1990), 13–102. On the growth of the seminar, see H. Heimpel, "Über Organisationsformen historischer Forschung in Deutschland," *Hundert Jahre Historische Zeitschrift, 1859–1959*, ed. T. Schieder (Munich, 1959), 139–222. The seminars for classical philology which grew up before and alongside those for history fostered similar developments.

Gibbon's footnotes could win them a reputation for both impudence and erudition. Their apparatus proved that they had used their private libraries well and inspired some others to work and write in similar ways. But in the new university system of nineteenth-century Germany, which rewarded original hypotheses more lavishly than eloquent narratives, footnotes and documentary appendices could make one more famous than one's text, and critical arguments could win more imitators than the constructive ones. No wonder that so many bright young men, like Heinrich Nissen, chose problems of source-criticism as the subjects for their well-annotated doctoral dissertations: content and form matched each other at last.[5]

In the late nineteenth and twentieth centuries, finally, the sources needed to produce footnotes became readily accessible to young men—and women—who did not come from families rich enough to provide them with private research libraries. The archives of the major European states opened reading rooms where scholars could work regularly, making all—or almost all—of their documents available to accredited readers. National libraries, similarly, made the published collections of primary sources available in their domed, public reading rooms to men and women of letters who would never have had the money or the social credentials to use them in the private libraries of previous centuries. Eminent professors used persuasion, blackmail, and offers of positions elsewhere to make their governments cough up the money for working collections where

5. See H. W. Blanke, "Aufklärungshistorie, Historismus, and historische Kritik. Eine Skizze," in *Von der Aufklärung zum Historismus. Zum Strukturwandel des historischen Denkens,* ed. H. W. Blanke and J. Rüsen (Paderborn, 1984), 167–186, with the comment by W. Weber, 188–189, and Blanke's reply, 189–190.

their students could read the printed sources, primary and secondary, in one place. The Berlin rooms of the *Monumenta Germaniae Historica,* for example, with their elaborate collections of reference works and primary texts, became a historical laboratory, the counterpart, for the human sciences, of the Cavendish. The low salaries paid to the young collaborators in this project caused endless anguish. Nonetheless, those who could make their way through the stone jungles of Berlin to the Preussische Staatsbibliothek mastered literature and technique with a new ease.[6] After World War II, the vast budgets of the West German universities enabled historical institutes across the country to establish similar collections for their students.

Slowly but inevitably, similar resources became available to young historians throughout the West. One story may stand for many. The English medievalist F. M. Powicke came to study history at Owen's College in Manchester, later the University of Manchester, in 1896. Soon after he arrived, the enormous library of the historian E. A. Freeman, which had been presented to the university some years before, was made available to students:

> Then, in 1898 a new library, the Christie library, was opened and a room in it was set apart as a study and classroom, with Freeman's books all round it, accessible. There, in that room, the student, now in his third and last year, was guided into the mysteries of two special subjects, by Tout on Italy in the fifteenth century, by Tait on the Roman Republic in the time of Cicero. He read many books and realized what original authorities were and how they should be used. He discovered what it meant to handle the folios of Muratori, to study the

6. H. Fuhrmann, with M. Wesche, *"Sind eben alles Menschen gewesen." Gelehrtenleben im 19. und 20. Jahrhundert* (Munich, 1996).

Venetian ambassadors, and read Machiavelli and Guicciardini and Comines in the original. It was a bewildering, but also a wonderful experience.[7]

The excitements of the footnote had reached industrial Manchester; two generations later, they would even capture industrializing Oxford.

No amount of access to sources, published or unpublished, has proved capable of settling all of history's unanswered questions. Neither the publication of massive series of diplomatic and political records about the origins of World War I nor that of vast quantities of information about the course of World War II has prevented historians from arguing without end. Documentation, moreover, never reaches completeness. Even modern archives seek to protect their users—or at least the less privileged ones—from certain forms of document. Still, anyone who attends a modern university in the West can learn, as easily as Powicke did, to handle the basic primary and secondary sources and cite them wherever apposite. The routines of advanced student life described in Chapter 1 ensure as much, despite the differences between national styles of research and training. Footnotes no longer hold much mystery for those determined to learn how to produce them.

Sadly, the footnote's rise to the status of a standard scholarly tool has been accompanied—in many cases—by its stylistic decline to a list of highly abbreviated archival citations. Ranke, supposedly the alchemist who created the modern historical apparatus, in fact disliked footnotes and did not compose them

7. F. M. Powicke, *Modern Historians and the Study of History* (London, 1955), 20–21. In the same book, Powicke offers detailed profiles of his teachers, T. F. Tout and J. Tait.

with the care and ingenuity that went into his original research or the writing of the appendices to his books. Footnotes flourished most brightly in the eighteenth century, when they served to comment ironically on the narrative in the text as well as to support its veracity. In the nineteenth century, they lost the prominent role of the tragic chorus. Like so many Carmens, they found themselves reduced to laborers and confined to a vast, dirty factory. What began as art became, inevitably, routine.

In a brilliant passage, Gibbon dissects the five volumes of the *Origines Guelficae,* the collection of documents which Leibniz undertook for the Dukes of Hanover: "The hands of the several workmen are apparent; the bold and original spirit of Leibnitz, the crude erudition and hasty conjectures of Eccard, the useful annotations of Gruber, and the critical disquisitions of Scheid."[8] One could say much the same—if one could write such sentences—of the footnote. A palimpsest, it reveals on examination research techniques framed in the Renaissance, critical rules first stated during the Scientific Revolution, the irony of Gibbon, the empathy of Ranke, and the savagery of Leo—as well as the slow growth of publishing conventions, educational institutions, and professional structures which reshaped historians' lives and work.

Ranke's history of research practices and their exposition in historical writing has turned out to be self-justification rather than accurate description. That should not occasion surprise; in a Protestant culture virtue naturally associates itself with claims of novelty and reform. But the story also has a number of larger morals. Considered at the level of practice, rather than

8. Gibbon, *Miscellaneous Works,* III, 365.

theory, the development of history looks gradual rather than legato, more evolutionary than revolutionary. Part of the story is certainly recognizable. Historians picked up their techniques, then as now, in smash-and-grab raids on the glittering shop-windows of other disciplines, and continued to employ these long after they had forgotten the theoretical reasons for doing so. They also managed to forget well-founded objections and qualifications; without oblivion, history could not continue to be written. But the glacial history of practice challenges the dramatic tale of seismic disciplinary changes traditionally proclaimed in prefaces and manifestoes and later retold in many histories of historiography. No accumulation of footnotes will necessarily make it possible to bring the two stories together.[9]

The story of the footnote also underlines the fact that not all significant changes in modern intellectual disciplines result from the search for personal or institutional power so often invoked to explain, for example, the rise of modern science. Certainly, some distinct stages in the rise of historical culture reflect power struggles. For example, a passion for documentary evidence and rigorous proof characterized both the historical scholarship of the later sixteenth and that of the early nineteenth century. Each period witnessed a massive confrontation between long-standing institutions and radical attackers. In the sixteenth century, defenders of the old practices of the medieval church, sanctioned by tradition rather than texts, and of old social forms, protected by memory and tradition rather than written history and law, confronted innovative Reformers of the church and aggressive reformers of the state. In the early

9. Cf. J. Levine, *Doctor Woodward's Shield* (Berkeley, Los Angeles, and London, 1977).

nineteenth century, lovers of the Ancien Régime confronted
votaries of the Revolution that had shattered it. In each case
both attackers and defenders of entrenched practices tried to
find evidence for their positions in the past. The rapid development of new techniques in research and argumentation was
directly connected with the wider world of struggle over land
and belief. But the story of the footnote also had many participants whose private wealth and personal independence freed
them from the need to attack or defend institutions, to find
disciples or organize against enemies. Personal quirks and id-
iosyncrasies as well as larger social formations helped to bring
about what was, in the end, a shift of form and practice within
a literary genre.

The story of the footnote, finally, sheds a new light on the
nature of history as a literary enterprise. In recent years, some
scholars have argued, influentially, that history is nothing more
than a form of imaginative literature—a narrative like a novel.
Others have contradicted them, insisting that historians not
only write elegant paragraphs but pursue erudite research.[10]
Neither side, however, has answered what seems an essential
question: what role does research play in the writing of historical narratives? Leon Goldstein argues, in his well-informed and
provocative study *Historical Knowing,* that history consists of a
superstructure and an infrastructure. The former consists of
"that part of the historical enterprise which is visible to non-
historian consumers of what historians produce," the latter of
"that range of intellectual activities whereby the historical past

10. See e.g. A. Momigliano, "The Rhetoric of History and the History of
Rhetoric: On Hayden White's Tropes," *Settimo contributo alla storia degli studi
classici e del mondo antico* (Rome, 1984), 49–59.

is constituted in historical research." Goldstein rightly points out that most work on the philosophy of history has concerned itself with the superstructure, and he offers an attractive model of how to analyze the infrastructure as well. Helpful first-hand analyses of historians' citation practices make plain how seriously Goldstein takes the task of showing that history is an investigative discipline as well as a form of story-telling.[11]

But even Goldstein fails to make the central rhetorical point that emerges from the present inquiry: modern history is modern precisely because it tries to give a coherent literary form to both parts of the historical enterprise. Goldstein argues that history's superstructure, its narrative form, has not developed in any vital way over the centuries; only the ever-expanding infrastructure, with its burgeoning new methods, new questions, and new sources, has changed radically with time. In fact, however, the history of the footnote shows that the form of historical narrative has mutated over and over again in the last several centuries. It has done so, moreover, because historians have tried to find new ways to tell the story of their research as well as those of their subjects, on separate levels and at different tempos. The history of historical research cannot usefully be separated from that of historical rhetoric: even the best-informed efforts to achieve that separation distort the developments they seek to clarify. Historical texts are not simply narratives like any other; they result from the forms of research and critical argument that footnotes record. But only the literary work of composing such notes enables the historian to

11. L. Goldstein, *Historical Knowing* (Austin and London, 1976), esp. 140–143; cf. L. Gossman, *Between History and Literature* (Cambridge, Mass., and London, 1990), chap. 9. Cf. M. Cahn, "Die Rhetorik der Wissenschaft im Medium der Typographie: zum Beispiel die Fussnote" (forthcoming).

represent, imperfectly, the research that underpins the text. To study the footnote is to see that strict efforts to distinguish history as art from history as science have only their neatness to recommend them. In the end, they shed little light on the actual development of modern historiography. A full literary analysis of modern historical writing would have to include a rhetoric of annotation as well as some version of the existing rhetorics of narration.

Historians' practices of citation and quotation have rarely lived up to their precepts; footnotes have never supported, and can never support, every statement of fact in a given work. No apparatus can prevent all mistakes or eliminate all disagreements. Wise historians know that their craft resembles Penelope's art of weaving: footnotes and text will come together again and again, in ever-changing combinations of patterns and colors. Stability is not to be reached.[12] Nonetheless, the culturally contingent and eminently fallible footnote offers the only guarantee we have that statements about the past derive from identifiable sources. And that is the only ground we have to trust them.[13]

Only the use of footnotes and the research techniques associated with them makes it possible to resist the efforts of modern governments, tyrannical and democratic alike, to conceal the compromises they have made, the deaths they have caused, the tortures they or their allies have inflicted. It is no coinci-

12. Cf. N. Z. Davis, "On the Lame," *American Historical Review*, 93 (1988), 572–603.

13. I agree strongly with the discussion of problems of historical knowledge offered by R. Chartier, "Zeit der Zweifel," *Neue Rundschau*, 105 (1994), 9–20 at 17–19. Cf. also A. B. Spitzer, *Historical Truth and Lies about the Past* (Chapel Hill and London, 1996).

dence that Cardinal Evaristo Arns, the protector of the lawyers who exposed the use of torture against the citizens of Brazil, had learned the historian's craft at a high level in Paris in the 1950s.[14] Only the use of footnotes enables historians to make their texts not monologues but conversations, in which modern scholars, their predecessors, and their subjects all take part. It is, again, no coincidence that the most elaborate set of historical footnotes ever written—a set of four layers, footnotes to footnotes to footnotes to footnotes—occurs in an early publication of the Warburg Institute.[15] The luxuriant thickets of annotation characteristically planted by the Institute's first members were no routine assemblage of the relevant and the irrelevant, the essential and the trivial. They provided a written counterpart to the experience of working in the Warburg library itself, where the encounter with traditions juxtaposed in radically new ways was meant to shock readers into creativity.[16]

Many kinds of footnotes, in many kinds of histories, administer the same salutary lessons. No one has described the way that footnotes educate better than Harry Belafonte, who re-

14. E. Arns, O.F.M., *La technique du livre d'après Saint Jérôme* (Paris, 1953) (a dissertation supervised by P. Courcelle). See L. Weschler, *A Miracle, a Universe* (New York, 1990).

15. H. Junker, "Ueber iranische Quellen der hellenistischen Aion-Vorstellung," *Bibliothek Warburg. Vorträge, 1921–1922* (Berlin and Leipzig, 1923), 125–178 at 165–171.

16. See E. W[ind], "Introduction," *A Bibliography on the Survival of the Classics,* I (London, 1934), v–xii. The historian's apparatus also protects the results of his or her original research against the all-encompassing thesis arrived at much later. It retains obdurate nuggets of source material that refuse to be refined down—and whose presence forces the historian to reconsider or modify conclusions or even to undertake new investigations. Cf. C. Wright Mills, "On Intellectual Craftsmanship," *The Sociological Imagination* (New York, 1959), 195–226.

cently told the story of his early reading of W. E. B. Du Bois: "I discovered that at the end of some sentences there was a number, and if you looked at the foot of the page the reference was to what it was all about—what source Du Bois gleaned his information from." Footnotes first inspired the young West Indian sailor to read critically.[17]

Footnotes guarantee nothing, in themselves. The enemies of truth—and truth has enemies—can use them to deny the same facts that honest historians use them to assert.[18] The enemies of ideas—and they have enemies as well—can use them to amass citations and quotations of no interest to any reader, or to attack anything that resembles a new thesis. Yet footnotes form an indispensable if messy part of that indispensable, messy mixture of art and science: modern history.

17. H. L. Gates, Jr., "Belafonte's Balancing Act," *New Yorker,* 26 August and 2 September 1996, 135. Belafonte also recalls how the citation codes Du Bois used stimied his first efforts at self-education: "So when I was on leave, going into Chicago, I went to a library with a long list of books. The librarian said, 'That's too many, young man. You're going to have to cut it down.' I said, 'I can make it very easy. Just give me everything you got by Ibid.' She said, 'There's no such writer.' I called her a racist. I said, 'Are you trying to keep me in darkness?' And I walked out of there angry."

18. See P. Vidal-Naquet, *Les assassins de la mémoire* (Paris, 1987).

INDEX